Catholic School Leadership

A volume in
Research on Religion and Education
Larry Burton and Anthony J. Dosen, *Series Editors*

Catholic School Leadership

edited by

Anthony J. Dosen
DePaul University

Barbara S. Rieckhoff
DePaul University

INFORMATION AGE PUBLISHING, INC.
Charlotte, NC • www.infoagepub.com

Library of Congress Cataloging-in-Publication Data

Names: Dosen, Anthony J., editor. | Rieckhoff, Barbara S., editor.
Title: Catholic school leadership / edited by Anthony J. Dosen, Barbara S.
  Rieckhoff.
Description: Charlotte, NC : Information Age Publishing, Inc., 2016. |
  Series: Research on religion and education | Includes index.
Identifiers: LCCN 2015031393| ISBN 9781681232713 (pbk.) | ISBN 9781681232720
  (hardcover) | ISBN 9781681232737 (ebook)
Subjects: LCSH: Catholic schools–United States–Administration. | Catholic
  Church–Education–United States. | School management and
  organization–United States. | Educational leadership–United States.
Classification: LCC LC501 .C3482 2016 | DDC 371.071/273–dc23 LC record
available at http://lccn.loc.gov/2015031393

This book is dedicated to the memory of our friend and colleague
Reverend Stephen J. Denig, C.M., Ed.D.
Born June 14, 1948
Ordained a Priest May 17, 1975
Died May 22, 2013

Professor of Education
Niagara University
Niagara, New York

Steve spent his life as a secondary teacher and administrator, professor, researcher, and a tireless advocate of Catholic education.

Requiescat in pace!

CONTENTS

Series Editors' Introduction ix

Acknowledgments xi

Introduction.. xiii

1 Leadership in a Catholic Key.. 1
   Anthony J. Dosen

2 What Makes a Catholic School Catholic Anyway? 19
   Anthony J. Dosen

3 Untangling the Structure of Catholic Schools................................ 35
   Anthony J. Dosen

4 Catholic Schools by the Numbers 49
   Anthony J. Dosen

5 The Foundations of Curriculum in Catholic Schools 63
   Anthony J. Dosen

6 Funding the Mission: An Examination of Financial Issues
   and Funding Efforts in Catholic Schools 81
   Frank Montejano

7 Recruiting and Retaining Students 107
   Barbara Stacy Rieckhoff

8 Faculty Development 133
Sr. Patricia Helene Earl

9 Understanding the Role of the Pastor 151
Barbara Stacy Rieckhoff

10 Operational Vitality 165
Barbara Stacy Rieckhoff

Afterword 185
Anthony J. Dosen and Ronald Hoover

About the Contributors 193

Index 195

SERIES EDITORS' INTRODUCTION

Catholic School Leadership is the latest addition to the *Research in Religion and Education Series*. This book, which examines the work of the Catholic school leader; whether principal, president, or pastor; presents a comprehensive guide for those preparing for leadership in Catholic schools or those who are already engaged in this work. Throughout this text educational theory is woven with philosophical, theological and pastoral insights, written in a style that is accessible to scholars, students of Catholic education and practitioners.

The administration of Pre-K–12 Catholic schools becomes more challenging each year. Catholic school leaders, not only have the daunting task of leading a successful learning organization; but they also are called to serve as the school community's spiritual leader and the vigilant steward who keeps the budget balanced, the building clean, and maintains a healthy enrollment. Each of these tasks can be a full time job, yet the Catholic school principal takes on these tasks day after day, and year after year, so that teachers may teach as Jesus did.

The goal of this book is to provide both beginning and seasoned Catholic school leaders with insights that will help them to meet these challenges with a sense of confidence. This text provides research-based approaches for dealing with issues of practice, especially those tasks that are not ordinarily taught in educational leadership programs. The book helps to make sense of the pastoral side of Catholic education, in terms of structures, mission, identity, curriculum, and relationships with the principal's varied constituencies.

Catholic School Leadership, pages ix–x
Copyright © 2016 by Information Age Publishing
All rights of reproduction in any form reserved.

Catholic schools, like other religious-based schools, must remember that they are not just another educational option. The Catholic school has a rich history and an important mission. Historically, education of the young in the Catholic tradition goes back to monastic and cathedral schools in the Middle Ages. In the United States, Catholic schools developed as a response to anti-Catholic bias that was rampant during the nineteenth century. Catholic schools developed to mo e their immigrant and first generation American youth from the Catholic ghetto to successful careers and lives in the American mainstream. However, most importantly, Catholic schools have brought Christ to generations of youngsters. It remains the continuing call of the Catholic school to be a center of Evangelization—a place where Gospel values live in he lives of faculty, students and parents. This text attempts to integrate the unique challenges of the instructional leader of the institution with the historical and theological underpinnings of contemporary Catholic education.

The book's editors, Anthony J. Dosen and Barbara Rieckhoff, both have extensive experience in Catholic schools and have continued to examine aspects of Catholic school leadership as associate professors of Educational Leadership at DePaul University. Dosen is a Vincentian priest with extensive experience teaching and administering secondary schools run by his community. His research background extends into areas such as Catholic identity in both Catholic K–12 schools and Catholic higher education, and the impact of the digital divide on Catholic schools. Rieckhoff, a successful Catholic school principal at the elementary school level with experience in reinvigorating a Catholic school that was in need of turn around. Both her research and service interests focus upon mentoring recently appointed Catholic school principals as well as looking at the effects of school improvement in Catholic schools that were part of a partnership with DePaul University. Sr. Patricia Helene Earl contributed a chapter examining faculty development within the context of Catholic education. Dr. Frank Montejano contributed a chapter entitled, "Funding the Mission." His work comes from the unique perspective of both a scholar and practitioner.

This book began and was approved by Lyndon Furst, Andrews University, and Stephen Denig, Niagara University. They provided important critiques that added value to this texts final production. During the course of the book's production, Lyndon Furst retired from the editorship of the *Research in Religion and Education* series and Stephen Denig passed away. This book is the last work under Furst and Denig's watch and the first book that we have been pleased to add to the series. We look forward to working with future authors who will submit manuscripts to this series.

—**Larry Burton**
Anthony J. Dosen

ACKNOWLEDGMENTS

The editors wish to thank our students who work in Catholic schools as teachers and administrators. You shared your lived experience with us, and therefore helped us to be better grounded in the realities of Catholic schools. We hope that our work will support you in your work.

The editors are grateful to our colleagues Sr. Mary Patricia Earle, IHM and Dr. Frank Montejano for their chapters in this volume. We are also grateful to Ron Hoover, an alumnus of DePaul, who shared his insights and reflections on his Catholic school leadership practice in the Afterword. Your work has enriched our work.

Thanks also to our colleagues at DePaul University for your support as we worked on this volume. We are also grateful for the support and encouragement that we received from colleagues in the Catholic schools community, especially members of Catholic Higher Education in Support of Catholic Schools (CHESCS) and colleagues from the National Catholic Education Association (NCEA).

Thank you to the editors of the Research in Religion and Education book series, Lyndon Furst and Fr. Steven Denig, C.M., who originally approved the concept of the book, and Dr. Larry Burton who has succeeded Lyndon as editor. Thank you as well to the staff at Information Age Publications (IAP) for your work in bringing this work to publication. We appreciate your help in bringing this project to fruition.

Finally, I am grateful to Fr. Steven Denig, C.M., who worked with me on developing this project and volunteered to be co-editor, and to Dr. Barbara Rieckhoff who graciously stepped into the editorial role upon Steve's untimely death last year. I am grateful for your advice, your willingness to collaborate on this volume and many other works over the years, and most importantly for your friendship.

—Anthony J. Dosen, C.M., PhD
Associate Professor, Educational Leadership
DePaul University

—Barbara Stacy Rieckhoff, PhD
Associate Professor, Educational Leadership
DePaul University

INTRODUCTION

The administration of Pre K–12 Catholic schools becomes more challenging each year. Catholic school leaders not only have the daunting task of leading a successful learning organization, but also serving as the school community's spiritual leader and the vigilant steward who keeps the budget balanced and the building clean and maintains a healthy enrollment in the school. Each of these tasks can be a full-time job, yet the Catholic school principal takes on these tasks day after day, year after year, so that teachers may teach as Jesus did.

As principals throughout the United States take on this leadership role, they approach the tasks with fear and trepidation. Alumni whom I know who administer Catholic schools feel well prepared to lead a successful learning organization. At moments they become intimidated by the challenges of a site based management system that plunges them into such diverse roles as marketing and development experts, building and maintenance specialists, and accountants who possess the power to change pennies into dollars. However, the role that truly scares these novice principals is the role of spiritual leader of the building. Their cry sounds very much like the cry of Jeremiah. "Ah, Lord God! ... I know not how to speak; I am too young" (Jer. 1:6, NAB).

The goal of this book is to provide both beginning and seasoned Catholic school leaders with some insights that might help them to meet these challenges with a sense of confidence. The words in this text provide research-based approaches for dealing with issues of practice, especially those tasks that are not ordinarily taught in educational leadership programs. This text

Catholic School Leadership, pages xiii–xvi
Copyright © 2016 by Information Age Publishing
All rights of reproduction in any form reserved.

helps to make sense of the pastoral side of Catholic education, in terms of structures, mission, identity, curriculum, and relationships with the principal's varied constituencies. It also provides some insights into enrollment management issues, finances and development, and the day in, day out care of the organization and its home, the school building.

As a Catholic school leader, you must remember that the Catholic school is not just another educational option. The Catholic school has a rich history and an important mission. Historically, education of the young goes back to the monastic and cathedral schools of the middle ages. In the United States, Catholic schools developed as a response to anti-Catholic bias that was rampant during the nineteenth century. Catholic schools developed to move their immigrant and first-generation American youth from the *Catholic ghetto* to successful careers and lives in the American mainstream. However, most importantly, Catholic schools have brought Christ to generations of youngsters. It remains the continuing call of the Catholic school to be a center of evangelization—a place where gospel values live in the lives of faculty, students, and parents.

The Catholic school, as an evangelizing institution, first and foremost becomes a place where all who enter encounter Christ. They encounter Christ in the curriculum, the order of the day, the prayer, the recreation, and most importantly in one another. Students must see the face of Christ in their classmates. Teachers must see the face of Christ in their students, the parents of their students, and in their colleagues. This is especially true of the student who is the thorn in their side. Christ is present! Do we see him, or are we blinded to him?

This is the gift of Catholic education, especially in the United States. A major concern is often raised that many of our Catholic schools do not have very many Catholic students in them. How can it be a Catholic school without Catholic students? It seems that Catholic school leaders, their teachers, and all the varied constituencies of Catholic education must see in this situation a new moment of evangelization. Educators and students, parents and staff members each in their own way present Christ to the community at large. This is our goal as a school community. We also provide students with safe places in which they can learn, with an enriched curriculum and grow up to be the person that God is calling them to be. But most importantly, Catholic schools become the place where students encounter Christ.

The authors of the chapters that follow all have experience in Catholic K–12 schools as teachers and administrators, some of us have moved into higher education, while one of our colleagues continues to serve as the principal of a Catholic elementary school. I asked one of my former students to reflect upon his role as an administrator in a Catholic school. I am grateful to him for his insights, enthusiasm, and honesty in addressing these issues. You will see his work with a commentary by the author in the Afterword of this text.

Know that as you continue your journey as a Catholic school leader, you are not alone. The Lord goes with you. Just as God promised Jeremiah, so He too promises us:

> See, I place my words in your mouth!
> This day I set you over nations and over kingdoms,
> To root up and to tear down, to destroy and to demolish,
> To build and to plant. (Jer. 1: 9b–10)

As we wrote this text, the authors sought to provide you, the reader, with insight and confidence. While we certainly wish you success in your work as a Catholic school leader, we wish to remind you of the words of Mother Theresa of Calcutta who said, "God does not look for success, only fidelity." May you always be faithful to the mission!

—**Fr. Anthony J. Dosen, CM**
College of Education
DePaul University, Chicago

CHAPTER 1

LEADERSHIP IN A CATHOLIC KEY

Anthony J. Dosen

VIGNETTE

Jane Deveraux is the principal of St. Patrick's Elementary School. She arrives at St. Pat's at 6:45 a.m., opening her office door; she checks her voice mail messages. Mercifully, there are no messages, no need to find a substitute today. As she walks through the first floor of the building, Jane notices a puddle of water on the floor near the boys' washroom. The janitor is not in yet, so Jane goes to the custodian's room and gets the mop and bucket and begins cleaning up the water. As Jane is mopping, Ms. Jensen, the first grade teacher, enters the building and sees her in action. Jane looks up, smiles and says, "The joys of being a Catholic school principal!" They share a knowing smile as Ms. Jensen heads to her classroom.

It is now 7:15 a.m. and the other teachers began to arrive. The students begin arriving 15 minutes later, and are in their assigned places by 7:45 a.m. Attendance is taken, and the student body begins the procession to the parish church for Mass. At Mass, Jane assists Fr. Janus, the pastor, with the distribution of communion.

After Mass, Jane returns to her office, but just for a few moments. She is off to Mr. Jackson's 7th grade social studies class for a scheduled

Catholic School Leadership, pages 1–18
Copyright © 2016 by Information Age Publishing
All rights of reproduction in any form reserved.

1

observation. After the observation, she returns to the office where she finds Jill, a mischievous third grader who was "sent to the office" for causing a disturbance in class. Jane has a conversation with Jill, after which Jill promises to behave better in class. Jane then sits at her desk and begins to map out the agenda for the faculty meeting that is scheduled for later in the week. Jane looks at the clock and realizes it is time to do principal's story time with Ms. Jenson's first graders. This is Jane's favorite time of the day—quality time with the first graders! Today's book is the kids' favorite, *The Cat in the Hat.* After story time, Jane walks through the halls, scanning the building. She is listening to the symphony of lessons coming from the classrooms while keeping an eye on the building's floors, walls, and ceilings, checking for potential maintenance issues. As she ends her tour, Jane comes down the front stairwell and approaches the office. Her secretary reminds her that it is almost lunchtime—time to go to the cafeteria, visiting with both faculty and students. She reminds Jack to clean up around his seat, shares a story with several fifth graders, and checks in with faculty to see how their day is going. As the students return to class, Jane prepares her tray and returns to the office for a quick lunch while she sorts through her mail.

Today's mail includes a thick package from the Office of Catholic Schools. "Yikes! It's the annual report. When will downtown send out these surveys electronically?" Jane looks at her calendar and sets aside several hours to work on the report. Fr. Janus stops by to talk about tuition scholarships for several students, asking if the funds have arrived from the donors. As is typical, Fr. Janus sits down and regales Jane with several stories that had little to do with the school or parish and then updates her on several upcoming events at the parish. Fr. Janus excuses himself as the end of the school day quickly approaches. Jane leaves her office and goes out the front door of the school, chatting with parents who have gathered to pick up their children at the end of the day. Jane chats with one parent about her son's struggle with getting along with his classmates and suggests to another parent that his idea for a fundraiser should be added to the PTA agenda for the next meeting.

Here come the students! It's a time of blessed chaos. Jane greets students, unable to hold back her smile. As the dust settles, Jane returns to the office and tackles some paperwork, including writing several letters and reviewing the monthly budget report. It's now 5:30 p.m. Jane, tired from a full day, closes the door to her office and stops at the grocery store on the way home. At the store, one of the preschoolers, who is in the store with his mom, yells out, "Look mommy, there's the St. Pat's lady!" Jane smiles; she is happy to be associated with St. Patrick's!

INTRODUCTION

Principals of Catholic schools are called to be instructional leaders and so much more. They, like their public school colleagues, are instructional leaders. Their primary task is to provide a culture and resources that enhance the instruction of each child in their care. Above and beyond this, Catholic school principals also hold the position of leadership in an organization that is decidedly self-contained. Catholic schools are an example of site-based management, a type of management that places the Catholic school principal as a leader, rather than a mid-level manager. On another level, the Catholic school principal is also a spiritual leader. Whether or not they are ordained, these principals function as pastoral leaders. They are each charged with the spiritual welfare of their individual school. Thus the Catholic school principal is an instructional leader, a pastoral leader, and the chief executive officer of the educational organization called the Catholic school—in all its varied aspects. Those who want to take on the role of Catholic school principal might justifiably think twice. This chapter provides an understanding of how these varied responsibilities are integrated together and become a cohesive and compelling vocation.

THE NATURE OF CATHOLIC SCHOOLS

One must understand Catholic schools within the context of a community. Catholic schools are outgrowths of parish and diocesan communities, they are learning communities, and they are, by their nature, communities of faith. Therefore, anyone who desires to become a principal of a Catholic school must first understand that he or she is undertaking leadership of a community and not a corporation. Sergiovanni (1994), in his book *Building Community in Schools,* looks at school communities (both public and private) from the perspective of two opposing terms: *gemeinschaft* and *gesellschaft.* While the terms might seem a bit pretentious, the underlying concepts clearly speak of two approaches to how we live together in this world.

> *Gemeinschaft* translates to "community" and *gesellschaft* translates to "society." The terms are attributed to the German sociologist, Ferdinand Tönnies. Writing in 1887, he used the terms to describe the shifting values and orientations that occurred as we moved first from a hunting and gathering society to an agricultural society, and then on to an industrial society. Each of the societal transformations resulted in a shift away from *gemeinschaft* toward *gesselschaft*; away from a vision of life as sacred community and toward a more secular society. (Sergiovanni, 1994, p. 6)

According to Tönnies (1887/1957, p. 42), *gemeinschaft* exists in three forms: kinship, place, and mind. *Gemeinschaft* of kinship relates to the unity that we experience as members of a family—not just one's immediate family, but one's extended family. Expanding from one's family, there is a *gemeinschaft* of place: a community that is based upon one's sharing of a common locale, whether that locale be a school, neighborhood, town, or country. Finally, there is a *gemeinschaft* of mind: a community that is based upon common and shared values and beliefs. By contrast, *gesellschaft* is a movement away from shared values, into a world that is focused upon contractual relationships. Tönnies saw this as the key characteristic of the transition from farming communities to an industrial society. Perhaps Thomas Hobbes' sense of a social contract might be instructive in understanding the nature of *gesellschaft*. Individuals enter into contractual relationship—relationships that are, more often than not, *quid pro quo*, calculated where one receives what one wants while offering up as little as is possible.

Contemporary society, and, by extension, schooling in the United States, leans heavily toward *gesellschaft*. Has such an overemphasis on the contractual been of service to students in American schools? Sergiovanni (1994) suggests that this over-emphasis needs to be balanced with schools that are truly communities of mind (*gemeinschaft*). Sergiovanni certainly is not suggesting that one must banish all expressions of *gesellschaft*. Rather, he suggests that schools need to find a balance. If community, as defined by *gemeinschaft*, needs to be found again in public schools, how much more so does it need to be found within Catholic schools? This is the foundation upon which leadership in Catholic schools is built. The principal is, first and foremost, the leader of a community.

Most Catholic schools speak of themselves as a *family*, such as "the St. Patrick's family." Therefore, it should not be surprising that this conversation about Catholic school leadership begins by distinguishing between communities (*gemeinschaft*) and the industrial/societal approach (*gesellschaft*). Catholic schools are communities of place and of mind. Most Catholic schools, especially at the elementary school level, are focused around their local community and the local parish. At the secondary school level, the local community is usually wider (part of the city or a town, diocese, or region), but it is equally as location bound. But Catholic schools are not merely bound by location, they are also communities of mind—communities that are bound together by shared values and beliefs. Even when students matriculate who are not baptized Catholics, they are choosing this school because of their sense of affiliation with the shared values and beliefs of the school. As stated above, Sergiovanni (1994) was not suggesting that the school was an isolated community in the midst of an industrial, *quid pro quo* society. Principals, especially Catholic school principals, need to be astute in their business dealings with the diocese, state educational offices, and their vendors. This is especially important when the principal is dealing with the financial issues of the school. Therefore, it is the principal's primary responsibility to be a leader of the community, but the principal must also be equipped to deal with the business dealings that are essential to the good running of the school.

LEADING AND MANAGING

The effective Catholic school principal is, at one and the same time, both a leader and a manager. Some do not bother to make a distinction between the two terms, but this can be a critical mistake, especially for the principal. While leaders and managers both work with people and are concerned with achieving organizational goals, there are significant differences. The overall goal of management is to promote order and consistency—certainly qualities that are essential in making schools places where teaching and learning can take place. By contrast, leadership pushes the organization toward change and forward movement. The leader provides a sense of mission and vision for the organization, through good communication and relational skills; the leader aligns people for the mission and accomplishment of the vision, while motivating and inspiring people along the way (Northouse, 2010). When speaking about the distinction between leadership and management, Bolman and Deal (2008) focus upon the value-add of a manager who is also a leader, as opposed to a manager who is not capable of leading:

> Leadership is often confused with management. But a person can be a leader without being a manager, and many managers could not "lead a squad of seven-year-olds to the ice-cream counter" (Gardner, 1989, p. 2). Bennis and Nanus (1985) suggest that "managers do things right, and leaders do the right thing" (p. 21)—managers focus on execution, leaders on purpose. A managerially oriented navy officer gave a ringing endorsement of his more leaderlike successor: "I go by the book, he writes the book." (p. 343)

In a taped lecture, Deal and Peterson (1996) spoke of the school leader's movement from the management function to the leadership function as moving a pencil along the outside of a mobius strip (Figure 1.1). At one moment the pencil is on the outside of the strip, then, without moving the pencil off the strip, the pencil is on the inside of the strip. Similarly, school leaders seamlessly move from one function to the other.

If one examines the activities of Jane, the principal in the vignette at the beginning of this chapter, it is clear that she must be both a manager and

Figure 1.1 Mobius strip.

a leader in order to meet the needs of her daily work. Deal and Peterson (1994) speak of the

> possibility that principals can be both leaders and managers, can create both meaning and order. They can be both supports of change and defenders of the status quo. Principals can find a balance point between being traditional or innovative, tight or loose, inflexible or creative. Principals can embrace paradoxes ad puzzles of their work as the fulcrum for creating new approaches to leadership. (p. 40)

The principal must be capable of maintaining order so that the primary work of the school—that is, teaching and learning—can take place in an uninterrupted fashion. The work of management is the work of schedules, budgets, organizational charts, rules, policies, and procedures. All of these factors play a critical role in the smooth operation of any school. However, at the same time, the principal must be a visionary, an individual who is capable of seeing beyond the immediate, challenging the *status quo,* and looking out beyond the immediate crisis, toward the long-term future of the school and of the children.

Bolman and Deal (2008), in their classic book, *Reframing Organizations,* speak of the various ways in which leaders examine organizations. Reviewing structural, human resource, political, and symbolic frameworks, they recommend that effective leaders not merely choose one approach over the others, but that leaders constantly examine their organizations from all four frameworks. In doing so, it provides leaders with the tools to critically examine every situation. To quote an old adage, "when the only tool one has is a hammer, everything looks like a nail!" According to Bolman and Deal (2008),

> Multiframe thinking requires moving beyond narrow, mechanical approaches for understanding organizations. We cannot count the number of times managers have told us that they handled some problem the "only way" it could be done. Such statements betray a failure of both imagination and

courage and reveal a paralyzing fear of uncertainty. It can be comforting to think that failure was unavoidable and we did all we could. But it can be liberating to realize there is always more than one way to respond to any problem or dilemma. (p. 19)

Jane, the principal in the vignette, must engage her organization on a number of levels. She is attentive to the structural needs of her organization. She works on budgets and paperwork. She is attentive to the demands of the school's schedule and her schedule within the school. She is also attentive to the good order of the building, keeping order by assisting a teacher in providing a focused and nondisruptive learning environment, by meeting with the recalcitrant third grader.

However, Jane is also a principal who realizes that she must be attentive to the needs of her staff (human resource frame). She is in the classroom, observing teachers and actively involved in the primary grades' reading project as a participant. She is also available at lunch hour to informally check in with her teachers and students. She is taking the pulse of her staff. Politically, Jane is negotiating aspects of the budget with her pastor, Fr. Janus. She purposely works at building coalitions with the pastor, with her teachers, and with the parents. Notice how Jane goes out of the building before the final bell of the day, casually chatting with parents. This is coalition building.

Finally, Jane is a symbolic leader. Catholic school principals represent more than themselves: They are representatives of their school, the parish, and more widely, the Catholic Church. Both their actions and their voices must speak to the mission of the Catholic community's school. Jane exudes the mission from the start of the day to the end of the day, both formally and informally. Whether it is cleaning up the water puddle in the building before the day begins, attending and ministering at the all-school liturgy, reading *The Cat in the Hat* to the first graders, or just being present, Jane is demonstrating what St. Patrick's School is about and that she is fully engaged. She becomes the symbol, a sacrament (if you will) of St. Patrick's. The preschooler prophetically proclaims, "There's the St. Pat's lady!"

SCHOOL MANAGEMENT

The Catholic school principal is responsible for a variety of managerial activities: personnel management, financial management, and institutional management. In each of these areas, the principal is expected to maintain an orderly and stable environment in which the school can successfully accomplish its mission of teaching and learning, and specifically, teaching and learning in a Catholic key. Most of the skills that are taught in an introductory level school administration or principalship class adequately outline these skills. What follows is not so much a listing of what Catholic school principals manage, as it is how they might manage effectively.

The research is clear that successful management, whatever the organization, must be attentive to the needs of the people in the organization. Douglas McGregor (1957/2001) coined the terms "Theory X" and "Theory Y" denoting two opposing ways of managing people, either presuming that people will not do their assigned tasks (Theory X) or trusting people to do their assigned duties (Theory Y). McGregor clearly falls in favor of the Theory Y approach. According to McGregor, Theory Y holds the following principles:

1. Management is responsible for organizing the elements of productive enterprise—money, materials, equipment, people—in the interest of economic ends.
2. People are *not* by nature passive or resistant to organizational needs. They have become so as a result of experience in organizations.
3. The motivation, the potential for development, the capacity for assuming responsibility, the readiness to direct behavior toward organizational goals are all present in people. Management does not put them there. It is a responsibility of management to make it possible for people to recognize and develop these human characteristics for themselves.
4. The essential task of management is to arrange organizational conditions and methods of operation so that people can achieve their own goals *best* by directing *their own* efforts toward organizational objectives (McGregor, 1957/2001, p. 46).

While McGregor is writing from an industrial perspective, it is important for those of us in schools—especially Catholic schools—at the beginning of the 21st Century to see the continued wisdom in his conception of Theory Y. The attitude of managers toward those that work with and for them varies. Despite the years, and research studies, that have passed since the 1950s, some managers continue to hold in contempt all in their employ. The secret to effective management—which in turn will lead to effective leadership—lies in the attitude managers have toward their workers.

Frederick Herzberg (1968/2001) examines the ways that managers motivate employees. His findings about what motivates are vitally important, especially to Catholic school leaders. In his study he determines those factors that lead to satisfaction on the job, what he calls *motivators*, and those factors that lead to dissatisfaction on the job, what he calls *hygiene*. Comparing the hygiene and motivator factors side by side, from the greatest satisfaction/dissatisfaction to the least, proves enlightening (Table 1.1).

TABLE 1.1 Comparison of Motivators and Hygenic Factors as Described in Frederick Herzberg's Work

Motivators (Extreme Satisfaction)	Hygiene (Extreme Dissatisfaction)
Achievement	Company policy and administration
Recognition	Supervision
Work itself	Relations with Supervisor
Responsibility	Work Conditions
Advancement	Salary
Growth	Relationship with peers
	Personal life
	Relationship with subordinates
	Status
	Security

What motivates people? Most individuals ordinarily consider the hygiene factors, such as salary and job security as real motivators. In reality, most people find themselves most upset about those very factors when they are dissatisfied with their job. The factors that are listed in the motivator side of the table are those that provide people with the greatest impetus to continue being productive. For Catholic school principals, where salary can never be mistaken for a prime motivation, Herzberg's motivator factors give Catholic school principals an insight into what truly keeps their teachers and staff returning year after year.

If we take the term *school* to mean all the people who make up the institution, rather than the building that houses those people, then the critical skills for effective school management are good communication skills. These communication skills include not just speaking and writing well, but also listening. While principals must be clear in both written and spoken expression, it is also critical that they also have the ability to carefully listen to their various constituencies. Communication skills are not only critical to the managerial process, but they will fold over into effective leadership as well.

SCHOOL LEADERSHIP

While principals are called to be good managers in the name of the school community, managing finances, personnel, physical space and time, principals are also called to be keepers of the mission and the vision. They are keepers of the mission and vision of schooling in a democracy, of effective schooling for all children, and, in Catholic schools, of holistic schooling within the context of the Catholic Church's own educational mission.

Managers maintain organizational stability; leaders spur organizations to newer and deeper ways of living the mission.

Sergiovanni (2006), in his work on the principalship, speaks of a values approach to defining the role of the principal. This approach outlines the role of the principal by using a clear set of standards that are to be met in leading the school and with particular markers that define the school's organizational health:

> A values approach seeks to identify thick visions and then translate these visions into images of what we want the school to be like. Thick visions are more than mission statements, more than catchy prose, more than inspirational words. They are working documents that state publicly what is important, why it is important, what our obligations are, and how we get there. Thick visions are contracts, even covenants, that spell out our roles and responsibilities to the school and its vision. These images include goals and pathways that help a school celebrate its direction and help that school create the frameworks, structures, norms, and other means to succeed. (p. 26)

The call of Christ, echoed so often by St. John Paul II, goes to the heart of the leader's mission. "When he (Jesus) finished speaking he said to Simon, 'Put out into deep water and lower your nets for a catch'" (Luke 5:4[1]). The leader is one who "puts out into deep water," and the leader's strength in the midst of feeling inadequate to the challenge, not unlike Peter, are found in Jesus' words, "Do not be afraid" (Luke 5:10). The research on transformational leadership, servant leadership, and authentic leadership meld together to provide the Catholic school leader with a solid foundation for building a meaningful practice that is focused upon mission.

THE CATHOLIC SCHOOL LEADER AS A TRANSFORMATIONAL LEADER

James MacGregor Burns (1978) coined the term *transformational leadership*. In his book, *Leadership*, he distinguishes between transactional and transformational leadership, defining transactional leadership as a *quid pro quo* relationship, or a "you scratch my back, and I will scratch yours." Transformational leadership, in contrast, is built upon the premise that

> whatever the separate interests persons might hold, they are presently or potentially united in the pursuit of "higher" goals, the realization of which is tested by the achievement of significant change that represents the collective or pooled interests of leaders and followers.... Transformational leadership is more concerned with *end-values*, such as liberty, justice, equality. (pp. 425–426, emphasis in original)

At the heart of transformational leadership is the joining together of each person's interests into a common interest. While each individual has his or her own interests, these interests are placed aside in order to serve a higher, common interest. In Catholic philosophical language, this common interest is also known as the "common good."

In describing transformational leadership, Bass (1985) expanded upon the work of Burns (1978) by changing the emphasis from the needs of the leader to the needs of followers. These follower needs are encapsulated in the four "I's" of transformational leadership:

1. Idealized influence
2. Inspirational motivation
3. Intellectual stimulation
4. Individualized consideration (Northouse, 2010)

Idealized influence, sometimes understood as *charisma*, describes the leader as one with whom followers connect. They relate to the leader and see the leader as an example to be followed. Secondly, transformational leaders inspire followers. Their inspirational motivation provides the followers with high expectations, moving the followers to commit to the shared vision of the organization. The leader provides the focus from which the group moves forward on their common mission. Thirdly, transformational leaders provide intellectual stimulation. Followers are encouraged to be creative and develop new ways of approaching problems. Transformational leaders develop and use the intellectual capacity of their followers, rather than presuming their followers have nothing to offer the organization in reaching its goals. Finally, transformational leaders demonstrate individualized consideration. These leaders care about their followers, offering them whatever particular coaching or advice they might need in order to be successful (Northouse, 2010).

Kouzes and Posner (2002) flesh out the qualities described as transformational leadership by citing five practices that point to effective leadership:

1. Model the way
2. Inspire a shared vision
3. Challenge the process
4. Enable others to act
5. Encourage the heart

One begins to see a pattern of motivating, strengthening, and permitting followers to accomplish the work at hand evolving as a focused strategy in the development of transformational leadership. These common themes repeatedly appear in the literature of effective transformational leadership.

The major principles in Kouzes and Posner (2002) again are directed toward how leaders provide the support their followers need in order to accomplish the mission of the institution. For example, in inspiring a shared vision (Principle #2), the leader begins by envisioning a future that is filled with possibilities. Oftentimes, especially in our contemporary setting, it is easy to either look backward to the "good old days," or to look forward with a sense of dread as to what might be coming next. Leaders who are transformational are able to see a future that is hope-filled, exciting, and worth pursuing. It is this vision that is the gift that leaders give to their followers. Leaders call their followers to imagine a future with them. This is the message of the Kingdom that Jesus preached. Jesus continues to light the imagination of his followers with the vision of "kingdom values." Catholic school leaders, in their own way, inspire their faculties, students, and local communities to build a small corner of that Kingdom in their individual schools.

Effective leadership is marked by a willingness to challenge the *status quo* (Principle #3). Effective leaders search for ways to foster continued growth and improvement in their schools and thus create an environment where experimentation and taking risks is permitted, where small wins add up to larger wins, and more importantly, the norm is to learn from one's mistakes, rather than to avoid mistakes by not taking risks. The ability to allow for the possibility of meaningful change and growth cannot take place unless leaders are able to help their followers act. The primary task of good leadership is not to do the job by oneself but to provide an atmosphere that provides followers with the support to accomplish the common task (Principle #4). These supports are both intrapersonal (developing a sense of competence, confidence and accountability for accomplishing the task) and interpersonal (providing the means for meaningful collaboration). This support requires attentiveness on the part of the leader (Principle #5). Leaders must recognize the contributions of their followers, providing recognition and appreciation for the unique gifts of each follower; at the same time, the community must celebrate as it progresses toward its goals. The leader is not just getting a job done, but the leader is also creating a new culture, a new community. It is this community that must be celebrated.

It is in the first principle, modeling the way that leaders do their personal work, whereby they have the inner strength to carry out the other principles. At the surface, modeling the way is about leadership's own ability to give example. Exemplary behavior flows from finding one's own voice. What is it that leaders believe about the school in their charge? How do leaders see their own strengths and weaknesses? How might they be examples of both good leadership and good followership? In finding their own voices, leaders are able to begin calling others to the institution's mission. If leaders are committed to developing their own voice and sense of mission, they will be able to inspire others to share in that mission.

Surveys of leadership theory (Northouse, 2010; Yukl, 2009) describe other leadership theories, such as servant leadership, authentic leadership, and distributed leadership that work in tandem with transformational leadership. Each of these particular theories highlights different aspects of transformational leadership, and each of these theories has aspects that commend them to leaders of Catholic schools.

SERVANT LEADERSHIP

Robert Greenleaf coined the term *servant leadership* in 1970 (Dosen, 2011; Greenleaf, 1977). Greenleaf's insights about the nature of leadership provide a serious challenge to traditional, transactional ideas of leadership, while reinforcing the transformational leadership theory's focus on the role of followers. According to Greenleaf, the concept of servant leadership was implanted into his psyche during his senior year of college, when a professor challenged Greenleaf and his classmates:

> There is a new problem in our country. We are becoming a nation that is dominated by large institutions—churches, businesses, governments, labor unions, universities—and these big institutions are not serving us well. I hope that all of you will be concerned about this. Now you can do as I do, stand outside and criticize, bring pressure if you can, write and argue about it. All of this may do some good. But nothing of substance will happen unless there are people inside these institutions who are able to (and want to) lead them into better performance for the public good. (Greenleaf, 1977, pp. 1–2)

Greenleaf makes use of Herman Hesse's novel, *The Journey to the East* (1972), as his entry into the concept of servant leadership. In this novel, Leo, who was the servant of the group as they journeyed, was later revealed as the leader of the organization that sponsored the journey. The servant was truly the leader. Catholic school administrators might be more familiar with the scriptural bases that recommend servant leadership.

> You know how among the Gentiles those who seem to exercise authority lord it over them; their great ones make their importance felt. It cannot be like that with you. Anyone among you who aspires to greatness must serve the rest; whoever wants to rank first among you must serve the needs of all. The Son of Man has not come to be served but to serve—to give his life in ransom for the many. (Mark 10:42–45)

> Anyone among you who aspires to greatness must serve the rest, and whoever wants to rank first among you must serve the needs of all. (Matthew 20:26–27)

> Do you understand what I just did for you? You address me as Teacher and Lord, and fittingly enough, for that is what I am. But if I washed your feet—I

who am Teacher and Lord—then you must wash each other's feet. What I just did was to give you an example: as I have done, so you must do. (John 13:12–15)

Whether one chooses to enter into the concept of servant leadership by way of Herman Hesse or the Gospels, what remains clear is that leadership is conceptualized from a framework of caring and tending one's followers, rather than exercising authority over them. This is a novel perspective. Oftentimes, those who are leaders see themselves primarily as "the boss" and not "the servant." However, this topsy-turvy approach to leadership must enter into Catholic school leaders' understanding of how they lead. Catholic school leaders lead because they desire to be of service to the community. Their service is their exercise of leadership in the school community.

AUTHENTIC LEADERSHIP

Authentic leadership, as a leadership theory, has arisen at the dawn of the 21st century in response to the dearth of honesty and integrity in both business and political dealings at the end of the 20th century and the beginning of the 21st century. The Enron scandal and the scandals of Illinois gubernatorial politics over the past several administrations are examples of why American citizens, consumers, and followers, more generally conceived, demand that their leaders be persons of integrity. The mantra of the 1960s, "distrust authority," has become a reality in the first decades of the 21st century. According to Northouse (2010),

> Authentic Leadership is "a pattern of leader behavior that draws upon and promotes both positive psychological capacities and a positive ethical climate, to foster greater self-awareness, an internalized moral perspective, balanced processing of information, and relational transparency on the part of leaders working with followers, fostering positive self-development." (Walumbwa et al., 2008 as cited in Northouse, 2010, p. 94)

If followers, whether citizens or consumers, are demanding basic integrity from the captains of industry and their political leadership, then it should come as no surprise that parishioners, parents, teachers, and students would expect similar from the leadership of their Catholic schools.

While research on authentic leadership is still in its earliest stages and its theoretical framework is yet to be formulated in a substantive way, followers are demanding integrity of their leaders. According to Northhouse (2010), this integrity is manifest by the following qualities:

1. There is a clear sense of purpose. Authentic leaders know what they are about and where they are going.
2. Leaders act from a clear set of values. Authentic leaders have a moral compass and use it!
3. Relationships are critical. Authentic leaders understand that their work is not merely about bottom lines, but about people.
4. Self-discipline is key. Authentic leaders must be capable of self-directed behavior.
5. The authentic leader must demonstrate heart. Authentic leaders are committed.

It is not difficult to see how authentic leadership might be a compelling leadership framework for the Catholic school leader. The varied constituencies of Catholic schooling demand those chosen to the principal's role to be paragons of integrity. Catholic principals are called to be principled leaders.

DISTRIBUTED LEADERSHIP

Distributed leadership, like authentic leadership, is a newcomer to the world of leadership theory. Often, distributed leadership has been described as another way of describing shared, team, or democratic leadership. Spillane (2005) disagrees with these facile comparisons and describes distributed leadership from the perspective of practice.

> [L]eadership *practice* is viewed as a product of the interactions of school leaders, followers, and their situation...the distributed perspective defines it as the interactions between people and their situation. These interactions, rather than any particular action, are critical in understanding leadership practice. (Spillane, 2005, p. 144)

Unlike other theoretical frameworks, the interactions between leaders and followers rather than persons, roles, and functions define leadership. These interactions and interdependencies between individuals in the school organization provide a framework for describing how schools function. The benefit of distributed leadership is that it is a reminder that leadership is not a simple function of the leader speaking and the followers following, but rather it is a complexity that bears careful and critical analysis. The question it seeks to answer is how these varied interactions that take place in the school building work together and how our activities as a school community work together for the benefit of our students.

Spillane (2005) does not offer distributed leadership as a panacea for school reform, but rather views it as a way of understanding and describing what is happening in school leadership. Distributed leadership, as of this writing, is still in its infancy as a descriptive theory. Principals should continue to keep an eye on this way of thinking about leadership to see how it might help them diagnose what is happening within their school communities.

CONTEMPORARY LEADERSHIP THEORIES AND THE WORLD OF THE CATHOLIC SCHOOL PRINCIPAL

As one reads the all-too-brief overview of the theoretical frameworks of transformational, servant, authentic, and distributed leadership, readers may find themselves shaking their head, saying quietly, "Yes, yes, this is something that I should keep in mind, but who can do all the things that are recommended in these theories?" The readers and their writer look at the ideal and may feel a twinge of reluctance or, perhaps, fear as they reflect on the reality of their personal life stories. The lives of real school leaders working in Catholic schools are filled with challenges, unexpected events, crises, but also consolations and joy. Leaders of Catholic schools may feel even more compelled to a sense of perfectionism because of the nature of their vocation. Principals must approach the task, the vocation of leading a Catholic school, with an openness to build something together with faculty, parents, students, pastor, and the parish or wider church community.

Transformational and distributed leadership remind leaders that they are not alone in the task of education. Schooling is a team sport! The task of the leader is to develop leadership among all the constituencies within the school. The goal of transformational leadership is to foster that type of leadership, while the goal of distributed leadership is to remain aware of the interactions among the constituencies as they seek to accomplish the goal—the holistic education of children in the Catholic tradition. Servant leadership provides Catholic school principals with a rock solid foundation. The one who wishes to lead must be the servant of the rest. The word "administration" comes from the Latin *ad ministrare*, which means "to minister." Leadership in Catholic schools is first and foremost a ministry. Authentic leadership reminds Catholic school leaders that they must be themselves, and their very selves must be grounded and rooted in a life of virtue.

In closing, perhaps the advice of Kouzes and Posner (2010) in their recent book *The Truth about Leadership* might prove helpful. Kouzes and Posner's ten things that everyone wants to know about leadership are:

1. You make the difference.
2. Credibility is the foundation of leadership.
3. Values drive commitment.

4. Focusing on the future sets leaders apart.
5. You can't do it alone.
6. Trust rules.
7. Challenge is the crucible for greatness.
8. You either lead by example or you don't lead at all.
9. The best leaders are the best learners
10. Leadership is an affair of the heart.

The goal of this chapter was not to provide you with easy answers to leadership and leading Catholic schools. Rather it has been to provide you with a tapestry of ideas and thoughts about how individuals have approached the practice of leadership and to offer some suggestions as to how these ideas might influence your practice as leaders in Catholic schools. The author hopes that you will continue to read books on leadership and reflect on how what is being offered might impact your school setting.

NOTE

1. All scriptural texts are taken from *The New American Bible* (New York, NY: J. P. Kennedy and Sons, 1970).

REFERENCES

Bass, B. M. (1985). *Leadership and performance beyond expectations.* New York, NY: Free Press.

Bolman, L., & Deal, T. (2008). *Reframing organizations: Artistry, choice, and leadership* (4th ed.). San Francisco, CA: Jossey-Bass.

Burns, J. M. (1978). *Leadership.* New York, NY: Harper & Row Publishers.

Catholic Biblical Association of America. (1970). *The New American Bible.* New York, NY: P.J. Kenedy & Sons.

Deal, T., & Peterson, K. (1994). *The leadership paradox: Balancing logic and artistry in schools.* San Francisco, CA: Jossey-Bass Publishers.

Deal, T. & Peterson, K. (Writers). (1996). *Principals: Leaders of change.* [Movie]. Video journal of education, (5,7) (Available from Linton Professional Development Corporation, Salt Lake City).

Dosen, A. (2011). Servant leadership. In H. Barker & M. G. Gibbs (Eds.), *Discussions in leadership theory* (pp. 29–47). Laurel, MD: Capitol College Innovation and Leadership Institute.

Greenleaf, R. K. (1977). *Servant leadership: A journey into the nature of legitimate power and greatness.* New York, NY: Paulist Press.

Hesse, H. (1972). *The journey to the east.* New York, NY: Bantam.

Herzberg, F. (2001). One more time: How do you motivate employees? In W. Natemeyer & J. T. McMahon (Eds.), *Classics of organizational behavior* (3rd ed., pp. 81–95). Long Grove, IL: Waveland Press. (Original work published 1968)

Kouzes, J., & Posner, B. (2002). *The leadership challenge* (3rd ed.). San Francisco, CA: Jossey-Bass Publishers.

Kouzes, J., & Posner, B. (2010). *The truth about leadership: The no-fads, heart-of-the-matter facts you need to know.* San Francisco, CA: Jossey-Bass Publishers.

McGregor, D. (2001). The human side of enterprise. In W. Natemeyer & J. T. McMahon (Eds.), *Classics of organizational behavior* (3rd ed., pp. 41–49). Long Grove, IL: Waveland Press. (Original work published 1957).

Northouse, P. (2010). *Leadership: Theory and practice* (5th ed.). Thousand Oaks, CA: Sage Publications.

Sergiovanni, T. (1994). *Building community in schools.* San Francisco, CA: Jossey-Bass Publishers.

Sergiovanni, T. (2006). *The principalship: A reflective practice perspective* (5th ed.). Boston, MA: Pearson Education.

Spillane, J. P. (2005). Distributed leadership. *The Educational Forum, 69*(2), 143–150.

Tönnies, F. (1957). *Gemeinschaft und Gesselschaft* [Community and Society] (C. P. Loomis, Ed. & Trans.). New York, NY: Harper Collins. (Original work published in 1887).

Yukl, G. (2009). *Leadership in organizations* (7th ed.). Englewood Cliffs, NJ: Prentice-Hall.

RECOMMENDATIONS FOR FURTHER READING

The texts listed below are, to the author's mind, classics that are worth reading. He has purposely avoided the works that were cited in this chapter while composing this list. His hope is to give you some works above and beyond what you experienced in the chapter. This being said, the author certainly would recommend the materials in the works cited section for your continued study as well.

Bolman, L., & Deal, T. (1995). *Leading with soul: An uncommon journey of spirit.* San Francisco, CA: Jossey-Bass.

Collins, J. (2001). *Good to great.* New York, NY: Harper Collins.

Goleman, D., Boyantzis, R. & McKee, A. (2002). *Primal leadership: Realizing the power of emotional intelligence.* Boston, MA: Harvard Business School Press.

Heifetz, R. (1994). *Leadership without easy answers.* Cambridge, MA: Harvard University Press.

Sergiovanni, T. (1992). *Moral leadership: Getting to the heart of school improvement.* San Francisco, CA: Jossey-Bass.

CHAPTER 2

WHAT MAKES A CATHOLIC SCHOOL CATHOLIC ANYWAY?

Anthony J. Dosen

INTRODUCTION

In 2012, after several years of work, a representative committee made up of superintendents and representatives of religious communities, Catholic publishing, and Catholic higher education presented American Catholic schools with *National Standards and Benchmarks for Effective Catholic Elementary and Secondary Schools* (2012). The work, supported by the National Catholic Educational Association and sponsored by two Jesuit institutions, Loyola University Chicago and Boston College, became the first clearly articulated and agreed-upon set of standards for Catholic education in a long time.

Among these standards are items that deal directly with mission and identity, governance and leadership, academic excellence, and operational vitality. In short, all those elements necessary for a Catholic school to be Catholic and for a Catholic school to be a successful academic institution. As Lorraine Ozar, the chair of the committee that established these standards, states:

> The publication of these effectiveness standards gives the entire Catholic
> community a common framework of universal characteristics of Catholic

Catholic School Leadership, pages 19–34
Copyright © 2016 by Information Age Publishing
All rights of reproduction in any form reserved.

identity and agreed upon criteria for Catholic school excellence. With this framework, we can and must hold ourselves accountable for the excellence and rigor, faith and nurturance that have been the hallmark of Catholic education, and which we must now guarantee for future generations. (*National Standards*, 2012, p. iii)

The committee drew upon a number of sources and various Church documents on Catholic schools to outline the defining characteristics of Catholic schools. These defining characteristics form the foundation upon which the standards and benchmarks rest. The author makes use of these defining characteristics to provide an outline for describing the mission and identity of Catholic schools.

CHARACTERISTICS OF CATHOLIC SCHOOLS

Catholic schools should be marked by the following characteristics.

- The Catholic school must be centered in the Person of Jesus Christ.
- The Catholic school must contribute to the evangelizing mission of the Catholic Church.
- The Catholic school is distinguished by excellence.
- The Catholic school is committed to educate the whole child.
- The Catholic school is steeped in a Catholic worldview.
- The Catholic school is sustained by Gospel witness.
- The Catholic school is shaped by communion and community.
- The Catholic school is accessible to all students.
- The Catholic school is established by the expressed authority of the bishop.

Examining these characteristics, the reader should be struck by the very first characteristic; the Catholic school must be centered in the person of Jesus Christ. While this statement seems obvious, it is still striking when seen on paper. Catholic leadership (bishops, priests, religious, lay leaders) certainly would agree with this statement, but because it is so obviously presumed, it could very well remain hidden. Yet the center of Catholic schooling truly is Christ. The Catholic school, at heart, is Jesus' own mission of proclaiming the Good News of the Kingdom, handed on to the apostles at the Ascension: "Go, therefore and make disciples of all nations... teaching them" (Matthew 28: 19–20[1]).

The mission of Catholic schools is to proclaim the Gospel, which is the heart of the Church's own mission, and in doing so to sustain the Catholic school by a Gospel witness. As will be discussed in greater detail below, the challenge of Catholic schools, at any level, is to make Christ present by a consistent witness of Gospel values not only on the part of Catholic school leaders and teachers, but also all who have a role in the school—maintenance, kitchen staff, administrative assistants, and, yes, the students, as well.

Catholic schools that are centered in Jesus Christ and His mission are schools that must be accessible to all students, committed to the education of the whole child, distinguished by excellence, and steeped in the Catholic tradition. These four characteristics each find their foundation in Christ and his own mission. Catholic schools must be accessible to all students, if they wish to be centered in Jesus Christ.

It was Jesus who went out to the poor and the marginalized of his day and brought them into his company. Similarly, Catholic schools are by their inherent nature called to be inclusive. Scanlan (2008) has described how Catholic schools have skirted this call to inclusivity by marginalizing racial minority students, English language learners and special education students. Scanlan makes use of Catholic social teaching to remediate this situation. In seeking to educate the whole child, Catholic schools profess the unique personhood of each child. Children, and adults, are not seen as pawns in the hands of society, but rather as children of God, redeemed by Christ and deserving of an education that develops all aspects of their lives. This education is to be distinguished by its excellence. Christ, who turned the water into wine at Cana of Galilee, did not produce an inferior wine, but rather "the good wine" (John 2:10). This education marked by excellence, inclusivity and holistic breadth is steeped in the Church's tradition. The history of the Catholic Church is marked by various faith-filled artists and scholars who studied all aspects of God's creation and using their own creativity created art, music and literature. These intellectual and creative works were preserved in monasteries and universities throughout the centuries and serve as a base from which future generations might learn about God and the world He created.

Finally, Catholic schools, while focused on Christ and attentive to the children in their care, are a part of a wider reality, the Church. The ecclesial nature of the Catholic school is manifest in how Catholic educators go about their work. It is a work of community building and welcoming. Catholic schools become the place where children experience the Church at their own level of understanding. As an ecclesial structure, the Catholic school is a Catholic school because of the bishop declaring it to be so. The bishop, as chief pastor and teacher, has the primary responsibility of determining whether a particular school is truly holding true to its mission. This is the bishop's canonical obligation. It should be seen as a guarantee that there is truth in what the Catholic school says it is.

The distinguishing characteristics highlighted by the *National Standards* (2012) are excellent sign posts to examine the questions of mission and identity. The chapter continues with some definitions of *mission* and *identity* and how these two concepts relate to organizations, in general, and Catholic schooling, in particular. The remainder of this chapter will examine each of the distinguishing characteristics of Catholic schooling and draw out the implications of these distinguishing characteristics as markers for the mission of Catholic schooling and the Catholic identity of Catholic education.

MISSION AND IDENTITY

The terms *mission, vision,* and *identity* can be quite confusing to individuals who are novices to the field of organizational theory. *Mission* speaks to the purpose of the organization (Yukl & Lepsinger, 2005). In the case of Catholic schools, the *mission* should explain the school's purpose, why it should exist, and what makes it different from other schools, both public and private. In the previous section, the author focused on the concept of the Catholic school centering itself in the person of Jesus Christ. This declaration distinguishes the Catholic school from both public schools and private non-sectarian schools and provides a framework for what the founders of the school envision as the inherent uniqueness of the school. Each of the distinctive characteristics noted above should demonstrate aspects of the Catholic school's unique mission.

Organizational or institutional identity is defined as "that which members believe to be central, enduring, and distinctive about their organization" (Whetten & Godfrey, 1998, p. 33). It would seem that this definition of *identity* mirrors what has been said about the definition of *mission.* In a very real sense, the questions that we are answering are "here is who we are," and "here is what we do." The Catholic school's mission and our identity should meld together quite easily. Sometimes, this may not be the case.

One of the interesting questions that arise in studying organizational identity is whether the identity comes from the leadership to the group, or whether the group as it interacts with the mission and one another creates the unique organizational identity of the institution. Those who hold to the former believe that the "boss" sets the identity of the organization and the "subordinates" carry out, either grudgingly or ungrudgingly, what the "boss" has predetermined. Those who hold the latter believe that the organizational identity is created by the interaction and commitments of the group. The leader's role in this type of setting is to guide and influence the setting (Whetten & Godfrey, 1998).

Taking the latter stance expressed above, the Catholic school leader is confronted with some interesting questions. As principal/leader of the Catholic school, it is your responsibility to shepherd the school's mission and identity. If your faculty and staff create an identity peculiar to your school, how can guarantee the school's Catholic identity? In this particular case, the mission is articulated. Here is what a Catholic school, or here is what Catholic schools in this diocese hold as their mission. What does a principal do when the organizational identity, or school climate/culture, is not in agreement with the school's mission?

This question creates more than a little angst not only in Catholic school principals, but also in parish priests and diocesan bishops. On one level, Catholic identity, which should move hand-in-hand with the mission of the Catholic school, is disrupted. Do the external constituents of the school—parents, potential parents, local community members, local clergy and others—notice this inconsistency? If they do, the principal might go to a quick fix, whereby the faculty are told of the situation and they attempt to put up a "good front" or to polish the school's image, as it were. What results is that the school begins to live a lie. There is inconsistency between the identity of the organization (the internal identity) and the image of the organization (how it is viewed from external sources).

The role of the Catholic school leader is gently, yet firmly, to guide the mission and the identity into conformity. This is the very real pastoral function of the Catholic school leader. They are the faith leaders of the school community. The principal, precisely as faith leader, is to call all members of the school community to living out the faith that allows Christ to be the center not only of the school community, but also of their individual lives.

Vision is intimately connected with direction. Where are we, as a school/faculty going? An apt way of describing organizational vision is to imagine wagon trains heading across the United States from the east coast to the western frontiers of the 19th century. These wagon trains employed scouts who would venture ahead and determine the safest passage to the wagon train's destination. Similarly, the Catholic school principal is called to look ahead and determine which direction the school community needs to take. This might require taking the time to reflect on where the school community is and what the school community envisions as its mission, and determining where the differences between the two lie. A visionary leader is able to call people to be the best that they can be. This means that the principal, as leader, must recognize the gaps in the faculty's aspired mission and their current situation. The principal then calls and directs the faculty to a new place.

To conclude, it is worth remembering the following. The mission of the school describes what we do. The identity of the school, especially its Catholic identity, describes who we are as a group/organization. The vision of the school is where we hope to be in the future. The final part of this chapter examines the distinguishing characteristics one more time, with the task of examining what they hold for the mission and identity of the Catholic school.

THE ECCLESIAL MISSION AND IDENTITY
OF CATHOLIC SCHOOLS

Centered in the Person of Jesus Christ

If Christ is not the center of the school, then the school should not be called *Catholic*. Christ is the rock foundation on which the edifice is built; any other foundation is sand (see Matthew 7:24–29). In professing that Catholic schools are centered in the person of Jesus Christ, they must mirror those Gospel values proclaimed by Christ. Each person must be seen as a child of God, made in His own image and likeness. This anthropological assumption presumes that each person has an innate dignity that must be respected. According to Groome (1996),

> The core of Catholic anthropology—its theological understanding of the human condition—is often described as a 'realistic optimism' about us. It recognizes our capacity and "proneness" for sin, but insists that we are essentially more good than evil. Though "fallen," our divine image and likeness was never totally lost through original sin. Rather we retain our innate capacity for good and for God. Practically this means that people are always in need of God's grace *and* have the capacity, with God's help, to make a positive contribution to our personal and common welfare. (p. 109)

The Catholic position falls between the two extremes of saying that human beings are capable of salvation on our own, known as the heresy of *Pelagianism,* and saying that human beings are totally depraved, as is the case with the radical reformers. Thus, each must respect the other, even the child who is the thorn in the side. St. Vincent de Paul (1581–1660) reminded his followers that one must see the face of God in the poor. Similarly, teachers and administrators must see the face of God in their students (see Matthew 25:31–46).

Contributing to the Evangelizing Mission of the Church

In the Catholic school, students, as well as all the adults in the building, must not only encounter Christ as the center of the school, but must also find themselves transformed by this encounter. Those who encountered Christ during his earthly life were changed. They had heard "Good News." They were changed by the very encounter with Christ. This is the essence of the evangelizing mission of the Church. Do the students, parents, and teachers who walk the halls of the Catholic school, interact in classrooms, libraries, meetings and liturgical celebrations find Christ, and find they are different because of the experience?

Catholic schools have strong catechetical programs. Certainly this is seen as one of the hallmarks of Catholic education (McLaughlin, 1996; National Conference of Catholic Bishops [NCCB], 1973; *National Standards*, 2012). But this sense of evangelization is not the mere transmission of catechetical data, but rather an encounter with the Risen Christ. As Reck (1991) cites, the Catholic school "is a place of evangelization, of authentic apostolate and of pastoral action—not through complementary or parallel or extra-curricular activity, but of its very nature: its work of educating the Christian person" (RD #33 in Reck, 1991, p. 22).

Catholic schools are unique in that faith imbues the curriculum. While the shallow protests that "there is no such thing as Catholic physics," expounded by educators such as Sr. Jacqueline Grennan in the 1960s, were once popular (Dosen, 2009), a more measured viewpoint might favor that the wonders one might find in physics helps students to "find God in all things."[2] Evangelization in Catholic schooling is evidenced in an academic rigor, critical thinking, and creativity. Denig and Dosen (2009), citing Groome's (1996), work found

> the curriculum of Catholic education must reflect and promote three commitments: 1) to affirm students' basic goodness, in order to promote their dignity, to honor their fundamental rights, and to develop their gifts to the fullest—as God's reflections; 2) to educate people to live responsibly, with God's help, for the fullness of life that God wills for self and others—as responsible partners; and 3) to convince and mold people to live lives that are worthwhile and have historical significance, so that their every good effort advances he well-being of all. (p. 143)

Sustained by Gospel Witness

The Catholic school, centered in the person of Christ and contributing to the evangelizing mission of the Church, finds its sustenance in the Gospel witness. The Catholic school is "guided and driven by a clearly communicated mission that embraces a Catholic identity rooted in Gospel Values" (*National Standards*, 2012, p. 2). What is the nature of this sustenance? It is the message of Jesus handed on generation to generation in the life of the Church. It is the Word of God, broken open for us, for our nourishment. As the disciples on the road to Emmaus declared upon recognizing Christ in the breaking of the bread, "Were not our hearts burning within us while he spoke to us on the way and opened the scriptures to us?" (Luke 24:32). The Gospel witness is twofold; it is the Word of God proclaimed and it is the living out of that word in the daily life of those who proclaim the Word.

There cannot be preaching without a life that models Gospel witness. A story from the life of St. Francis of Assisi demonstrates this preaching in action aptly. One day St. Francis invited on of the young friars who had just joined the community to join him in preaching in a neighboring town. The young friar was elated. He was going to preach with Francis, his hero. The day finally arrived, and the young friar excitedly accompanied Francis as he walked to the outskirts of the town. His expectations rose higher and higher as they entered into the town and continued to walk toward the center of town. Suddenly, the young friar felt his heart sink. They had walked through the town and were now on the outskirts of the opposite side of town, but Francis had not said a word. Crestfallen, the young friar said to St. Francis, "I thought we were coming to this town to preach. What happened?" St. Francis said in reply, "We did preach. We must always preach, and when necessary use words."

The preaching of the Gospel that the school community engages in and the evangelizing in which they participate with the Church are predicated first, and most importantly, in this reality. The example adults in the building give to the students and the standards of behavior to which we hold our students must be firmly connected to Gospel values. Additionally, the students in the building oftentimes become examples of Gospel values for the adults of the school and parish community as well.

Shaped by Communion and Community

Catholic schools are not just a collection of students, faculty, and parents, but rather they are a community of believers who have set out on a mission of growing in knowledge, maturity, and grace. Catholic schools are gatherings of a local church, under the pastoral (and administrative) leadership of the principal. In the bishops' statement on Catholic education, *To Teach as Jesus Did*, the bishops spoke to the nature and importance of community in Catholic Christian education.

> Community is at the heart of Christian education not simply as a concept to be taught but as a reality to be lived.... Formed by this experience, they (the students) are better able to build community in their families, their places of work, their neighborhoods, their nation, their world. (NCCB, 1973, #23)

In building community in our schools, there is no one cookie cutter approach, but there are some definite hallmarks that will be clearly demonstrated when a school has been successful at building community. Reck (1991) offers the following list.

> Schools are called to the following conditions which build community and a supportive climate:
> - Everyone agrees with the educational goals.
> - All cooperate in achieving the educational goals.

- Interpersonal relationships are based on love and Christian freedom.
- Families are welcomed.
- The local church is an active participant.
- Civil society—local, national, and international—is included. (Reck, 1991, p. 25)

Groome (1996) believes that Catholic schools, although they are not parishes, should be exemplars of Christian faith lived out in community.

> As such, it is to share in the traditional tasks of a Christian community, albeit in an educational way. Since the earliest days, the Church has recognized that the mission of God's reign in Jesus entails at least four historical tasks: to teach, preach and evangelize the *word* of God in scripture and tradition (*kerygma*); to *witness* as a community of faith hope and love in the world (*koinonia*); to *worship* God in prayer and communal liturgy (*leitourgia*); and to care for human *welfare* (*diakonia*). (p. 116, emphasis in original)

Catholic schools must not relegate these programs to the religion department or the school's chaplaincy efforts. These efforts should be part and parcel of the school community's living its daily life—from liturgy, into the daily life of the school, and moving beyond the school in order to impact the wider community in which the school resides. Thus, the school, as a microcosm of the Church, moves from worship into service. It is the Eucharist that plays a critical role in the formation of the Catholic school community. The Eucharist, which is the source and summit of our life as a Church, draws students, faculty, and parents together in ways that provide them with the spiritual resources for building community.

In this author's experience, one of the most heart wrenching experiences of students' lives is when their school closes. Catholic educators know that they have been successful in fostering community in their school when students spontaneously declare that they feel like they are losing their home. Many Catholic school principals have told their students that they are a school family. It should not be surprising when students in the midst of this type of traumatic situation tell their teachers and administrators that they feel like they have been thrown out of their home. Community is built in the everyday moments, in the small interactions that take place, seemingly unnoticed. Administrators should never underestimate the importance of the casual exchanges we have with faculty, parents, and especially students.

Established by the Authority of the Bishop

Of all the characteristics of Catholic education, this one seems at first look to be out of place. The other characteristics speak to what school leaders, teachers, students and parents observe and live in their day-in and day-out lives in a Catholic school. The fact that a Catholic school is established by the authority of the diocesan bishop seems oddly out of place. Perhaps, it is more juridical and less pastoral. Yet this establishment is an outgrowth of community and communion. The Diocesan Bishop, as the chief teacher and pastor, has the responsibility of guaranteeing that the Catholic faith is being proclaimed faithfully in the Church's institutions. His approval indicates that the Catholic school is in communion with the wider Church.

Canon 803 states:

§1. A Catholic school is understood as one which a competent ecclesiastical authority or a public ecclesiastical juridic person directs or which ecclesiastical authority recognizes as such through a written document.

§3. Even if it is in fact Catholic, no school is to bear the name *Catholic school* without the consent of competent ecclesiastical authority. (Beal, Coriden, & Greene, 2000, p. 956)

Therefore, Catholic schools are Catholic because they have the approval of the diocesan bishop. This issue will be discussed in greater detail in the following chapter.

EDUCATIONAL MISSION OF CATHOLIC SCHOOLS

Committed to Educate the Whole Child

Holistic development is marked by a sense of "total wellness"—that active process by which an individual becomes aware of and makes choices toward a more balanced existence (Beutow, 1988, p. 81). Total wellness challenged Catholic schools to assist students not only in becoming technologically competent, but also in providing them with a sense of hope as they confront the uncertainty of contemporary life, and to find community in the midst of a large, highly complex society (Bryk et al., 1993). (Denig & Dosen, 2009, p. 145)

Educating the whole child is a deeper concern than preparing a student to enter the world of work. It involves helping the individual to create a meaningful life, to construct a worldview that moves beyond the pragmatic and into the realm of understanding oneself and others. Educators have professed for many years that the goal of education in a democracy was to guarantee an enlightened electorate. Beutow (1988) described this holistic approach as helping individuals to choose a more balanced existence.

John Dewey (1915/1990) describes what he believes should be the nature of schooling, in general, moving from a focus upon the teacher and the textbook to a focus upon the child. This focus is not a matter of allowing the child free access. Rather, it is the opportunity to begin with the child's natural experience and to build the curriculum upon this focus. Here are Dewey's own words from *The School and Society*:

> If we take an example from an ideal home, where the parent is intelligent enough to recognize what is best for the child, and is able to supply what is needed, we find the child learning through the social converse and constitution of the family. There are certain points of interest and value to him in the conversation carried on: statements are made, inquiries arise, topics are discussed, and the child continually learns. He states his experiences, his misconceptions are corrected. Again the child participates in the household occupations, and thereby gets habits of industry, order and regard for the rights and ideas of others, and the fundamental habit of subordinating his activities to the general interest of the household. Participation in these household tasks becomes an opportunity for gaining knowledge. The ideal home would naturally have a workshop where the child could work out his constructive instincts. It would have a miniature laboratory in which his inquiries could be directed. The life of the child would extend out of doors to the garden, surrounding fields, and forests. He would have his excursions, his walks and talks, in which the larger world out of doors would open to him. (Dewey, 1915/1990, pp. 34–35)

From Dewey's approach, we begin to see that the world becomes the classroom and that the child engages that world and makes sense of it as her own person. The child's engagement is not at his whim. Rather, the child is subordinate to the family's agenda. Similarly, the child in the classroom must be engaged in such a way that she is connected to and engaged in the learning that is taking place. Exploratory lessons, experiential learning, constructivist learning, and the flipped classroom, to name but a few approaches, are all outgrowths of Dewey's basic insight.

Dewey's philosophical bent does not allow him to speak to the issue of the child and his religious and spiritual development. Yet, this naturally fits into the framework of what Dewey suggests in *The School and Society*. Catholic schools, which hold as a tenet, that the parents are the primary teachers of the child—especially in matters of faith, see the faith development of children as critical to the conception of holistic education.

Bryk (1996; Bryk et al., 1993) describes this holistic education as character education that is informed by the school's mission of the human and spiritual formation of their students and the transmission of the Catholic cultural tradition. Bryk et al. (as cited in McLaughlin, O'Keefe & O'Keefe 1996) speak to the underlying reasoning for championing the education of the whole child.

> The Second Vatican Council emphasized that part of the continuing mission of the Catholic school was to teach faith and morals. Prevalent in the mission statements of Catholic schools is the phrase "education of the whole person." A Catholic education today stresses that each person, no matter how rich or poor, no matter how academically gifted or challenged, no matter what one's national heritage nor what color of the spectrum is one's skin, all are equal in the eyes of God. Each student has dignity and worth; because each one is a "person-in-community." (Bryk et al.,1996, p. 33)

The Catholic school seeks to support the development of the whole child by influencing not only what students know, but also what kind of people they will become. This is the responsibility of every faculty member on staff (Denig & Dosen, 2009).

Steeped in a Catholic Worldview

The curriculum of Catholic schooling, whether in primary school or graduate school, must show the connection between an individual area of study and the believer's faith life. It is important to realize that many of history's greatest scientists, artists, and literati were believers and that their beliefs were integrated into their faith. If one believes that truth is a universal, then truth must somehow be united. There cannot be a separate scientific truth and a different religious truth. This bifurcation of truth occurred as the result of a post-Enlightenment philosophy that limited truth solely to the observable, and cut out the possibility that there could be a universal Truth.

The curriculum of Catholic schooling cannot be limited to a secularist curricular approach that might allow for religious education as a discrete disciplinary study that is one of many possibilities but is not allowed to appropriately permeate and inform other areas of study. Rather, Catholic schooling seeks to "find God in all things." What are the moral implications of Shakespeare's great plays? The Catholic school teacher allows the budding scientist to marvel at the beauty of creation while observing the heavens through a telescope or watching cells divide and grow under the microscope. It is seeing the mirror of the perfection of God in mathematical precision and learning how unique yet similar peoples of different nations are through the study of foreign language and social studies. Catholic education is about the integration of faith and life, faith and knowledge. It truly is finding God in all things.

A wonderful text that speaks to this issue at the undergraduate level is *Teaching the Tradition: Catholic Themes in Academic Disciplines* (Piderit & Morey, 2012). While this work engages the academic disciplines of undergraduate and professional school programs, the examples that individual authors present in their particular disciplines can provide insight to both middle school and secondary school teachers in varied disciplines.

Accessible to All Students

The question of the accessibility of Catholic Education to all students is a multifaceted issue. Over the years we have not always been as accessible as other schools. In some cases, we have, quite legitimately, denied children access because we were unable to meet their particular needs. The conversation has now turned from our not being able to meet these needs to how might we meet their needs. A second issue is whether or not we would accept non-Catholic children into Catholic schools. There has been a level of belief that Catholic schools are for Catholic children only. However, we have invited non-Catholic children and their families to join our school communities from the earliest days. In a blog from the Archdiocese of Washington DC, Deacon Curt Turner wrote,

> "We don't teach them because THEY are Catholic; we teach them because WE are!" I have heard this quote attributed to the former Archbishop of Washington, James Cardinal Hickey. Apparently, this was the Cardinal's response to a question of why Catholics should support a Catholic school that doesn't have many Catholics among its student body. (Turner, 2014, n.p.)

If the mission of the Catholic school is evangelization, then we must be ready and willing to invite others to hear the *good news* as it is proclaimed in Catholic schools at every level.

The reputation of Catholic schools at one point in our history was similar to the reputation of charter and magnet schools today. Their opinion of Catholic schooling was that they took the qualified and left the lower-achieving students to the public system. In an era prior to Public Law (PL) 94-142, each school attempted to teach students as best they could and disqualified others from attending schools because their disabilities were such that the schools could not offer them anything. This changed in 1975 with PL 94-142. States received grants to provide a free and appropriate public education for all students with disabilities (Pierangelo & Giuliani, 2007). At this point in educational history, special education programming expanded, and Catholic schools who believed they had children who qualified for special education recommended that students attend the local public school.

Catholic schools have made use of the resources that came from Title I (US DOE, 2014) for a variety of remedial and tutorial programs for low income and low achieving students prior to this time, and they continue to do so. Unfortunately, many times the classroom in which the public school

Title I teacher works is by law mandated to be stripped of its religious symbols, such as crucifixes.

In the past decade, Catholic schools have begun developing special education programming, if not in each school, perhaps regionally, to serve the needs of all children in a Catholic school environment. While Title I funding and teachers continue to be a part of the landscape of Catholic schools, slowly a new day is beginning to dawn in terms of a more full inclusion in Catholic schools.

In the end, one needs to ask, why is it important for us to envision Catholic schools as accessible to all students? It is not about a marketing strategy for increasing enrollments, but rather what Catholics believe about the human person. Catholics believe that humans are made in the image and likeness of God. Therefore, if we believe that humans are made in the image and likeness of God, then these images of God are to be treated with reverence and respect. Groome (1996) reflects that Catholic education, in light of who we are as human beings, must reflect and promote three commitments:

- To affirm students' basic goodness, to promote their dignity, to honor their fundamental rights, and to develop their gifts to the fullest—as *God's reflection.*
- To educate people to live responsibly, with God's help for the fullness of life that God wills for self and others—*as responsible partners.*
- To convince and mold people to live as if their lives are worthwhile and have historical significance, that their every good effort advances the well-being of all—*as history makers.* (p. 111)

Catholics believe in the innate goodness of humanity, but are realistic in their understanding of the effects of sin. The lives of Catholic Christians are spent in the hope that good conquers evil in Christ.

CONCLUDING THOUGHTS

The mission and identity of Catholic schooling is formidable. The Catholic school community is called to live and proclaim the Gospel in the midst of a world that increasingly proclaims other values. McLaughlin (1996) identifies three issues that need to be examined in terms of tending the identity and mission of the Catholic school:

1. What is the true content of religious education in Catholic schools? Have school leaders and teachers whittled away the dogmatic side of the coin?

2. There are a wide range of views regarding various elements of Catholic faith. What is truly a matter of faith and what is not? How do we go about teaching those things that are not agreed upon by all Catholics?
3. Do we have enough teachers who will be good role models of Catholic virtues and values?

These are the knotty questions that Catholic school leaders, as faith leaders, must engage and work through with their faculties and other constituencies. If Catholic school leaders do not spend time on these issues, they might have a very nice school, but will it be Catholic?

NOTES

1. All Scripture references in this chapter taken from New American Bible, revised edition. (2010). Washington, DC: Confraternity of Christian Doctrine, Inc.
2. This saying is ascribed to St. Ignatius of Loyola, founder of the Jesuits.

REFERENCES

Beal, J., Coriden, J., & Green T. (2000). *New commentary on the code of canon law.* New York, NY: Paulist Press.

Bryk, A. (1996). Lessons from Catholic high schools on renewing our educational institutions. In McLaughlin, T., O'Keefe, J. & O'Keefe, B. (Eds.), *The contemporary Catholic school: Context, identity and diversity* (pp. 25–41). London, England: Falmer Press.

Bryk, A., Lee, V., & Holland, P. (1993). *Catholic schools and the common good.* Cambridge, MA: Harvard University Press.

Buetow, H. (1988). *The Catholic school: Its roots, identity, and future.* New York, NY: Crossroad.

Denig, S., & Dosen, A. (2009). The mission of the Catholic School in the pre-Vatican II era (1810–1962) and the Post-Vatican II Era (1965–1995): Insights and observations for the new millennium. *Journal of Catholic Education, 13*(2). Retrieved from http://digitalcommons.lmu.edu/ce/vol13/iss2/2

Dewey, J. (1990). *The school and society. The child and the curriculum.* Chicago, IL: University of Chicago Press. (Original work published 1915)

Dosen, A. (2009). *Catholic higher education in the 1960s: Issues of identity, issues of governance.* Charlotte, NC: Information Age.

Heft, J. (1991). Catholic identity and the future of Catholic schools. In *Catholic schools for the 21st century: The Catholic identity of Catholic schools.* Washington, DC: National Catholic Education Association.

Groome, T. (1996). What makes a school Catholic? In T. McLaughlin, J. O'Keefe, & B. O'Keeffe (Eds.), *The contemporary Catholic school: Context, identity and diversity* (pp. 107–125). London, England: Falmer Press.

McLaughlin, T. (1996). The distinctiveness of Catholic education. In T. McLaughlin, J. O'Keefe, & B. O'Keeffe (Eds.), *The contemporary Catholic school: Context, identity and diversity* (pp. 136–154). London, England: Falmer Press.

National Conference of Catholic Bishops. (1973). *To teach as Jesus did*. Washington, DC: U.S. Catholic Conference.

National Standards and Benchmarks for Effective Catholic Elementary and Secondary Schools. (2012). Retrieved from www.catholicschoolstandards.org

Piderit, J., & Morey, M. (2012). *Teaching the tradition: Catholic themes in academic disciplines*. New York, NY: Oxford University Press.

Pierangelo, R., & Giuliani, G. (2007). *Special education eligibility*. Thousand Oaks, CA: Corwin Press.

Reck, C. (1991). Catholic identity. In *Catholic schools for the 21st century: The Catholic identity of Catholic schools*. Washington, DC: National Catholic Education Association.

Scanlan, M. (2008). The grammar of Catholic schooling and radically "Catholic" schools. *Journal of Catholic Education, 12*(1). Retrieved from http://digitalcommons.lmu.edu/ce/vol12/iss1/8

Turner, C. (2014). We don't teach them because they are Catholic. Retrieved from http://blog.adw.org/2010/04/we-don%E2%80%99t-teach-them-because-they-are-catholic-we-teach-them-because-we-are/

U.S. DOE. (2014). Improving basic programs operated by local educational agencies, Title I. Retrieved from http://www2.ed.gov/programs/titleiparta/index.html

Whetten, D., & Godfrey, P. (Eds.). (1998). *Identity in organizations: Building theory through conversations*. Thousand Oaks, CA: Sage Publications.

Yukl, G., & Lepsinger, R. (2005). Improving performance through flexible leadership. *Leadership in Action* (March/April, 2005) cited in *Roundtable Viewpoints: Organizational Leadership*. Munro, J (ed.). Dubuque, IA: McGraw-Hill Company, 2008.

RECOMMENDATIONS FOR FURTHER READING

Dewey, J. (1990). *The school and society. The child and the curriculum*. Chicago, IL: University of Chicago Press. (Original work published 1915)

McLaughlin, T., O'Keefe, J, & O'Keeffe, B. (Eds.). (1996). *The contemporary Catholic school: Context, identity and diversity*. London, UK: Falmer Press.

National Conference of Catholic Bishops. (1973). *To teach as Jesus did*. Washington, DC: U.S. Catholic Conference.

National Standards and Benchmarks for Effective Catholic Elementary and Secondary Schools (2012). Retrieved from www.catholicschoolstandards.org

Piderit, J., & Morey, M. (2012). *Teaching the tradition: Catholic themes in academic disciplines*. New York, NY: Oxford University Press.

CHAPTER 3

UNTANGLING THE STRUCTURE OF CATHOLIC SCHOOLS

Anthony J. Dosen

INTRODUCTION

One of the most difficult questions for new principals in Catholic schools is "Who do I report to, and when do I report to them?" Catholic education is often spoken of as the largest system of education in the United States after the public school system. But the question remains, is Pre-K–12 Catholic education really a system, or is it rather a loose confederation? In a world of diocesan superintendents, school boards, boards of directors, diocesan bishops, pastors of parishes, and superiors of religious congregations that sponsor elementary and secondary schools, one is left with a maze of "bosses." So, the question remains, to whom does the principal report? The goal of this chapter is to look at the structure of Catholic schooling in the United States and to untangle the knots so as to get a clearer picture of the lines of authority in Catholic schools.

Catholic School Leadership, pages 35–48
Copyright © 2016 by Information Age Publishing

CATHOLIC SCHOOLS AND CANON LAW

In order to clearly understand the governance of Catholic schools, it is helpful to look to the Church's law, also known as Canon Law, in order to understand how the Church understands Catholic schooling and what types of regulations and responsibilities are placed upon all types of Catholic schools.

The primary principle in Catholic education is that the parents are the primary teachers of their children. Parents are reminded of this responsibility during the introductory rites of the Sacrament of Baptism. Canon Law states:

> §1. Parents and those who take their place are bound by the obligation and possess the right of educating their offspring. Catholic parents also have the duty and right of choosing those means and institutions through which they can provide more suitably for the Catholic education of their children, according to local circumstances. (Canon 793)

In the next canon, the Church affirms its duty and right of educating as a part of the "divinely entrusted" mission of the Church. The duty of implementing Catholic educational institutions and programs rests with pastors.

> §2. Pastors of souls have the duty of arranging everything so that all the faithful have a Catholic education. (Canon 794)

The primary responsibility of arranging Catholic education assigned to pastors of souls falls primarily to bishops and parish priests. It is their duty to implement a plan of Catholic education for all the faithful. Reciprocally, it is the responsibility of the faithful to assist pastors in this task by being supportive in their promotion of these programs and serving as coordinators of the Church's efforts.

As has already been expressed in Chapter 2 of this text, the goal of a Catholic education is to provide a holistic education of each individual. In Canon 795, this is clearly explicated:

> Since true education must strive for complete formation of the human person that looks to his or her final end as well as to the common good of societies, children and youth are to be nurtured in such a way that they are able to develop their physical, moral, and intellectual talents harmoniously, acquire a more perfect sense of responsibility and right use of freedom, and are formed to participate actively in social life. (Canon 795)

These canons provide a background that describes the rights and responsibilities of parents, pastors, and those who are engaged in the work of the school. It is the right and responsibility of the parents, as the first teachers of their child, to provide their children with education in the faith. It is the right and responsibility of pastors, both bishops and priests, to provide adequate assistance in the form of schools and programming so that the teaching mission of the Church may be available to the faithful. Finally, it is the responsibility of all who are employed in Catholic education, clerics, religious and laity, to see that students receive a truly holistic education that prepares them as both Christians and citizens who are capable of discerning and acting in the name of the common good.

Canonically, a school can be called *Catholic* when the following criteria are met:

§1. A Catholic school is understood as one which a competent ecclesiastical authority or a public ecclesiastical juridic person directs or which ecclesiastical authority recognizes as such through a written document.

§2. The instruction and education in a Catholic school must be grounded in the principles of Catholic doctrine; teachers are to be outstanding in correct doctrine and integrity of life.

§3. Even if it is in fact Catholic, no school is to bear the name *Catholic school* without the consent of the competent ecclesiastical authority. (Canon 803)

The first point states that a Catholic school must be under the direction of competent ecclesiastical authority (the diocesan bishop or by extension the parish priest) or a juridic person. The term *juridic person* can be a difficult one to understand. According to Canon Law,

A juridic person . . . is an artificial person, distinct from all natural persons or material goods, constituted by competent ecclesiastical authority for an apostolic purpose, with a capacity for continuous existence and with canonical rights and duties like those of a natural person (e.g., to own property, enter into contracts, sue or be sued) conferred upon it by law or by the authority which constitutes it. Like a civil-law corporation, it is a legal construct which can and must be conceived of apart from the natural persons who constitute it, administer it, or for whose benefit it exists. (Kennedy, 2000, p. 154)

It might be easier to state what a juridic person is not. A juridic person is not a real person; rather, it must be looked at more as a corporation. For example, religious communities would be an excellent example of a juridic person. The juridic person is the community, not its provincial superior or the local superior. So, Catholic schools are either under the direction of the diocesan bishop, as is the case with diocesan high schools; the parish priest, as is the case with parochial schools; or under the direction of a recognized religious community, such as the Franciscans, Jesuits, Vincentians, or

Daughters of Charity. Alternatively, a diocesan bishop can declare a Catholic school run under the direction of the laity as a Catholic school by a written declaration to that effect.

Again, as has already been discussed in Chapter 2, Catholic schools must be grounded in Catholic doctrine. A Catholic school cannot ignore doctrine in its educational programming. Catholic doctrine must undergird the curriculum. Doctrine must be a concern not just for the principal, but for the teachers as well. All who minister in a Catholic school must proclaim the Gospel, not only in word, but also in the manner of their life. Finally, a Catholic school, even if it has a solid curriculum steeped in Catholic doctrine and faithful Catholic teachers, cannot be considered Catholic unless the diocesan bishop declares it so. The diocesan bishop is the sole arbiter of what is Catholic in his diocese, and his approval is essential for a school to be declared a *Catholic school.*

The remainder of the canons in the section on schooling speaks to the bishop's and parish priests' obligation to be attentive to the work of the Catholic schools entrusted to their care. This means that they should be attentive that all Catholics are able to avail themselves of the church's aid in receiving a Catholic education—whether in a Catholic school or through other types of programming—and that they should be especially attentive to the needs of the people in their territory and offer appropriate educational programing to meet their particular needs. It is significant to note that this type of appropriate programming includes not only elementary and secondary schools and religious education programs, but also technical schools and other types of schooling.

CIVIL LAW AND THE CATHOLIC SCHOOL

The state requires that all children attend school. The precedent for mandatory school attendance finds its origin in the common law doctrine of *parens patriae,* which describes the state as the "father of all persons." That is, the state is responsible for the welfare of both the commonwealth and individual citizens.

> Few cases have defined "private school" as used in compulsory attendance laws. Precise definition is lacking perhaps partly because in several jurisdictions children are not required to attend either public or private schools but must obtain "equivalent instruction." Although vaguely defining the term "equivalent" as meaning "equal," the court generally refers to the qualifications of the instructor and the available teaching materials as the primary criteria for determining equivalency of instruction. (Alexander & Alexander, 1985, p. 219)

Therefore, the state does have authority to determine whether a private school, religious or otherwise, meets the criteria of a school that is considered *equivalent* to the public schools in the state. This in part explains why the state board of education sends out evaluation teams to private elementary and secondary schools to examine academic and health records of students, to certify the qualifications of teachers, and to assess the safety of the physical plant.

In the 1920s, the state of Oregon legislated that all children between the ages of eight and sixteen were required to attend public schools. This was seen as an attempt to block private school attendance, including religious schools. A suit was brought against the state by the Society of Sisters of the Holy Names of Jesus and Mary, who ran a Catholic school and Hill Military Academy. It seems that the legislation was an attempt on the part of the state to regulate potential inclusion of Bolshevism and communism into the curriculum. The suit did not challenge the state's power

> [t]o reasonably regulate, inspect, supervise, and examine all schools, teachers, and pupils and to see that nothing was taught that was inimical to the public welfare.... In ruling in the plaintiffs' favor, in *Pierce*, the United States Supreme Court decided the case on the grounds that the state cannot, through improper regulation, deprive a business corporation of its patrons or customers. The law deprived the corporations of a liberty protected by the Fourteenth Amendment, according to the court. (Alexander & Alexander, 1985, p. 220)

While neither parents nor children were appellants in this particular case, the Court did go on to reaffirm the rights of both the parent and the child:

> The fundamental theory of liberty upon which all governments in this union repose excludes any general power of the state to standardize its children by forcing them to accept instruction from public teachers only. The child is not the mere creature of the state; those who nurture him and direct his destiny have the right, coupled with the high duty to recognize and prepare him for additional obligations. (*Pierce v. Society of Sisters,* in Alexander & Alexander, 1985, p. 220)

Thus the Supreme Court, while not asked to rule on the issue, reaffirmed the right of parents to choose the type of education their child would receive.

THE ORGANIZATION OF CATHOLIC SCHOOLING
AT THE DIOCESAN LEVEL

Since the diocesan bishop, as the chief pastor, is responsible for education in his diocese, it is logical that most dioceses would have some sort of office for education. Depending upon the diocese, this office is organized in different ways. In some dioceses, all of the educational ministries, including Catholic schools, of the diocese fall under one person, either a vicar or secretary for education. In other cases, there is a superintendent of Catholic schools who is responsible for all of the Catholic schools within the diocese. The other model is the diocesan director of religious education, who is responsible for all of the catechetical programming in the diocese both in parish programs and in the Catholic schools (McDonald & Schultz, 2013). The mandate for each of these positions differs from one another. The largest umbrella is that of the secretary (or vicar) of education. This position requires the holder to oversee all educational programming at the diocesan level. It serves as an umbrella position that includes Catholic schools, parish religious education programming, adult education, and any other educational initiatives that a diocese is undertaking. By contrast, the positions of superintendent of schools and diocesan director of religious education have a much more limited scope. The superintendent is responsible solely for the Catholic schools of the diocese and serves in a manner similar to the superintendent of a public school district, with some very clear distinctions. Similarly, the diocesan director of religious education is responsible for supervising and assisting parish programs of religious education, as well as school catechetical programs.

A major distinction between most Catholic diocesan offices of education and the central offices of public school districts is in the number of personnel in their respective offices. According to McDonald and Schultz (2013), 16 diocesan education offices are staffed by the superintendent with no other personnel in the office, while another 50 are staffed by the superintendent and one support person. Even one of the largest of the diocesan offices of Catholic schools, the Archdiocese of Chicago (2012), has approximately 34 staff members, including the superintendent and associate superintendent. The archdiocese comprises all of Cook and Lake Counties in Illinois. In contrast, Chicago Public Schools, which services only the city of Chicago has 14 members on its leadership team at the district office and a total of 1,558 staff members in central/regional offices (Chicago Public Schools, 2014).

Catholic superintendents, as a group, found that the three issues that require the greatest amount of attention from their office are articulation of the mission, professional development, and leadership formation. The issues that ran closely behind these top three were issues of curriculum and personnel issues (Cattaro & McDonald, 2010).

The work of Catholic school superintendents is different from that of their peers in the public school districts. While public school superintendents have authority to make personnel decisions, in terms of hiring and firing, Catholic school superintendents ordinarily do not share that authority.

In the case of parochial schools, the authority to hire and fire is handed over to the pastor of the parish, or alternatively in other Catholic schools it is the responsibility of either the board or the sponsoring congregation. In some dioceses, authority over personnel is assigned to the superintendent by the bishop, but the norm seems to be either the pastor or the school's sponsoring congregation.

The work of the Catholic school superintendent can be viewed primarily as mission related and coordinating policies and programs. The superintendent offers advice to individual schools and their leaders, but in the end, the individual school is left to make its own decisions. In exceptionally difficult and critical situations, the superintendent may intervene in disputes that arise between boards and administrators, or pastors and principals. The superintendent's role is also to broker arrangements for federal funding dollars that should, by law, come to the Catholic schools in their diocese. In larger public school districts, the clout of the superintendent of Catholic schools can free resources where the principal in an individual school may be unable to penetrate the walls of bureaucracy. An integral part of the superintendent's role is to provide the schools of the diocese with information concerning trends in education and to coordinate a common set of goals in addressing these trends.

The Catholic superintendent's role is tending the big picture. The day-in, day-out running of Catholic schools and their supervision is left to individual principals and their administrative teams in those schools that have a leadership team. Thus, while the superintendent is responsible for vision and coordination, the individual principal has responsibility and authority to administer the individual school in ways that best meet the needs of the particular situation. In this sense, Catholic schools have been practicing site-based management long before it ever became popular.

ADMINISTERING THE INDIVIDUAL CATHOLIC SCHOOL

There is a scene from the movie *Blazing Saddles* that aptly describes the nature of the site-based approach of Catholic school management. In this particular scene, the future sheriff of Rock Ridge is heading west at the end of a long wagon train. When the Native Americans attack the wagon train, the other wagons circle. However, the wagon containing the young Bart's family is not allowed into the midst of the circling wagons, so they take their lone wagon and ride in a circle by themselves! This, to my mind, is an apt image of Catholic schooling. We are each in our own wagon, but when difficulties come, we each circle our own wagon, and do not join the others in the protective circling of the wagons.

Individual Catholic schools need to look beyond the short-term competition for student enrollment and begin to look for ways that we might support one another. Oftentimes it is easy to allow another school to be out on their own, while each of us quietly thank God that it is not us in this situation, and yet we are a little fearful that the next crisis will hit closer to home. Collaboration among Catholic schools in the diocese or a given area is the way to success.

A SHORT HISTORY OF ORGANIZATIONAL MODELS FOR CATHOLIC SCHOOLS

The traditional model of Catholic schooling, beginning in the 19th century, is the parochial school model. The structure consisted of a parish school consisting of grades 1–8, and occasionally grades 1–12, under the direction of a community of religious sisters, with one sister serving as principal—and occasionally serving as a teacher as well. The school, as everything else in the parish, was supervised by the pastor. The system was self-sustaining for many years, even during the most tumultuous times in 19th and 20th century history, only to be a victim of its own success in the decades after the Second Vatican Council. As the number of children in schools expanded in the years after the Second World War, the number of sisters, brothers, and priests who taught in schools could not keep up with the skyrocketing enrollments (see Chapter 4). After the Council, and in the midst of the uncertainty that it engendered, there was an exodus of religious and priests from their vocations. This exodus, along with the decreasing numbers of students as the baby boom subsided, found many Catholic classrooms only partially filled, and more lay teachers were hired to take the place of sisters, brothers and priests who were no longer available to teach in the schools. Thus, the old system of the parochial school began its decline. Parishes were no longer able to subsidize parish schools given the increase in costs and the decrease in tuition revenues brought about by fewer students enrolling in Catholic schools. Thus it was inevitable that schools began closing.

The earliest attempts at solving the fiscal and enrollment crises was to combine parish schools; thus, one building would be used rather than two, and there would be sufficient students to fill the classrooms. In these earlier attempts, the parish community, whose campus was shuttered, behaved as if the school had been closed and not combined. Most of the families from the shuttered school sent their children to places other than the newly formatted school. To add to the confusion, pastors of the parishes where the school was combined began to take on the role of landlord, rather than pastor. They did not see their role as being a support to the educational program—especially from a financial point of view. Similarly, their colleagues who had shuttered their school saw their role in Catholic education as no longer required. Therefore, the parish staffs seemed to back away from the new multi-school campus (personal conversation, 1999).

From these earliest attempts at reconfiguration of parish schools developed a number of new approaches to school configuration and governance. Haney (2010) outlines several models that received an award from the National Catholic Education Association's SPICE (Select Programs for Improving Catholic Education) program. Among these reconfigurations were models in which groups of parish schools were organized into a regional configuration, administered by a single administrative body. The new system is civilly incorporated but linked under the diocese. The schools are separated from the individual parishes and seen as a new entity. The parishes maintain the pastoral care for the system. The parochial school (parish school) is still alive, but in many cases suffering, primarily from financial strain. However, other models of schooling have shown promise. Haney (2010) highlights models of reconfiguration that include both elementary and secondary schools into a geographic system that is supported by all the parishes in the area (e.g., Chippewa Area Catholic Schools and Risen Christ Catholic School) or are supported by the diocese (St. Augustine Schools).

GOVERNANCE IN CATHOLIC SCHOOLS

The governance structure of Catholic schools before the Second Vatican Council most often was limited to the collaboration of the sister principal and pastor of the parish. The pastor, being the *juridic person*, had the final say in school matters, as in all other pastoral matters. Oftentimes, the pastor and/or principal would seek the advice and input of parents through PTA types of programming. In time, both Catholic elementary and secondary schools moved toward the foundation of school boards. Fr. O'Neil D'Amour, superintendent of Catholic schools in Marquette, Michigan from 1954 until his death in 1968, is considered the founder of Catholic school boards (Hunt, 2004). Seeing the school board as a viable way of professionalizing Catholic education in the second half of the 20th century, he pushed for boards in every Catholic school in the country, believing that by the 1970s over 90% of Catholic schools would be run by school boards. While his dream never became a reality on the timeline that he had set, school boards have become a part of the life of Catholic schools, whether the school is parochial, diocesan, or private.

There are three categories of boards: advisory, consultative, and limited jurisdiction (Haney, 2010).

Advisory. An advisory board is a body that participates in the decision-making process by formulating, adapting, and recommending policy to the person with authority to enact it. The authority does not have to accept the board's advice.

Consultative. A consultative board is a body that participates in the policy-making process by formulating, adapting, and recommending policy to the person with authority to enact it. The person with authority is required to consult the board before making decisions in designated areas, but is not bound by the board's advice.

Limited Jurisdiction. A board with limited jurisdiction, also called a policy-making board, is a body that participates in the policy-making process by formulating, adapting, and enacting policy. The board has been delegated final authority to enact policy regarding certain areas of institutional operation, although its jurisdiction is limited to those areas of operation that have been delegated to it by the constitution and/or bylaws and approved by the delegating Church authority. (Haney, O'Brien, & Sheehan, 2009, pp. 69–70 in Haney, 2010, p. 200)

In each of these board structures, the authority of the diocesan bishop or *juridic person*, whether pastor or religious community, is upheld. In the first case, the *advisory board* has the sole mandate of offering advice. This advice does not have to be sought after. The head of the school, whether diocesan bishop, pastor, or religious congregation, is free to exercise authority over the school; however, it has the advisory board as a body that offers advice, if it is desired. In the case of the *consultative board*, the authority that has jurisdiction over the school has a limited responsibility to seek consultation on particular matters. Seeking consultation, however, does not mean that the authority must follow this advice. The *board of limited jurisdiction* has authority to make policy decisions within a specified range of issues. The nature of these decisions is outlined in a document known as the board's *bylaws*. The board of limited jurisdiction comes closest to the image that Fr. O'Neil D'Amour contemplated about school boards in the 1960s.

In each case, the rights of the diocesan bishop, his delegate, the local pastor, or the juridic person are upheld. In the case of the board of limited jurisdiction, the authority of the diocesan bishop/juridic person is maintained in those areas which are of primary importance—that is, faith and morals. In other areas of governance, they share authority with members of the board.

The school board has taken on new responsibilities, such as development activities, building and grounds maintenance, enrollment activities, and long term planning. In order for boards to be effective, they need to recruit board members with a rich diversity of gifts. While earlier school boards were made up of a committee of parents with children in school, the contemporary board is made up of a diverse group of individuals with various skill and talent sets. The recruitment net is cast wider, looking for expertise in finance, maintenance, marketing, fundraising, and educational issues. A board is only as strong as its membership. Therefore, board membership needs to expand into, if not beyond, the local community.

THE PRESIDENT–PRINCIPAL MODEL
IN SECONDARY SCHOOLS

The rule, rather than the exception, states that Catholic secondary schools are led by a team of a president and a principal. This model is fairly new, making its appearance in the late 1980s. "The President/Principal model represents an evolutionary change in Catholic secondary school administration from a 'mom and pop' organizational structure to a 'professional bureaucracy'" (James & Vercruysse, 2005, p. ix). The model mirrors the administrative model of the small college. The president is seen as the presiding officer and the external face of the institution, while the principal serves in the role of provost or academic dean with responsibilities for the academic and extracurricular programming. Both share responsibility for the identity and ethos of the school.

Br. William Dygert (2000) conducted a survey of Catholic secondary schools that employed the president–principal model. Dygert surveyed presidents and principals in Catholic secondary schools in 1997. A total of 358 surveys were distributed, 179 to presidents and 179 to principals. The return rate was 60%, with a total of 57% (204) able to be used (110 presidents and 94 principals).

When asked why the president–principal model came into being, the group responded (in rank order of importance): development and fundraising (97%); to enable the principal to be the instructional leader (92%); and public relations (89%) (Dygert, 2000, p. 18). Respondents clearly described the roles of president and principal and assigned both a number of important shared roles (see Table 3.1). The underlying reason for moving toward the president–principal model was the exponential increase in the principal's responsibilities that developed in the two decades after the Second Vatican Council. The head of school was responsible not only for the education of students, but also for the financial stability of the school, public relations, enrollment management, and fund raising, along with any and all programs and facilities related to the school. The job simply became too complex for one person.

As one looks at the job descriptions of presidents and principals, several factors become quite clear. The president is the external face of the school, while the principal presides over all of the academic and extracurricular programming. The president handles all matters that are not

TABLE 3.1 Principal Roles of President and Principal

President's Role	Principal's Role	Shared Role
Development	Inside person/day-to-day operations	Spiritual leadership
Executive for School Board	Educational/Academic leadership	Personnel Management
Outside person/overall responsibility		Institutional Management
Chief Spokesperson		Maintain identity of religious order
Business/Financial management		Board policy implementation
Board Policy Development		

directly related to the academic programs and student life, such as physical plant, fundraising, alumni relations, and budgeting, to name but a few of the tasks. The president and principal share responsibility for the mission of the Catholic school the school's climate, strategic planning, and facilities scheduling (Dygert, 2000).

One who chooses to take the position of principal, or president for that matter, in the president–principal model must be aware of the parameters of the job description for the particular position for which they are applying. The task descriptions listed in Table 3.1 are generalizations of the nature of the position. It is critical that a candidate for a leadership position at the high school level carefully examine the job description for the position for which she is applying. Are you comfortable with the responsibilities that are listed? More importantly, are you able to share authority with another individual? The president–principal model is only as successful as the two individuals who hold the positions are able to collaborate. Dygert (2000) found, "The three conditions which respondents almost unanimously agreed are very important to the success of the model, that is, mutual trust and respect, a spirit of cooperation and collaboration, and compatible educational philosophies and values" (p. 29).

If one wishes to be successful in a president–principal model setting, the parties need to trust one another. If one party or the other has questions about whether or not he can trust the other, then it is better not to take the position (or hire the individual for the open position). While the president and principal may have different strengths and talents and differing tasks, they must have similar philosophical perspectives and values, for the work of leading a school is built upon this foundation.

SOME CONCLUDING THOUGHTS

Catholic schools are an important component of the Catholic Church's universal mission. As was stated in Chapter 2, they are centers of evangelization and serve as a special Christian community within the context of parish communities. The specialness of the school is not that it is preferential, but rather that it becomes a distinct community with particular obligations under both Church and civil law. The diocesan bishop has authority over Catholic schools (see Canon 803 above) in his role as the chief teacher of the diocese. Principals of Catholic schools must be collaborative with both diocesan and parish administrators, especially among the clergy. The ecclesial goals of Catholic schooling can be achieved only by a collaborative effort among all parties: school administration, faculty, parents, parish priests, and the diocesan administration.

This collaboration must extend to members of the various boards that serve as a governing body of the school. The reason these individuals join the board is their interest in the success of the school. We must envision each of these individuals as potential partners who will share in the struggle and joy of the school's journey. Finally, although not spoken of in the context of governance, the administration of the Catholic school must be attentive to the local community in which it lives and serves. How can the school serve its local community?

The governance task is to create the best school for the children under our care and those who will come after them. Greenleaf (1977), in his book, *Servant Leadership*, sees the institution (in particular, churches, universities, and businesses) as servant:

> This is my thesis: caring for persons, the more able and the less able serving each other, is the rock upon which a good society is built. Whereas, until recently, caring was largely person to person, now most of it is mediated through institutions— often large, complex, powerful, impersonal, not always competent, sometimes corrupt. If a better society is to be built, one that is more just and more loving, one that provides greater creative opportunity for its people, then the most open course is to *raise both the capacity to serve and the very performance as servant* of existing major institutions by new regenerative forces operating within them. (p. 49)

Leaders are called to remember why their organization exists: to serve the children of our community. In the end, it is not about an individual's power base or career trajectory; it is about being the servant of the other.

REFERENCES

Alexander, K., & Alexander, M. D. (1985). *American public school law* (2nd ed.). St. Paul, MN: West Publishing Company.

Archdiocese of Chicago. (2012). *Official directory of the Archdiocese of Chicago*. Chicago, IL: Author.

Canon law society of Great Britain. (1983). *Code of Canon Law*. Grand Rapids, MI.: Eerdmans.

Cattaro, G., & McDonald, D. (2010). *Diocesan educational administrative leadership survey 2009: A national profile of the Catholic superintendency*. Washington, DC: National Catholic Educational Association.

Chicago Public Schools. (2014). Stats and Facts. Retrieved from http://cps.edu/About_CPS/At-a-glance/Pages/Stats_and_facts.aspx

Dygert, W. (2000). The president/principal model in Catholic secondary schools. *Journal of Catholic Education, 4*(1). Retrieved from http://digitalcommons.lmu.edu/ce/vol4/iss1/10

Greenleaf, R. K. (1977). *Servant leadership: A journey into the nature of legitimate power and greatness*. Mahwah, NJ: Paulist Press.

Haney, R. M. (2010) Design for success: New configurations and governance models for Catholic schools. *Journal of Catholic Education, 14*(2). Retrieved from http://digitalcommons.lmu.edu/ce/vol14/iss2/4

Haney, R., O'Brien, S., & Sheehan, L. M. (2009). *A primer on educational governance in the Catholic Church* (2nd ed.). Washington, DC: National Catholic Educational Association.

Hunt, T. C. (2004). D'Amour, O'Neil C. (1919–1968). In T. C. Hunt, J. A. Ellis & R. J. Nuzzi (Eds.). *Catholic schools in the United States: An encyclopedia* (Vol. I, pp. 209–210). Westport, CT: Greenwood Press.

James, J. T., & Vercruysse, R. J. (2005). *Development of the president principal model in Catholic high schools*. Washington, DC: National Catholic Education Association.

Kennedy, R. (2000). Commentary on Chapter II Juridic Persons. In J. Beal, J. Coriden, & T. Green (Eds.), *New commentary on the code of Canon Law* (pp. 154–176). New York, NY: Paulist Press.

McDonald, D., & Schultz, M. (2013). *The Annual statistical report on schools, enrollment and staffing: United States Catholic elementary and secondary schools 2012–2013*. Washington, DC: National Catholic Educational Association.

RECOMMENDATIONS FOR FURTHER READING

Heft, J. L. (2011). *Catholic high schools: Facing the new realities*. New York, NY: Oxford University Press.

James, J. T., &. Vercruysse, R.T. (2005). *Development of the president principal model in Catholic high schools*. Washington, DC: National Catholic Education Association.

McCullough, M. K., Graf, V., Leung, B., Stroud, M., & Orlando, M. (2008). *Building community through school success teams*. Washington, DC: National Catholic Educational Association.

Shaughnessy, M. A. (2004). *Policy formation in Catholic education: A guide to legal issues*. Washington, DC: National Catholic Educational Association.

Sheehan, L. (1990. *Building better boards: A handbook for board members in Catholic education*. Washington, DC: National Catholic Education Association.

CHAPTER 4

CATHOLIC SCHOOLS BY THE NUMBERS

Anthony J. Dosen

VIGNETTE

Charlie is preparing for his first day of kindergarten at St. Edward's School, and his parents and grandparents are each reminiscing about their wonderful experiences of Catholic elementary school. Both sets of Charlie's grandparents were graduates of St. Edward's, as were his parents. Grandma Rossi recalled the gentleness of Sr. Mary Luke, who seemed like a giant to grandma as a kindergartener; she remembered Sr. Luke as a gentle giant. Grandpa Dijon said it was the sisters who made the Catholic school what it was. "There we were 40 fourth graders in front of Sr. Maria Goretti, and there was no horseplay. We knew *Sister was in charge!*" Charlie's parents spoke of their memories of Catholic schooling, such as service projects and all-school liturgies. They reminisced about teachers such as Ms. Jones, the science teacher, and Mr. Phillips, the religion teacher. They remembered Sr. Maria Goretti as the kindly sister who tutored each of them during their first grade year, but she was the only sister that was left teaching in the school. There were fewer students in school during Ron and Clara Rossi's elementary school years. Their classes averaged about 20 to 25 students. Luckily, St. Edward's has maintained an average of about 25 students per

Catholic School Leadership, pages 49–61
Copyright © 2016 by Information Age Publishing
All rights of reproduction in any form reserved.

classroom, and so Charlie will be entering into his Catholic grade school experience with both finger paints and computer technology. The only sister he may see during his first years in school will be in a religion textbook. My, how things have changed!

HOW HAS CATHOLIC SCHOOLING CHANGED?

Catholic schools, like other aspects of the Church, seem like they have been around forever. However, in reality, while some things remain the same, Catholic schools are very different from their earlier history. The driving force behind Catholic schools, communities of religious sisters, has diminished in the decades following the baby boom. The number of Catholic schools as well as the number of Catholic school students has diminished since the heyday of Catholic schooling in the first half of the 20th century.

The Catholic schools in the United States at the secondary and collegiate level were founded under the auspices of various religious communities. Many of these institutions began as seminaries that added programs for laymen as well. The lay colleges helped to support the seminary programs and made use of the advanced seminarians, who served as professors for the lay students. Beginning in 1727, the Ursuline Sisters opened a school for women in New Orleans. Later, other schools for women were founded by communities of sisters. These nascent institutions of higher education were populated with students who were better considered secondary level students. It was not until the beginning of the 20th century that the secondary programs were separated from the higher education programs (Hennesey, 1981).

Elementary education was primarily under the care of local parishes. Among the earliest systemic foundations of Catholic elementary schools were those founded by Bishops Hughes and Kenrick in their battles with public school officials over an overly Protestant approach to bible reading and anti-Catholic propaganda in the public schools. At the Third Plenary Council of Baltimore in 1884, the bishops called for every Catholic parish in the country to build a parish school, so that every Catholic child might have the opportunity to attend a Catholic school. The bishops' plan to create an alternative school system "was a dream never fulfilled, but in no other nation at any time in history has any non-governmental agency attempted the massive educational program begun in 19th-century America by Roman Catholics" (Hennesey, 1981, p. 107).

Parish elementary schools were staffed by an expansive number of communities of sisters. Many of these sisters were immigrants who came to the United States with the plan of ministering to their fellow nationals as they came to the New World; others came as missionaries to the wilds of the

United States, and several communities, such as the Sisters of Charity (St. Elizabeth Ann Seton) and the Sisters of Loretto were unique foundations of the American church to assist in its educational apostolate.

In the second surge of immigration from central and southern Europe at the end of the 19th century, the church continued to grow in numbers, and gradually in influence. By the 1920s, Catholic schools dotted the landscape of the nation. Tables 4.1 and 4.2 demonstrate the vicissitudes of enrollment in Catholic elementary and secondary schools, by decade, from the 1920s through the beginning of the 21st century.

The 1920s were an advantageous time for the Church. The end of the First World War brought with it a new era of American Catholic confidence,

TABLE 4.1   Number of Catholic Elementary Schools by Decade (McDonald & Schultz, 2013)

Year	Number of Catholic Elementary Schools	Difference From the Start of the Previous Decade	% Diff
1920	6551		
1930	7923	1372	20.9
1940	7944	21	0.3
1950	8589	645	8.1
1960	10501	1912	22.3
1970	9366	−1135	−10.8
1980	8100	−1266	−13.5
1990	7395	−705	−8.7
2000	6923	−472	−6.4
2010	5889	−1034	−15.0

TABLE 4.2   Number of Catholic Secondary Schools by Decade (McDonald & Schultz, 2013)

Year	Number of Catholic Secondary Schools	Difference From the Start of the Previous Decade	% Diff
1920	1552		
1930	2123	571	36.8
1940	2105	−18	−0.8
1950	2189	84	4.0
1960	2392	203	9.3
1970	1986	−406	−17.0
1980	1540	−446	−22.5
1990	1324	−216	−14.0
2000	1221	−103	−7.8
2010	1205	−16	−1.4

albeit in isolation. Hennesey (1981) depicts this confidence as a certitude that was grounded in what has been called the "Catholic ghetto."

> The American Catholic community throughout its many-layered being grew in self-assurance and acquired a sense of chosen-ness theretofore reserved in America for those with better Puritan credentials. If this resulted in isolation from one or another aspect of surrounding culture, or from the whole congeries, this was for Catholics a source of pride, rather than distress. (Hennesey, 1981, pp. 221–222)

The decade of the 1920s saw a 20.9% increase in the number of Catholic elementary schools built, as well as a 36.8% increase in the number of Catholic secondary schools. During the 1930s, in the midst of the Great Depression, Catholic elementary schools marked a very small increase (21 schools) and an equally small decrease (18 schools) of secondary schools. This speaks to the high priority that bishops, pastors, and laity placed on the value of Catholic education. The consistent work and self-sacrifice of religious women and men throughout the Depression were responsible for not only the survival, but the continued flowering of the Catholic school *system.*

The baby boom at the end of the Second World War saw a major expansion in the number of Catholic schools throughout the decades of the 1940s and 1950s. Enrollments at every level of Catholic education, from kindergarten through undergraduate education, expanded at the speed of light. Similarly, there were increases in the number of candidates entering both seminaries and religious institutes of men and women. Even with the increased numbers of novices in religious communities and the number of seminarians being ordained, the number of teaching positions expanded beyond the number of priests and religious available to cover them (Dosen, 2009). By 1960, over 25% of the teaching force in Catholic K–12 education was made up of members of the laity (McDonald & Schultz, 2013). From the end of the 1960s until today, the number of lay faculty members has increased exponentially from 26.2% to an overwhelming 96.8% in 2013 (see Tables 4.3 and 4.4).

As the number of students rose through the 1950s and early 1960s, despite record numbers of seminarians and aspirants to religious life, the number of priests and men and women religious could not keep up with the enrollment bubble of the post-World War II baby boom. By the end of the 1960s, younger and middle-aged religious sisters, brothers, and priests left their communities in record numbers. Similarly, the large ordination classes of the previous decade were decimated with resignations from ordained ministry. Replacing those religious and priests who had retired or resigned in the 1960s and 1970s became even more difficult as the number of aspirants and seminarians also decreased, causing what has become known as the *vocation crisis.* The sisters who remained in their communities

TABLE 4.3   Number of Religious and Lay Teachers in Catholic Schools by Decade (McDonald & Schultz, 2013)

Year	Number of Religious Teachers	Percentage of Teachers Who are Religious	Number of Lay Teachers	Percentage of Lay Teachers
1920	45563	92.0	3942	8.0
1930	65601	90.4	6951	9.6
1940	73960	91.2	7097	8.8
1950	84925	90.1	9370	9.9
1960	112029	73.8	39873	26.2
1970	80615	48.4	85873	51.6
1980	42732	29.0	104562	71.0
1990	20020	14.6	116880	85.4
2000	11011	7.0	146123	93.0
2010	5749	3.7	148567	96.3

TABLE 4.4   Number of Religious and Lay Teachers in Catholic Schools by Year (McDonald, 2006, 2007, 2008; McDonald & Schultz 2010, 2011, 2013)

Year	Number of Religious Teachers	Percentage of Teachers Who are Religious	Number of Lay Teachers	Percentage of Lay Teachers
2006	7153	4.7	145349	95.3
2007	7064	4.4	152071	95.6
2008	6594	4.1	153481	95.9
2010	5749	3.7	148567	96.3
2011	5568	3.7	145905	96.3
2013	4853	3.2	146552	96.8

were also given opportunities previously unavailable to serve in the capacity of various pastoral ministries outside of the educational and healthcare apostolates. These phenomena begin to explain why the number of religious men and women working in schools diminished so drastically between 1960 and 1970, while the number of students had not yet dropped as drastically. But then Catholic schools experienced a drop in student enrollment.

A second factor that is often not appreciated is that the baby boom ended by the mid-1970s, and there were fewer children of school age than there were a decade earlier. Large Catholic families that were a part of the earlier decades of the American church's existence were being replaced with smaller, one- to two-child families. Therefore, there were fewer children in the pool of potential candidates for Catholic education.

PAYING FOR CATHOLIC EDUCATION TODAY

These two factors led to the increases in tuition at Catholic schools. As the enrollments declined and the number of lay faculty increased, Catholic schools—which have traditionally been tuition driven—were required to raise the tuition fees for students. What was approximately $30 per year for elementary school tuition in 1959 increased to about $300 by 1970, and by 2007 it had increased to approximately $3,159 per year. The tuition dollars, even at the 2007 school year level, do not come close to covering the cost per student. Student costs during that year amounted to $5,870 per pupil. This means that on average the Catholic elementary school subsidizes each pupil in the amount of $2,711, or approximately 46.2% of the total cost per child (Bimonte, 2008, p. 4).

Where does the school find the extra income that provides for each student's actual cost of education? As seen in Figure 4.1, fundraising (11.1%) and endowment (17.4%) make up the bulk of the non-tuition income, with parish subsidies (7.7%) and other income—such as interest, scholarships, and money received from ancillary school programs (e.g., extended day programs, cafeteria fees) make up the remainder (Bimonte, 2008, p. 17).

While the averages that Bimonte (2008) shared are reasonable averages, the new principal of a Catholic school must understand how the income of her particular Catholic school is developed. For example, Catholic elementary schools, as well as some Catholic high schools, are parish-based. Thus, the parish subsidy might be slightly higher than the percentage suggested above. In some cases, the parish school might become a strain on the parish's overall budget. This is, perhaps, one of the major concerns of pastors who are called upon to lead parishes with a

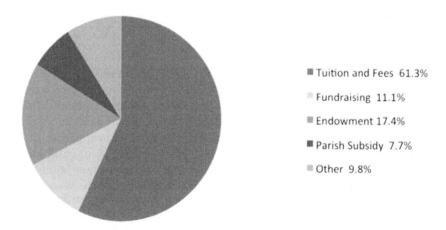

■ Tuition and Fees 61.3%

▨ Fundraising 11.1%

▦ Endowment 17.4%

■ Parish Subsidy 7.7%

▨ Other 9.8%

Figures 4.1   Catholic elementary school income from various sources.

parish school. Catholic high schools that are sponsored by religious communities do not have a parish community to help subsidize the parish school, and thus these schools must supplement their tuition income with a higher level of fundraising and endowment work. Those schools that are unable to do so often find themselves seeking funds from the sponsoring religious community. Over the years, religious communities funded these schools by the work of the members of their community who worked long hours for minimal pay and who took on other tasks, such as tutoring, piano lessons, and duties in local parishes in order to keep their school's tuition affordable. These same communities now seek to fund a number of works and support their retired members, with few younger religious entering their personnel pool. So if the community is asked to give funds, it will probably be a one-time gift, for the community's available funds may be minimal and they will be unable to support your high school. Whether one is a principal of a parochial elementary school or a private Catholic high school, the best financial advice one can offer is to wean your school off the parish or religious community's subsidy.

Looking at the expenses side of the school budget, the largest expense of the Catholic school remains salaries and benefits (62.7% salaries and 15.2% benefits), a total of 77.9% of the total budget (Figure 4.1). The remaining 22.1% of the budget is used for instructional materials, maintenance and repair, and other non-salary expenses (e.g., utilities, administrative costs, student services and activities). On average, the salaries of the highest-paid teachers in Catholic schools are approximately 26.2% less than their public school peers. This is a reality of which the reader is undoubtedly very much aware. While this percentage of difference might disappoint some Catholic school teachers, for savvy administrators it is a sign of teacher commitment to the mission. It is also a source for refuting those who say that the percentage of money spent on salaries is too high.

SO WHY ARE NUMBERS SO IMPORTANT?

Throughout this chapter, the reader has been presented all sorts of numbers: enrollment statistics over time, statistical descriptions of the number of teachers and administrators who are teaching in Catholic schools, and how finances are impacted by these various numbers. In brief, these various numbers provide the current situation of Catholic schools at the beginning of the 21st century.

The primary trend that is highlighted in the enrollment statistics described in the first part of this chapter is that student enrollment in Catholic education has been seriously declining since the 1970s. This has certainly impacted Catholic elementary and secondary schools around the United States. The

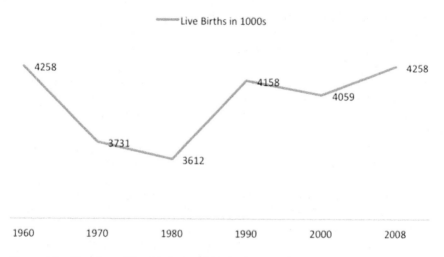

Figure 4.2 Number of live births in 1000s from 1960–2008. *Source:* U.S. Census Bureau, 2012).

lower enrollment numbers were first and foremost a factor of the end of the post-World War II baby boom. The number of live births dropped by 527,000 between the years 1960 and 1970, and the number of live births dropped to an even lower 646,000 from 1960 to 1980 (Figure 4.2). It was not until the 1990s that the population began to rebound, and it finally reached the 1960 level in 2008 (U.S. Census Bureau, 2012).

Secondarily, the number of religious congregations of men and women who once staffed schools diminished to the point of near extinction within the Catholic school system. The decline in the number of sisters, brothers, and priests who once staffed Catholic schools required an increasing number of lay teachers who, of necessity, were paid at a higher level than the religious. Most dioceses continue the custom of paying salaries on two scales: one for religious and the other for lay faculty. While this practice has been abandoned in most institutions of higher education and hospitals, as well as most private Catholic high schools run by religious communities, dioceses have been slow to grant equity to religious men and women for the work that they do. When the added costs of salaries are added to the price of tuition, the rate of tuition became too high for some families to afford Catholic education. According to DiFiore (2011), the increasing costs of Catholic parochial education rose at a greater rate than parish income between the years 1980 and 1993:

> One of the most perceptive analysts of Catholic Church and school finances nationally over the last two decades has been Joseph Claude Harris, an independent researcher from Seattle. He estimates that Catholic school oper-

ating costs increased at an average annual rate of 8.7% between 1980 and 1993—about twice the rate of inflation, while parish fiscal resources grew at a 3.1% annual rate. The average school that had cost $184,372 in 1980 required $547,838 to operate in 1993. In contrast, the average parish with a school had income of $348,000 in 1980 and $517,000 in 1993. (DiFiore, 2011, p. 4)

Were these the only factors impacting Catholic schools? Certainly not! One can find in the history of Catholic education in the 1960s–2010s a wide variety of other factors that can explain why there has been a downward turn in enrollments in the 1990s to the present, including such factors as the multiple lawsuits against clergy originating in this era regarding sexual abuse of minors and the mishandling of these cases by the chanceries. Secondly, there is the rise of charter schools in many of the urban centers. While the jury may be out on the overall success of charter schools, a free alternative to inferior public schooling is preferable to the Catholic school alternative that comes with a tuition bill each month.

USING DATA IN CATHOLIC SCHOOLS

Public education has pushed for its schools to make use of data to demonstrate the level of success that their schools are attaining. These accountability measures have pushed principals to learn how to analyze test data in order to increase the productivity of instruction in their schools. While this phenomenon of using data-driven decision making has grown out of federal policies such as *No Child Left Behind*, principals in both public and Catholic schools need to have a keen sense of what data are important and what might be learned from a careful examination of these data. It should be obvious how testing data and other measures of student achievement are critical for academic success. However, the savvy principal (or president) of the Catholic school (both elementary and secondary) should be using data to determine trends in enrollment, staffing, and financing their schools.

Principals should have a basic knowledge of statistics, good observational skills, and the ability to think critically about administrative problems. For example, if an elementary school principal begins to notice that the enrollments in her kindergarten classroom have been lower over the past two years, she could begin to look at some basic historical data. For example, how many of the students in our school are members of the local parish? If the enrollments in kindergarten have remained steady at 20 new students each year, and they have now fallen to 18 students, the principal can take several courses of action. He could just say that it is a trend and hopefully, next year will be better, or she could look at the data of how many students in the last five years were recruited from the parish.

Upon finding out that 85% of the students in the kindergarten class over the previous three years were recruited from the parish and 15% from outside the parish (either from another parish or non-Catholic students), she can now ask from where the current members of the kindergarten class and first grade class have come. If the records show that the parish has continued to send 17 students to the school as they have in previous years, then something has happened to the pipeline that brings students in from other places. Now the principal can begin to think about what has been happening differently either at the other parishes or within the local community that could have impacted the number of incoming students. It is also possible to project into the future by simply looking at the baptismal records for the past five years and at the baptismal records of the students who are currently enrolled in the school. How many children were baptized during each of the years that your current students were baptized? What percentage of the total baptized in the parish are enrolled in school? Examine the chart in Table 4.5.

At first glance, it has seemed that the enrollment of the school has remained stable, but the percentage of parishioners who enroll in the school has fluctuated widely. The critical question is whether the enrollment problem is really the result of having fewer students entering from outside the parish or not recruiting as many students as could possibly be recruited from each baptismal cohort. Now look at the Table 4.6, which will display the children who will be entering the school in the next five years. If one were to examine the hard enrollment numbers, without looking at the potential pool of candidates for admission to the school (that is, the number of children baptized each year), the principal could be lulled into a sense of security around enrollment numbers. By examining the baptismal records

TABLE 4.5 Fictitious Parish and School Numbers for Students in Elementary School Grades K–8

Year	Number of Children Baptized	Number of Children From This Group Enrolled in School	Percentage of the Total Baptized at the Parish Enrolled in the School
2000	35	17	48.5%
2001	36	17	47.2%
2002	36	18	50%
2003	32	17	53.1%
2004	33	17	51.5%
2005	34	18	52.9%
2006	37	18	48.6%
2007	39	17	43.5%
2008	41	17	41.5%

TABLE 4.6 Fictitious Parish Baptismal Numbers for Examining Potential Growth of Enrollment in the Next Five Years

Year	Number of Children Baptized	Percentage of Potential New Students Enrolled in School if the Number of Students Recruited Each Year is 17	Number of Potential New Students Enrolled in School if the Number of Students Recruited Remains at 48%
2009	37	46%	17
2010	40	42.5%	19
2011	41	41.5%	20
2012	42	40.5%	20
2013	41	41.5%	20

of children in the parish, one could begin asking some deeper questions: What is the enrollment potential from within the parish boundaries? By doing a similar study of the school's feeder parishes (those parishes with no parish school), one can also determine whether the recruitment efforts in these parishes are adequate. Perhaps the number of potential candidates from these other parishes could be increased as well.

Similarly, Catholic secondary schools can request from their feeder schools how many students are currently enrolled in K–8 grade. This can help to provide a long-term base enrollment plan and help to implement recruitment planning strategies. Another approach is to examine the ratio of students that matriculate from Catholic elementary schools versus public and other private schools. Does this alter your recruitment patterns? How might this alter your curriculum? Yet another alternative that one might examine is the number of students who matriculate into freshman year by zip code. Are students coming from one particular area more than others? Is your student body made up of students from across a wide area? What are the implications for extracurricular activities? for snow days? for recruitment?

Nothing is ever as easy as it seems. In the highly mobile society of the early 21st century, it is highly possible that a number of the families whose infants were baptized in the last five years may move out of the parish before they are able to matriculate into kindergarten or the first grade. In this case, another approach might be to examine the enrollments in the parish school against those of the parish religious education program. The metric that one could use is the realistic percentage of students enrolled in the parish school out of the cohort of active parishioners in that age group. The word "realistic" is cautionary. One should not state, as a matter of fact, that every child will enter the parish school. This is an "unrealistic" expectation, although, perhaps a hopeful one.

THE VALUE OF REFLECTING ON DATA

Principals are called to be good stewards of the resources that are put under their direction. Catholic school leaders might well take to heart the words of sacred scripture, "be shrewd as serpents, and gentle as doves" (Matthew 10:16, NAB). Our wise use of resources, human, material, and spiritual, are best tended by not just collecting data, but also making wise decisions based upon data. As noted above, data informs enrollment, financial, personnel issues as well as academic/curricular issues. Collecting data is useless without reflection and drawing conclusions from the data. All too often, standardized test scores are returned to individual schools (usually too late to be used effectively), and the results are locked in a file cabinet rather than analyzed and used as a way of focusing on particular curricular or instructional problems that the scores point toward.

Similarly, principals often do not examine basic demographic data to predict school enrollments for future academic years. How is it possible for schools that are dependent upon enrollments to survive without having a clear sense of the number of students in the potential pool? The number of students also provides an indication of your tuition income for each year. Determining the amount of tuition income that the school will collect in the upcoming school year becomes the first step in planning how expenses will be met in the upcoming school year. With the tuition income in mind, the principal can now reflect on how the remaining expenses for the year might be met.

Enrollments and finances have played a crucial role in the recent history of Catholic education in the United States. Unfortunately, for most of this time Catholic schools were impacted by the data, rather than using the data to provide an alternate history, possibly a bit more positive, than the current scenario. Catholic education has faced many storms in the past and will continue to do so in the future. Data can prove to be a helpful tool for making solid strategic decisions as Catholic school leaders face the future.

REFERENCES

Bimonte, R. (2008). *Financing the mission: A profile of Catholic elementary schools in the United States 2007.* Washington, DC: National Catholic Educational Association.

DeFiore, L. (2011). *Story of the storm: Catholic elementary schools from the 1960s to the present.* Washington, DC: National Catholic Education Association.

Dosen, A. (2009). *Catholic higher education in the 1960s: Issues of identity, issues of governance.* Charlotte, NC: Information Age Publications.

Hennesey, J. (1981). *American Catholics: A history of the Roman Catholic community in the United States.* New York: Oxford University Press.

McDonald, D. (2006). *United States Catholic Elementary and Secondary Schools 2005-2006.* Arlington, VA: National Catholic Educational Association.

McDonald, D. (2007). *United States Catholic elementary and secondary schools 2006–2007.* Arlington, VA: National Catholic Educational Association.

McDonald, D., & Schultz, M. (2008). *United States Catholic elementary and secondary schools 2007–2008.* Arlington, VA: National Catholic Educational Association.

McDonald, D., & Schultz, M. (2010). *United States Catholic elementary and secondary schools 2009–2010.* Arlington, VA: National Catholic Educational Association.

McDonald, D., & Schultz, M. (2011). *United States Catholic elementary and secondary schools 2010–2011.* Arlington, VA: National Catholic Educational Association.

McDonald, D., & Schultz, M. (2013). *United States Catholic elementary and secondary schools 2012–2013.* Arlington, VA: National Catholic Educational Association.

U.S. Census Bureau. (2012). Statistical abstract of the United States. Table 78. Retrieved from http://www.census.gov/prod/2011pubs/12statab/vitstat.pdf

RECOMMENDATIONS FOR FURTHER READING

The author recommends the following books, first, to help give a deeper understanding of using data in leadership and secondly, to help provide leaders with national data trends in Catholic schools.

Bimonte, R. (2008). *Financing the mission: A profile of Catholic elementary schools in the United States 2007.* Washington, DC: National Catholic Educational Association. *(This volume is updated every several years, you might want to look for the most recent editions at NCEA's publication site).*

DeFiore, L. (2011). *Story of the storm: Catholic elementary schools from the 1960s to the present.* Washington, DC: National Catholic Educational Association.

Holcomb, E. (1999). *Getting excited about data: How to combine people, passion, and proof.* Thousand Oaks, CA: Corwin Press.

McDonald, D. (2013). *The annual statistical report on schools, enrollment and staffing: U.S. Catholic Elementary Schools 2012–2013.* Washington DC: National Catholic Education Association. *(This volume like Bilmonte's above is updated regularly. You might want to look for the most recent editions at NCEA's publication site).*

Phillips, J. (2000). *How to think about statistics* (6th ed.). New York, NY: Henry Holt & Company, Inc.

CHAPTER 5

THE FOUNDATIONS
OF CURRICULUM
IN CATHOLIC SCHOOLS

Anthony J. Dosen

VIGNETTE

Mrs. Jankowski is interviewing candidates to replace the beloved fourth grade teacher, Mrs. Schmidt, who retired at the end of the last school year. Jennifer Gianetti, the candidate, when asked about how she would integrate faith into her classroom work responded, "I do not see any relationship between religion class and the rest of the classes." Surprised by this, Mrs. Jankowski stated, "Faith is the thread that weaves the curriculum together at our school." Unfortunately, each of the candidates for the fourth grade position responded to Mrs. Jankowski's question in the same general way. Her fear was that some of her current classroom teachers would not answer this question much better. How might Mrs. Jankowski and the written curriculum assist all teachers in integrating faith and knowledge?

Catholic School Leadership, pages 63–79
Copyright © 2016 by Information Age Publishing
All rights of reproduction in any form reserved.

THEOLOGICAL FOUNDATIONS

Christian education, in the Catholic tradition, has a history that goes back to the Gospel itself. Jesus' great commission to his disciples was to "Go, therefore, and make disciples of all the nations... Teach them to carry out everything I have commanded you" (Matthew 28:19–20[1]). The mission of the Church, from its inception, was educational. At different points in the Church's history, this mission of teaching was expressed in different ways, and it continues to be understood in different ways by different Christian communities. H. Richard Neibuhr (1951), a Protestant theologian and ethicist, examined the relationship of faith and culture in his classic work, *Christ and Culture.* Embedded in this work, Neibuhr offers a variety of alternative approaches to describing the relationship between Christian belief and "the world." While Niebuhr's work is not *per se* a theology or philosophy of education, it does provide the reader with a framework for understanding how particular Christian groups emphasize their values and approaches about Christian education (see Table 5.1).

At the core of Niebuhr's synthesis are the polar opposites of "Christ against culture" and "Christ of culture." In the case of "Christ against culture," the believer sees a break between faith and reason. For them, Jesus is all one needs. Everything else is rubbish. One does not need to look very far in today's contemporary context to find biology programs that are based upon *creationism* and a rigid unwillingness to attempt to use reason to integrate the realities of science and biblical faith. On the opposite pole, the believer seeks to accommodate faith with culture, to such an extent that faith dissolves in the face of the worldly culture's influence. At the extreme, what passes for Christian values becomes a tool for sustaining the culture's *status quo.* Neither of these extremes provides a very solid foundation for the curriculum of the Catholic, Christian school. However, the three frameworks that Neibuhr develops as a middle ground provides Christian educators with some viable ways of integrating sacred and secular knowledge, faith and reason, into the holistic curriculum of religious schools.

The three alternative frameworks of Niebuhr provide an interesting landscape from which Catholic and mainline Protestant educational philosophies developed. The Catholic tradition moves between the frameworks of "Christ above culture" (essentially a Thomistic approach) and "Christ the transformer of culture" (an Augustinian approach), while the Protestant tradition would move between "Christ the transformer of culture" and "Christ and culture in paradox" (Luther's approach).

The Catholic tradition, built upon the philosophical and theological traditions of St. Thomas Aquinas and St. Augustine, calls for a curriculum that allows for the divine to shine through the natural, an Incarnational world. In this world, the Word of God breaks through and allows creation to mirror

TABLE 5.1   Summarization of Niebuhr's Christ and Culture

Approach	Meaning	Theological Problems
Christ Against Culture	Affirms the sole authority of Christ over the Christian and resolutely rejects culture's claims to loyalty.	Disassociation of revelation and reason. Revelation (from God) and reason (culture)
Christ of Culture	Interpret culture through Christ, regarding those elements in it as most important that are most accordant with his work and person; on the other hand, they understand Christ through culture, selecting from his teaching and action as well as from the Christian doctrine about him such points as seem to agree with what is best in civilization.	Cultural answers to the Christ–culture problem show a consistent tendency to distort the figure of the New Testament Jesus.
Christ Above Culture	This is a synthesis of Christ and culture where the imperatives of nature and those of the gospel are recognized as divine imperatives, yet a partial and genuine discontinuity between them is also acknowledged, though the divine law is in part republication of the natural law. God reigns, nature is ordered, we are capable of understanding nature. Incarnational approach. (Approach of St. Thomas Aquinas)	Tendency to not engage in serious dialogue between divine and natural law. It becomes easier to give settled answers because the synthesis is completed.
Christ and Culture in Paradox	Accepts gospel ethics in radical form, not attempting to re-interpret them in some form natural to reason. Accepts the demands of nature and culture as inescapable and from God. The two cannot be unified simply, but the human person ignoring either side is subject to sin. (Martin Luther)	Body–Spirit dualism (Culture–Christ) is so pervasive that it seems impossible, or at least unseemly, to see Christ in culture.
Christ the Transformer of Culture	Creation: Human and world—living under the rule of Christ and creative power and ordering of the divine will. In the human fall, human nature becomes corrupted; this does not implicate all of creation (nature/culture), as with the dualists (see above). History is characterized as the continued interaction between God and humanity. (St. Augustine)	In some ways it becomes an optimistic form of dualism.

the creator. The world is charged with the possibility of Christ. In looking at the *Christ above culture* (approach of St. Thomas Aquinas) and the *Christ the transformer of culture* (approach of St. Augustine) approaches, we begin to see connecting points between the human/worldly and the divine. This is in stark contrast to the sharp division between nature and divinity found in the *Christ and culture in paradox* and the *Christ against culture* approaches. However, it does not provide the overly facile connections between nature and divinity that those who accept the *Christ of culture* model would endorse. The theological underpinning of a solid Catholic school curriculum is thus marked by "finding Christ in all things," a hallmark of the spirituality of St. Ignatius of Loyola.

STANDARDS AND BENCHMARKS

In March 2012, a task force of the National Catholic Education Association, under the leadership of Lorraine Ozar, presented the *National Standards and Benchmarks for Effective Catholic Elementary and Secondary Schools*. These standards and benchmarks were vetted nationally among diocesan superintendents, bishops, and university professors who are active in working with Catholic schools. These standards are beginning to be used as a clear criterion to evaluate Catholic K–12 schools for re-accreditation. In this chapter, the standards and benchmarks for academic excellence will be highlighted.

There are three standards that deal directly with academic excellence:

1. An excellent Catholic school has a clearly articulated, rigorous curriculum aligned with relevant standards, 21st century skills and Gospel values, implemented through effective instruction.
2. An excellent Catholic school uses school-wide assessment methods and practices to document student learning and program effectiveness, to make student performances transparent, and to inform the continuous review of curriculum and the improvement of instructional practices.
3. An excellent Catholic school provides programs and services aligned with the mission to enrich the academic program and support the development of student and family life (standards and benchmarks).

At first blush, as one looks at these standards, they might mistakenly believe that the first two standards are not that different from standards that are *de rigueur* for public school districts, with the notable exception of Gospel values. However, as one mines deeper into the benchmarks, it become obvious that this is not a thinly constructed standard, but rather one that calls the Catholic school community to be attentive not only to the basic skills, but also to the development of the child's critical analysis and moral judgment. It is a curriculum that is attentive to not only the intellectual but also the spiritual, affective, and social dimensions of the child's life.

The standards and benchmarks speak clearly to the educational purposes that the Catholic school seeks to attain. The Catholic school, like its public counterpart, seeks to provide a rigorous academic experience for all its students, based on content standards recommended by experts in the various academic disciplines. The distinguishing factor is certainly brought out in Benchmark 7.2, which states: "Standards are adopted across the curriculum and include integration of the religious, spiritual, moral and ethical dimensions of learning in all subjects" (Standards and Benchmarks, 7.2).

The curriculum of the Catholic school has as its overarching objective the integration of the religious within the curriculum, the development of a Catholic worldview. This does not mean a rigid adherence to a fundamentalist perspective that does not allow for a serious consideration of academic disciplines on their own merit. Rather, the Catholic approach seeks to demonstrate the interwoven patterns between creation and the Creator, between the human and the divine. St. Thomas Aquinas believed that grace built on nature. The Catholic approach to education allows for the proper development of each discipline, knowing that truth is one. Opposites cannot both be true, but one must discover where truth lies, rather than simply declaring one or the other false. This may mean that we live in a sense of uncertainty, but knowing that the truth, which is out of our reach, might with study eventually become clear. Notice that this approach does not fall into the extremes of Niebuhr's Christ against culture and the Christ of culture that were discussed above. Rather, it seeks to provide a middle ground that does not automatically downplay one conception of truth for another, but rather respects the rational process by which intellectual believers come to a rational faith.

This theological discussion sets a framework for Catholic education and offers insights into the uniqueness of the Catholic school program and provides direction regarding how we might organize the educational program. What follows is a framework for developing and evaluating curriculum in Catholic schools.

CURRICULAR FRAMEWORK: RALPH TYLER AND GRANT WIGGINS IN CONVERSATION

The National Standards and Benchmarks for Effective Catholic Elementary and Secondary Schools find a natural home in the work of Ralph Tyler (1949) and Grant Wiggins and Jay McTighe (2006). The standards and benchmarks answer the first two classical questions that Tyler (1949) proposes for developing an integrated curriculum:

1. What educational purposes should the school seek to attain?
2. How can learning experiences be selected that are likely to be useful in attaining these objectives?

These questions seek answers to the big questions: What should we teach and why should we teach it? This is the fundamental question that must be answered if the curriculum is to have a solid focus. Tyler's other questions are dependent upon the foundational question of what is worth teaching.

Wiggins and McTighe (2006) make use of a similar methodology in *Understanding by Design*. The *Understanding by Design* model is comprised of three stages:

1. Determining desired results: That is establishing goals, core understandings and knowledge. These goals must be big picture goals. With what kind of lasting learning should students walk away, at the end of the lesson, unit, semester, year?
2. Develop assessment evidence: Teachers need to move beyond merely giving quizzes and tests to assess student understanding and knowledge. What might be the performance tasks that students can use to demonstrate that they truly understand the core of the curriculum? If teachers, and schools, ask students to demonstrate their understanding and knowledge by developing a unique product or performance, the evaluators must have criteria that they are able to share with the students prior to the demonstration, that will provide them with a clear sense of what they need to accomplish in order to be successful.
3. Developing a learning plan: The learning plan becomes the map that provides curricular direction. Where is the lesson going? Have the students' prior learning and interests been taken into consideration? (Wiggins & McTighe, 2006, p. 28).

Essentially, Tyler (1949) and Wiggins and McTighe (2006) are proposing very similar approaches to curriculum development. The primary difference lies in Tyler's (1949) linear emphasis to curricular development, which begins with the social and philosophical foundations of curriculum design that is the answer to the question, "What educational purposes should the school seek to attain?" Wiggins and McTighe's (2006) approach truncates this question within the question of course goals, understandings, and knowledge (objectives). Secondly, Wiggins and McTighe move from the goals and objectives immediately into the development of assessments that are clearly aligned with the goals and objectives. Finally, they create the learning plans that will move the students to successfully attain the goals and objectives listed and demonstrate their mastery of the goals by assessments that move beyond mere paper and pencil tests into performance-based assessments.

For purposes of Catholic schools, it seems that a blend of *Understanding by Design* and Tyler's rationale provide a beneficial framework for developing a uniquely *Catholic* curriculum.

What Educational Purposes Should the Catholic School Seek To Attain?

Tyler (1949) begins answering the question of purpose by asking educators to consider the child *in toto* (needs, talents, abilities), the world in which the child lives, and what subject matter specialists consider essential learning for an educated person. While the Catholic school curriculum considers the intellectual development of each child as very important, it is not the whole picture. The Catholic school seeks to deal with the whole child, the socioemotional, the physical, as well as the spiritual and moral aspects of life. In a world that is increasingly focused upon money, power, and base satisfaction, viewing life from an egocentric prism, it becomes increasingly important to help students develop the social and emotional skills that allow them to consider the other person before themselves and to see the greater good in the common good. Thus the current world scene impels Catholic education to provide its students with the tools to create an alternate vision of *the good life*.

Philosophical Reflections

After reflecting on the nature of the child, society, and the academic disciplines, Tyler (1949) prescribes that these factors be examined in light of the school's educational philosophy and its psychology of learning. In Catholic education, the educational philosophy and psychology of learning are imbued with a theology that envisions a world that is Incarnational, an imagination that is sacramental, and an anthropology that speaks to the inherent goodness of the human person made in God's image.

> God created mankind in his image;
> in the image of God he created them;
> male and female he created them...
> God looked at everything he had made,
> and found it very good. (Genesis 1:27, 31a)

In the passage above, God is shown as creating humanity in His own image and likeness. This speaks to the nature of the human person as inherently good although damaged by original sin. In the end it is not the sin that wins, but rather the goodness of God with whom each person shares a likeness. In speaking of the Incarnational, Catholic belief focuses upon the reality that God became one of us, in Christ. God created us in such a way that He might take on our human nature. It reminds us that human nature has the capacity to hold the Divine. The human person, God's own creation, is given the dignity of being capable of sharing kinship with the Divine.

Sociologist Fr. Andrew Greeley (2000) speaks of a unique Catholic imagination. At the heart of this imagination was the Catholic's belief in sacrament. God is capable of manifesting Himself in natural elements: bread and wine, oil and water, the imposition of hands. Anyone who has encountered a beautiful sunset, a magnificent ocean view, or a newborn infant has had the opportunity to encounter God, in His wonderful creation. Gerard Manley Hopkins described this reality well when he wrote, "The world is charged with the Grandeur of God" (Hopkins, 1877, n.p.).

These theological principles form the backbone of a solid Catholic preK–12 curricula. Catholic education is not merely a theological or catechetical program with other academics as window dressing, but rather it becomes the Catholic student's encounter with the world through the lenses of a Catholic intellectual tradition that is as old as the Church. It does not shy away from the physical sciences or the social sciences; it encounters a world of beauty in the world of arts and letters; it is reflective and active, solitary and communal. It provides students with the reflective ability to encounter Christ in all things. The Catholic curriculum must be a program that is holistic, engaging, and Christocentric.

Learning Theory

In the Catholic tradition, students are seen as children of God, and as such are to be treated with dignity. The role of the teacher is to provide direction, example, and assistance to each child, so that each may grow and learn. Educators have various understandings of how children learn. Educators usually vary between behavioral approaches to learning with its variants on one side, constructivism on the opposite pole, with various types of cognitive field approaches in between. While most teachers will describe themselves as constructivists, in reality, informed observers might describe them as behaviorists. Some antiquated models of learning such as mental discipline, which describes learning as exercising the "muscle of the brain," were part and parcel of Catholic education in an earlier part of its history. Mercifully, this theory of learning has been abandoned for the most part.

Determining the Desired Results of Learning

The term *learning objectives* is falling into disuse in favor of the term *results of learning*. This is nothing new. Tyler (1949) warned:

Since the real purpose of education is not to have the instructor perform certain activities but to bring about significant changes in the students' patterns of behavior, it becomes important to recognize that any statement of the objectives of the school should be a statement of changes to take place in students. (p. 44)

Wiggins and McTighe (2006) use terms such as *desired result* or *achievement target and goal* in order to articulate the student-centered focus that Tyler (1949) was attempting to implement in his work six decades earlier. Thus, determining what desired results should result from instruction, one must focus upon outcomes. Outcomes refer

> to the priorities of a curriculum or an educational program. An outcome-based approach focuses on desired outputs, not the inputs (content and methods). The key question is results-oriented (What will students know and be able to do as a result of instruction?) rather than input-based (What instructional methods and materials shall we use?). (Wiggins & McTighe, 2006, p. 346)

These goals or desired outputs should not be anemic, weak little goals hardly worthy of your students' effort. They should be big and worthy goals. Management guru Jim Collins (2001) made use of the term *big hairy audacious goals* in speaking of what makes a company move from good to great. This should inspire the types of goals that faculty should create for their curriculum: goals that allow students to explore understandings, while gaining knowledge and skills. This is not spoon feeding students with a lecture/explanation of a concept, but rather helping them to explore the big picture and to contextualize their acquisition of knowledge and skills within the bigger goal. These goals move beyond mere memorization and recitation upon demand, toward the higher-order objectives that can only be assessed by application, analyzing and synthesizing data. These are the higher-order skills of Bloom's taxonomy, those skills that are not able to be assessed with simplistic multiple-choice examinations (Bloom, Krathwohl, & Masia, 1956).

To accomplish these inspiring goals and make certain that students have successfully met these goals, varied forms of assessment need to be employed. Unfortunately, the politicized culture of American public education views assessment as a one-dimensional, quantitative measurement that takes the form of standardized tests. Wiggins (1993) describes assessment as a way of providing the students with feedback on their level of mastery of a given objective or goal. In defining assessment, he provides the etymology of *assessment* as *assidere*, or "to sit with." When the reader encounters this etymology, they will undoubtedly question what sitting has to do with assessing student progress. However, Wiggins (1993) explains that in order to come to know what a student understands, the teacher must sit with student and take the time to observe and ask meaningful questions of the student.

At heart, Wiggins is recommending authentic forms of assessment as the way to ascertain what the student understands.

Authentic assessment evaluates student performance by asking students to demonstrate, using real-world situations, their ability to make use of what they have learned. Authentic assessments include performances; creating a product; solving a problem; or analyzing, synthesizing, or applying data to create something new. Wiggins (1993) suggests nine postulates for creating a meaningful assessment system. These postulates provide basic approaches that distinguish authentic assessment from the high-stakes standardized testing that has become the norm in American education. Wiggins' postulates are listed below.

> Postulate 1: Assessment of thoughtful mastery should ask students to justify their understanding and craft, not merely to recite orthodox views or mindlessly employ techniques in a vacuum ...

> Postulate 2: The student is an apprentice liberal artist and should be treated accordingly, through access to models and feedback in learning and assessment ...

> Postulate 3: An authentic assessment system has to be based on known, clear public, nonarbitrary standards and criteria ...

> Postulate 4: An authentic education makes self-assessment central ...

> Postulate 5: We should treat each student as a would-be, intellectual performer, not as a would-be learned spectator ...

> Postulate 6: An education should develop a student's intellectual style and voice ...

> Postulate 7: Understanding is best assessed by pursuing students' questions, not merely by noting their answers ...

> Postulate 8: A vital aim of education is to have students understand the limits and boundaries of ideas, theories, and systems ...

> Postulate 9: We should assess students' intellectual honesty and other habits of mind (Grant, 1993, pp. 47–63)

Students are apprentice "liberal artists." This is a marvelous image. Are teachers ready to allow their students to be historians, scientists, authors, and mathematical theorists? Perhaps it is not a matter of teachers impeding students in their pursuit of becoming liberal arts apprentices, as it is teachers not having the skills to create an environment that allows students the opportunity to move beyond being passive recipients of knowledge. Do teachers ask their students how they came to the conclusions that they have reached? Do teachers listen to students' questions and evaluate those questions to assess how students think? Do teachers provide students with clear expectations and rubrics regarding assessment projects? Have teachers provided students with the skills to critically examine their own work and go about correcting and perfecting their assessment projects? These are the skills that Catholic school principals must help their teachers develop if they expect their students to be successful.

While the author has seemed to disparage the current practice of objective multiple-choice examinations, he is not so naïve as to believe that these examinations will be abandoned any time soon. Objective examinations can be helpful when they are used in combination with other types of assessments, like those that have been discussed above. These types of examinations can be especially helpful when results are available to teachers in a timely fashion so that they can adjust their teaching in order to increase their students' success. The use of these examinations as lone sources of evaluation for student promotion or retention, or institutional effectiveness, is misguided, at best, in the eyes of this author.

Developing Effective Instructional Plans

Once teachers have a clear understanding of instructional goals and how students will be evaluated, the next step is to develop an instructional plan that allows students to develop the requisite knowledge, understanding, and skills to attain the goals students are expected to achieve.

In coming to understand a concept, students move through and integrate various ways of understanding. Wiggins and McTighe (2006) outline six facets of understanding: explanation, interpretation, application, perspective, ability to empathize, and metacognitive awareness. As teachers are preparing for instruction, it would be helpful for them to keep these facets in the forefront of their minds. In what ways might teachers help their students explain the big concepts they are studying in a particular unit? Listen to the students give examples of the concept. Are the examples they are giving appropriate interpretations of the concept? What types of activities might allow the students to apply their understanding in a practical *real-world* way? Are the students' applications on track or does the student seem uncertain, or tentative, as to how the concept might be applied? As students become more comfortable with the concept, allow them to experience, read, or hear other viewpoints and perspectives? How does the student handle different perspectives? How do students deal with others who hold positions that are different from their own? Are they able to be empathetic to another person's position? Finally, are students able to reflect on how they have come to understand the new material? Can they describe what they have learned and how they were able to learn it (Wiggins & Mc-Tighe, 2006)?

In order to begin the process of learning, students need to acquire skills that provide them with the appropriate tools to deal with new concepts. Perhaps the most basic skill students must develop is literacy. Schmoker (2011) states that academic success can be found by focusing upon three issues, a "reasonably coherent curriculum (*what* we teach); sound lessons (*how* we teach) and far more purposeful reading and writing in every discipline, or *authentic literacy* (integral to both what and how we teach)" (p. 2, emphasis in original). Schmoker's focus upon curricular coherence and sound lessons are addressed in the work of Wiggins and McTighe (2006). In choosing learning goals that are truly important, the faculty and principal cut through the morass of varied state and professional standards and choose those learning goals that are truly important—deleting those that are secondary. This allows teachers and students to have sufficient time to cover material in depth. In an attempt to meet "the standards," teachers often feel compelled to cover multiple standards in short periods of time. Often, teachers complain either that they need to cover the entire textbook before the end of the term or that they do not understand why students do not comprehend the course content, since the teacher clearly spent the entire class talking about it. The misconceptions are legion—for example, the textbook is the curriculum and it is to be followed at all costs. More often than not, teachers who are harried to cover an excess of content rely on the textbook as the curriculum rather than as a tool to enhance the written, negotiated curriculum. From an instructional perspective, some teachers believe that teaching is solely about verbal communication—"from my mouth to their ears!" Above was a discussion of how students can demonstrate their understanding of a concept. Students will not be able to demonstrate their understanding using any of the approaches suggested by Wiggins and McTighe (2006) by simply listening to the teacher lecturing at the front of the classroom. Therefore, teachers must re-envision themselves as facilitators of student learning rather than walking and talking encyclopedias of knowledge. This type of facilitation takes time and patience. It means allowing students to learn from their mistakes, not by merely giving them the right answer, but by guiding them to rethink their answer and find their mistakes.

Schmoker (2011) recommends that beyond the organizational issues of curricular and lesson planning, success is achieved by attention to helping students to develop *authentic literacy*, or the ability to read, write, and speak across the range of academic subjects. At one point or another, most secondary teachers have taken courses in teaching reading in the content areas. Schmoker (2011) is recommending is that educators actively engage in this process as a means to helping students at every grade level not only to read well, but also to analyze academic content at their appropriate ability level. This ability to gather data by careful and critical reading and to express ideas in both the written and the spoken word is the lynchpin that allows students to become serious learners—liberal artists, as it were. Providing students with the literacy skills that are necessary for understanding academic content and then providing students with opportunities to use this content in creative and meaningful ways is the true meaning of educational success.

FINAL THOUGHTS ON ACADEMIC COURSE WORK

The recommendations that have been made thus far in this chapter speak to why Catholic schools have been successful. Catholic educators have traditionally focused the academic curriculum of their schools on substantive goals; they believed that each student can be successful and thus pushed each student to excel, and if the student fell short, they worked with the student to assist them in achieving their goals.

The ideas of authentic assessment and a curriculum that engages students and helps them take ownership of their learning may not be as widespread in Catholic schools as they should be. Professional development and providing opportunities for teachers to observe other teachers—both within their own building and externally—are effective means of assisting teachers in developing these skills. Principals, as instructional leaders, must be ready and capable to assist both inexperienced and experienced teachers in creating the best academic program for all their school's students.

THE OTHER LEARNING THAT HAPPENS
IN CATHOLIC SCHOOLS

Catholic schools are committed to educating the whole child. Catholic school education is rooted in the conviction that human beings have a transcendent destiny, and that education for the whole person must form the spiritual, intellectual, physical, psychological, social, moral, aesthetic and religious capacities of each child. Catholic schools should develop and implement academic, co-curricular, faith-formation, and service/ministry programs to educate the whole child in all these dimensions. (Congregation for Catholic Education, 1977, p. 29)

This means that the principal, as both instructional and spiritual leader, must also have an active interest in the development of students' physical, spiritual, moral, emotional, creative, and interpersonal growth. Thus extracurricular activities, co-curricular activities, spiritual and religious activities, and any other interactions that take place in the school are under the purview of the principal.

In today's environment, extracurricular and co-curricular activities hang on the periphery of K–12 education. In urban public school systems, these activities are considered ancillary to the primary activity of teaching and learning, and often they are the first budget items cut in times of trial. Suburban districts in wealthier areas have extensive extracurricular and co-curricular programs that may or may not be a part of the overall educational mission of the district. Catholic schools must embrace every aspect of the school experience, whether it is sports, music, drama, scouting, or whatever one might imagine as an instructional moment, making it a teaching moment. Whether it is perseverance or teamwork, commendation or correction, the learning that takes place in these settings is critical to the Catholic school's overall mission.

This does not mean that every school, in order to be a Catholic school, must have extensive and comprehensive extracurricular or co-curricular programming. Rather, it means that the faculty, staff, parents, and administration at each school must find ways of meeting the particular needs of assisting their students' growth and development. In some cases, this means that the drama program is little more than a student-written and directed production of skits for the entire student body, rather than a finely honed drama program with several productions each academic year. Or it might mean interscholastic soccer, volleyball, and basketball teams with an intramural softball league, rather than a full schedule of every possible interscholastic sporting program known to K–12 education.

Students will develop confidence and skills in these varied activities, and this is important. However, just as important are the virtues and attitudes, such as collaboration, good sportsmanship, and acting with integrity, that students also learn in these activities. Principals, as well as all those involved in the supervision of these programs, must be certain that the Christian virtues and attitudes are held up as important. For often, winning the game or taking first in an artistic competition becomes a greater priority than the virtues of fair play, honesty, and good sportsmanship. It is critical that the adults model the way for the students, and that the principal (and pastor) model the way for the adults.

As has been stated earlier, the mission of Catholic education and Catholic educators is not only focused upon the whole child, but to take seriously the primary vocation of bringing students to encounter Christ. This is clearly stated in the *National Standards and Benchmarks* (2012).

> Catholic schools pay attention to the vocation of teachers and their participation in the Church's evangelizing mission (*The Catholic School on the Threshold of the Third Millennium,* #19).

Thus, the role of the principal is to coordinate this core mission of Catholic schooling. Sr. Patricia Helene Earle, IHM describes how the role of this critical aspect of Catholic school mission in the life and work of the Catholic school principal.

> As the leader of the school, the principal fosters and helps the faculty maintain the instructional quality of the school. The principal also manages the day-to-day operations of the school. However, because of the unique faith dimension of the Catholic school, the principal is also the spiritual leader of the school, along with the pastor and priests. . . . The principal sets the tone of the school. Thus, kin the area of spirituality it is vital that the principal initiate and model the importance of spirituality in his or her own life, while also empowering the faculty to value it, demonstrate its importance through their example, and guide their students to appreciate its importance in their own lives, age appropriately. (Earle, 2012, p. 3)

Of all the tasks that Catholic school principals encounter in their work, the spiritual dimension of the Catholic school seems to be the most intimidating. In light of tasks such as enrollment management, fundraising, and building maintenance, as well as being the building's instructional leader, this tends to be telling. Nowhere else in the principal's work world is there a place where the principal is as vulnerable and exposed as in the area of spiritual example. Many seem to repeat the cry of St. Peter, "Depart from me Lord, for I am a sinful man" (Luke 5:8) or the words of Jeremiah, "Ah, Lord God! . . . I do not know how to speak. I am too young!" (Jeremiah 1:7).

The challenge and the invitation of spiritual leadership in a school setting is to accept Christ's offer to take on this ministry and then to allow ourselves to remain both open and vulnerable. As principals share their faith with faculty, staff, and students, they slowly receive the strength that allows them to encourage and challenge and, most importantly, to accompany their school community on its faith journey. It is in the journey that the principal will experience her or his own continued growth in the spiritual life.

CONCLUSION

The Catholic school principal, as the instructional leader, is called to tend to the complete learning of each student. This includes the academic, socioemotional, physical, and spiritual development and learning of each child. This is greater than Howard Gardener's (2006) *Multiple Intelligences*, because it is not just about finding the student's strengths as a pathway to knowledge. Rather, the Catholic school principal helps the school community to see the integration of learning. The content students study in class is not disassociated from their lives, their interests, and their concerns.

Principals help teachers to help students to see the interrelatedness of learning. Most importantly, principals in Catholic schools help their academic community "to find Christ in all things" (Ignatian Spirituality, 2014).

NOTE

1. All Scripture references are taken from the New American Bible, revised edition (2010). Washington, DC: Confraternity of Christian Doctrine.

REFERENCES

Bloom, B., Krathwohl, D. R., & Masia, B. B. (1956). *Taxonomy of educational objectives: The classification of educational goals.* New York, NY: D. McKay.

Collins, J. (2001). *Good to great.* New York, NY: HarperCollins, Inc.

Congregation of Catholic Education. (1977). *The Catholic School.* http://www.vatican.va/roman_curia/congregations/ccatheduc/documents/rc_con_ccatheduc_doc_19770319_catholic-school_en.html

Congregation for Catholic Education. (1997). *The Catholic School at the Threshold of the Third Millenium.* http://www.vatican.va/roman_curia/congregations/ccatheduc/documents/rc_con_ccatheduc_doc_27041998_school2000_en.html

Earle, P. H. (2012). A Catholic school spirituality. In P. V. Robey (Ed.), *Scholarly essays on Catholic school leadership: Research and insights on attaining the mission of Catholic schools.* Arlington, VA: National Catholic Education Association.

Gardner, H. (2006). *Multiple intelligences: New horizons in theory and practice.* New York, NY: Basic Books.

Greeley, A. (2000). *The Catholic imagination.* San Francisco, CA: University of California Press.

Hopkins, G. M. (1877). "God's Grandeur." Retrieved from http://www.poetryfoundation.org/poem/173660

Ignatian Spirituality. (2014). *Finding God in all things.* Retrieved from http://www.loyolapress.com/ignatian-spirituality-finding-god-in-all-things.htm?class_id=13&parent_class_id=

National Standards and Benchmarks for Effective Catholic Elementary and Secondary Schools. (2012). Retrieved from www.catholicschoolstandards.org

Neibuhr, H. R. (1951). *Christ and culture.* San Francisco, CA: Harper and Row.

Schmoker, M. (2011). *Focus: Elevating the essentials to racially improve student learning.* Alexandria, VA: ASCD.

Tyler, R. W. (1949). *Basic principles of curriculum and instruction.* Chicago, IL: University of Chicago Press.

Wiggins, G. (1993). *Assessing student performance: Exploring the purpose and limits of testing.* San Francisco, CA: Jossey-Bass.

Wiggins, G., & McTighe, J. (2006). *Understanding by design* (2nd ed., expanded). Upper Saddle River, NJ: Prentice Hall Education.

RECOMMENDATIONS FOR FURTHER READING

English, F. W. (1992). *Deciding what to teach and test: Developing aligning, and auditing the curriculum.* Newbury Park, CA: Corwin Press.

Gardner, H. (2006). *Multiple intelligences: New horizons in theory and practice.* New York, NY: Basic Books.

Holcomb, E. L. (1999). *Getting excited about data: How to combine people, passion, and proof.* Newbury Park, CA: Corwin Press.

Schmoker, M. (2011). *Focus: Elevating the essentials to radically improve student learning.* Alexandria, VA: ASCD.

Wiggins, G., & McTighe, J. (2006). *Understanding by design.* (2nd ed., expanded). Upper Saddle River, NJ: Prentice Education.

CHAPTER 6

FUNDING THE MISSION

An Examination of Financial Issues and Funding Efforts in Catholic Schools

Frank Montejano

While earlier examining the issue of Catholic school sustainability, I conducted a case study of a K–8 Catholic school (we will call this school St. Leo) suffering from low student enrollment and depleted finances (Montejano, 2007a). During one of various meetings with the principal, I listened as she rattled off a list of seemingly desperate measures to secure enough funding to save the school. These included letters to noteworthy alumni and Hollywood celebrities who, according to the local narrative, had ties to the school and would certainly come to St. Leo's aid if only they knew the gravity of the situation. At that moment, St. Leo's future and the school's chance of securing funding remote appeared murky, as was the sense that these letters would ever reach their intended target, let alone bear fruit. And even if some emergency funding were to come the school's way, it begged the question: What next?

At the time, St. Leo was losing money; it had neither the infrastructure nor the needed human and other resources to build capacity in the school;

operating without foresight, the staff and administration instead focused entirely on the all-consuming task of keeping the lights on and the doors open. The skeletal staff was committed but could hardly be expected to take on more than they already had. Not surprisingly, the school principal was a novice administrator, rushed into a position of leadership after the previous principal left for a better paying, more secure position. The parish, with its own financial woes, could offer little more than spiritual guidance to the school.

The circumstances that surrounded St. Leo are familiar to Catholic educators, especially those administrators, teachers, and parents whose schools either have closed or sit on the edge of extinction. Consider that in 2009–2010, Catholic school enrollment in the United States decreased 3.3%, or 73,190 students, from the previous year (McDonald, 2010); and since 2000, 20% of the K–12 Catholic schools in the United States have closed; going back further, there are now fewer Catholic schools in the country than in 1920 (McDonald, 2010), despite a Catholic population that today is five times greater. What the above indicates is that beyond the decline in numbers of schools and students is the staggering loss in market share among Catholics themselves. The sobering trend shows that we can expect a significant number of Catholic schools to close in the coming years unless a very different course is charted.

At the same time, it is important to note that Catholic schools in parts of the country continue to be successful in terms of both student enrollment and finances. Yet many of these schools, often in affluent communities, are serving a decreasing portion of the population (Harris, 2000). Baker and Riordan (1998), for example, chronicled the continued success of Catholic schools in suburban communities, and the simultaneous decline in the inner city, referring to the phenomenon as the "eliting" of Catholic education. Many Catholic schools with financial and other human resources have been able to either adapt or successfully withstand the financial problems that have plagued others. Yet these data serve as a painful irony for those who have championed the Catholic schools' historical success in educating scores of immigrants. The underlying point is that while tuition-based models once served Catholic schools well, fewer of them are able to rely solely on the financial support of the schools' families for their survival.

A still smaller number of schools have refused to succumb to the statistical odds against them and have creatively tapped resources inside and outside the community to develop new revenue streams (see for examples Brown, 2005; James, 2007; Karp, 2009; Reid, 2003; Roberts, 2009; Zehr, 2003a, 2003b). Often beginning with a plan that emphasizes their purpose and value, they have built school programs that attract the interest of business and philanthropy, as well as key members of the local community. The ability of these school programs to adapt to the financial constraints facing Catholic schools, for the most part, will be the focus of this chapter.

The aforementioned meeting with the principal of St. Leo was one of several I conducted with a variety of the school's stakeholders, including personnel, parents, and benefactors (Montejano, 2007a). St. Leo's story has implications for how Catholic schools might develop a process to ensure a successful future and secure the funding necessary to further the mission. Throughout, I will apply many of the lessons learned, not only from St. Leo, but also from Catholic schools and dioceses throughout the country that have attracted and cultivated the interest of business, individuals, and other benefactors. These lessons will assist Catholic educators interested in answering the question of what should happen next for Catholic schools that require substantial funding beyond the tuition-driven models that have defined Catholic education for the better part of its existence.

The purpose of this chapter is to examine the financial challenges and needs to sustain Catholic schools both now and in the future, as well as provide Catholic school leaders with ideas to assist in creating a successful development program. Herein we will consider examples of successful Catholic school development models and their connection to guiding principles. Catholic schools interested in a development plan that secures their future must be purposeful: attuned to the mission, values, and identifying characteristics of the school; generative: focused on cultivating relationships and establishing partnerships; and sustainable: constructed in ways that change the culture in order to secure the long-range future. We might consider these principles the foundation, structure, and long-term solutions for the institution, although there should be fluid movement among them. These basic principles will serve as a guiding framework for schools interested in initiating and implementing a development program. We will examine not only what schools have done in areas of development, but also the perspectives of potential donors such as philanthropists, foundations, and business. At times, we will go beyond the field of education and look to examples in the business world for assistance. This chapter will also include an explication of a brief history of Catholic schools from a financial perspective.

The over-arching perspective here is that Catholic school leaders must chart a new direction for their schools (while being true to core values) before funding can be assured to levels that sustain Catholic education for the next 30 years and beyond. These leaders will need to conceive of and articulate a course that considers the *zeitgeist* and anticipates developments in the field of education, as well as movements in society; in other words, they will need to be innovative and at the same agile enough to adapt to changes in the educational environment. The broad stance I adopt is similar to that of O'Keefe, Greene, Henderson, Connors, Goldschmidt, and Schervish (2004): simply, Catholic schools must "innovate or perish" (p. 66). The goal of this chapter, then, is to assist Catholic schools in creating a development plan that is purposeful, generative, and sustainable.

Further, development in the context of the Catholic school is regarded as a ministerial component of the church's mission; educational leaders who are serious about securing the future of Catholic schooling should view its function through the lens of service to a church that has entrusted the faithful with a tremendous gift: an education rooted in discipleship and the education of the whole person. These elements distinguish Catholic education from other educational models and systems; in a commitment to stewardship, these elements need to be protected and nurtured. Development, in this sense, might be defined as the process of obtaining, maintaining, and developing financial, human, and other vital resources to secure the long-term future of the school in service to the educational ministry of the church.

Finally, it is important to reflect on this chapter's potential audience. I assume Catholic school leaders and others who read this will come from different starting points and have access to various levels of human and other resources. Some, for instance, may have a dedicated development person already in the school, while others can only dream of such a luxury. Yet I would argue that schools in either of the above circumstances would be able to initiate basic development plans with the help of, for example, a dedicated parent or parish volunteer. This point is echoed by Carol O'Day, the director of marketing and development (DMD) at St. Anne School, Santa Monica, California; she suggests the following as areas where schools might make headway without a dedicated development person (personal communication, January 21, 2011):

- creation of a school website;
- creation or updating of a school brochure;
- establishment of a school presence in the parish (at mass, via bulletin and pulpit announcements);
- launch of an electronic newsletter, for internal and external distribution and promotional purposes;
- development of databases for area preschools, baptismal records, alumni, local media, and donors;
- development and promotion of open house and other school events;
- cultivation of relationships with preschool directors (through faculty assignments and preschool alumni parents); and
- annual giving campaign and mailing to past donors, parishioners, alumni, area businesses.

The point is that even Catholic schools with very limited resources can, and should, find ways to address the long-term financial goals of the school.

With this understanding, I have tried to make this chapter of value to schools in a wide variety of circumstances. The framework is loosely structured so that schools can craft a development plan that is adapted to their particular needs. In other words, it is not presented as a step-by-step process, primarily because planning of this kind must serve the particular context in which the school resides; because the detailed elements of a development program depend heavily on the circumstances of the school, they are for the better part not scripted here. The examples presented in this chapter are more a sign that schools who commit themselves to the right development plan can flourish. It is my hope then that the structure and content will be of interest to a broad audience of Catholic school leaders, including principals, presidents, and diocesan leaders, as well as members of Catholic boards, foundations, and individual philanthropists.

A HISTORICAL/SOCIAL PERSPECTIVE ON THE FUNDING OF CATHOLIC SCHOOLING

It is helpful to first understand the Catholic schools' broader historical and social contexts as they relate to funding. The landmark events in the history of Catholic schooling are covered extensively in the literature (see Walch, 1996) and will not be rehashed extensively here, except to highlight the relevant issues that have impacted Catholic schools from a funding perspective. However, in order to contextualize the cultural milieu under which Catholic schools emerged, the recollection of a singular event during its formative period will be helpful.

The Eliot School Rebellion

In the mid-1800s, the common schools of the New England States maintained a distinctly Protestant ethos (McGreevy, 2003). One such school in Boston was the Eliot School for boys. According to McGreevy's (2003) account, the children in the school daily recited the King James Version of the Ten Commandments, which was a requirement of Massachusetts state law. When 10-year-old Catholic boy named Thomas refused to recite the King James Version of the Ten Commandments (preferring instead to recite the Catholic version), the principal beat his hands "with a rattan stick for half an hour until they were cut and bleeding" (McGreevy, 2003, p. 8). Young Thomas Whall's refusal and subsequent punishment became national news, highlighting for the burgeoning country the deep religious divide between Catholics and Protestants (McGreevy, 2003). The day after Whall's protest, the principal ordered all boys who refused to recite the Protestant version of the Ten Commandments to leave the school, and about 100 boys walked out. Within weeks of the incident, a small school for seminarians at the local St. Mary's parish was transformed into a school for boys. One year later, St. Mary's Institute enrolled 1,150 young boys, which made it Boston's largest Catholic school at the time (Guerra, 2004).

This event, known as the Eliot School Rebellion, illustrates the contentious climate and resulting fervor that led to the steady (and sometimes rapid) growth of Catholic schools in the United States for roughly 200 years. During that time, the need for a separate school system crystallized in the belief that a distinctly Catholic education for its immigrant families would counter the hegemony they experienced in the broader society (McGreevy, 2003). And in order to maintain their independence, these schools would be funded by faithful Catholics themselves, who would make the necessary sacrifices to build and maintain a private system under the guidance of the church.

The Growth of Catholic Schools

In support of this belief, the Third Plenary Council of Baltimore in 1884 mandated Catholic schools in parishes and made it binding for all Catholic children to attend (National Conference of Catholic Bishops, 1884). The document proclaimed that "near each Church where it does not exist, a parochial school is to be erected within two years. All Catholic parents are bound to send their children to the parochial school" (as cited in Guerra, 2004, p. 6). That mandate fostered continued Catholic school growth in the country, primarily in neighborhoods serving poor and immigrant families. At the turn of the 1900s it was estimated that one million children were attending Catholic schools (Youniss & Convey, 2000). Twenty years later, Catholic schools in the country nearly doubled as student enrollment grew to 1.8 million (Guerra, 2004).

Catholic schools grew continued to grow steadily throughout the century, and at their peak in 1965, five and one half million students attended a Catholic school, which translated to 12% of the nation's school-age population (Guerra, 2004). Access seemed hardly an issue, as 14,000 Catholic schools populated the country, also an all-time high (McGreevy, 1996). But a rapid decline in Catholic school enrollment ensued in the late 1960s (McLellan, 2000). By 1974, Catholic enrollment had declined 42% over a 10-year period, while the student population in the United States remained virtually the same (Ganley, 1979, as cited in McClellan, 2000). Prior to 1960, defending the Catholic faith was paramount (as evidenced by the Eliot School Rebellion). As such, schools were viewed by the faithful as a primary vehicle to carry out the church's mission, and the church leadership was also clear and universal in its support for Catholic schools, rallying its members to help build new schools throughout the country.

The Impact of Vatican II

For many, the election of a Catholic president in John F. Kennedy was evidence that Catholicism had become part of the American mainstream and no longer required its own school system (Youniss & Convey, 2000). But a more defining issue was one that significantly altered the course of the church itself. In 1962, Pope John XXIII convened the Second Vatican Council, which signaled the church's transition from a siege mentality to that of a new openness, or *aggiornamento;* it also meant that religious men and women would serve increasingly in ministries beyond the boundaries of the parish school, resulting in a mass exodus "of the greatest single work force in the church's modern period" (Dolan, 2010, p. 12). To wit, the numbers of sisters, brothers, and priests in Catholic schools decreased from 114,000 in 1965 to a mere 9,000 in 2002 (Steinfels, 2003).

The council also opened the gates to countervailing views that challenged the purpose and function of many of the church's institutions, including Catholic schools. Ryan's (1964) publication, *Are Catholic Schools the Answer?*, was one such response. Ryan (1964) contended that the Catholic school had outlived its mission to provide a distinctly Catholic education for recent immigrants. Specifically, she argued that the Catholic schools' need for disproportionate funding was unnecessary and should be directed to other, presumably more deserving, parish ministries. Her provocative stance framed a brewing debate about the role of Catholic schools in furthering the mission of the church, particularly in light of the finite financial resources available. Ryan's challenge essentially bridged the years between Catholic schooling's meteoric rise and the decline that would follow.

Financial Impacts Post-Vatican II

The suddenly increased role of the laity following Vatican II dramatically altered the financial structure of Catholic schools (Harris, 2000). Rising teacher salaries and benefits, along with operational and maintenance costs, began to impact Catholic schools in ways "much higher than the spreadsheets reveal," according to Walch (1996, p. 245). "In spite of belt tightening and other economies, few parishes can raise the funds necessary to maintain their own schools" (p. 245). At the same time, parish financial support to the schools began to decrease dramatically. In 1969, the first year the National Catholic Educational Association began collecting financial data, parishes contributed 63% of the cost toward its elementary schools (Bredeweg, 1980). In 1994 the percentage of parish financial support for the school had dropped to 25% (Harris, 2000). Once a church-funded endeavor, the cost of financing a Catholic school had clearly been passed on to the families themselves.

Additionally, the cost of operating Catholic schools increased at a faster rate than families' ability to pay. Between 1990 and 1994, for example, the operational costs for parish elementary schools increased at an average annual rate of 7%—nearly double the rate of inflation (Harris, 2000). The increased costs were not surprisingly passed on to the consumer. Examining growth over a 10-year period, an average tuition of $969 per child in 1990–1991 (Kealey, 1992) grew to $2,178 in 1999–2000 (Kealey, 2001), a greater than 100% increase in 10 years. The point is that participating families were required to allocate to the Catholic school ever-increasing portions of the family budget, creating tipping points for those who would choose a Catholic education but increasingly found it beyond their financial means.

The present financial turmoil could hardly be foreseen prior to 1960. In earlier times, families attending Catholic schools paid little or no tuition to attend the local parish school (Harris, 2000). The built-in support of the parish along with the minimal costs associated with running the Catholic school made it easy to do so. But the dramatic rise in costs increasingly placed the burden squarely on the family. At roughly the same time, parish giving declined even as the Catholic population increased (Center for Applied Research in the Apostolate [CARA], 2005).

Years later, Hallinan (2000) essentially revisited Ryan's (1964) dilemma about the need for Catholic schools given the finite resources available. While noting that the world of today is far different than the one into which Catholic schools were ushered, she looked at four areas in assessing the need for Catholic schools in the present era: student academic achievement, religious education, social development, and citizenship. In three of the areas (sans religious education), she compared relevant data on both public and Catholic education. She concluded that Catholic schools are at least as successful as their public school counterparts in each of the areas considered.

Examining a period from 2000–2005, the Center for Applied Research in the Apostolate (CARA) at Georgetown University conducted a study on the factors impacting Catholic schools in the United States (2005). Overall, the CARA researchers described the present outlook as "healthy" and "cautiously positive," despite a 5% drop in the number of Catholic schools within the period of their study. A key section of the report examined the issue of affordability. Parents with school-age children who had not enrolled a child in a Catholic school cited tuition costs and financial assistance as far more important than areas such as technological resources, after-school care, and extracurricular activities. Most parents also indicated that the provision of vouchers or tax credits would increase the likelihood that they would enroll their children in a Catholic school. The suggestion with respect to affordability is that while parents may find schools with particular technological and other resources attractive, the core of a Catholic education and basic financial concerns still have primacy.

James, Tichy, Collins, and Schwob (2008), in an attempt to determine statistical differences between open and closed Catholic schools, explored the relationship between school closure and selected financial and demographic variables for schools in the Archdiocese of St. Louis, Missouri. While examining a total of 138 schools in the archdiocese between 2000–2005 (99 open schools and 39 closed schools), they determined that enrollment change in the last year (up or down), tuition as a percentage of median adjusted household income, and enrollment rates (above or below 200) were variables that produced the most substantively meaningful differences between closed and open schools.

The findings of James et al. (2008) found application within the Archdiocese of St. Louis. They were able to classify 93% of the schools as either open or closed using the above criteria. They correctly classified 87.5% of those schools that closed. This led them to believe in the efficacy of developing an early warning system for schools. But a key element in their model was tuition costs in relation to families' household income. Echoing Harris' (2000) work, data collected by James et al. (2008) indicate that there is a clear tipping point at which families will no longer make the financial sacrifice to choose the Catholic school.

PURPOSEFUL: CRAFTING A VISION ROOTED IN MISSION

The above historical overview of Catholic schooling highlights the massive shift from a protected and valued entity to a vulnerable system threatened by archaic financial models, not to mention the advent of new models such as charters, which have proven to be attractive options for families that might otherwise choose a Catholic school (Zehr, 2002). The church's once marginalized standing, coupled with the widely held belief that Catholic schools were the best means of catechizing the faithful, led to a steady and sometimes rapid growth in its schools for more than 150 years. But in the last 50 years, a confluence of financial and organizational issues overwhelmed segments of the Catholic school population. While Catholic schools from a different era struggled to become relevant against the hegemony of their time, the challenge today is to remain relevant in an increasingly secularized society where new and attractive educational options abound. Archbishop Timothy Dolan of New York characterizes the new struggle in this way (2010):

> Today's anti-Catholicism hardly derives from that narrow 19th-century Protestantism. . . . Instead the Catholic Church is now confronted by a new secularization asserting that a person of faith can hardly be expected to be a tolerant and enlightened American. Religion, in this view, is only a personal hobby, with no implications for public life. Under this new scheme, to take one's faith seriously and bring it to the public square somehow implies being un-American. To combat this notion, an equally energetic evangelization—with Catholic schools at its center—is all the more necessary. (p. 1)

An Argument for Catholic Schools

Dolan's passionate assertion frames the importance of Catholic schools to contemporary society. It further reminds us of the distinctiveness of Catholic education. Rooted in mission, Catholic schools counter educational systems that advance—directly or indirectly—what Bellah et al. have coined *utilitarian individualism*, defined as a particular drive towards independence and mastery of the environment (Bellah, Madsen, Sullivan, Swidler, & Tipton, 1985). In other words, Catholic education's emphasis on values such as community, service, and social justice are among the core characteristics (see Groome, 1998) that make a Catholic education distinctive; its focus on a community of faith counters the narrative that education exists solely to climb the ladder of so-called success. For Catholic leaders, the ability to articulate for whom and to what end the Catholic school exists is vital in a society where more Catholics are marginally connected to church life, and thus less likely to make the choice for a Catholic school among myriad educational options (CARA, 2006).

Dolan's (2010) argument for why Catholic schools are needed today challenges each person interested in securing the future of Catholic education to do similarly. Any discussion about crafting a development program must begin with fundamental questions around what establishes an organization's heart. For instance, each Catholic school must ask: Who are we? Whom do we serve? Where are we going? What is best about us? And why should X support us (financial or otherwise) instead of Y? Answers to these questions, hardly a given, establish an organization's *raison d'etre*. These foundational questions are often positioned within a strategic planning process for the entire school program. Strategic planning is "a tool used by leadership to involve the community in designing the preferred future of the school" (Wincek & O'Malley, 1995, p. 3). Many such tools exist for Catholic schools (see Dwyer, 2009; Wincek & O'Malley, 1995) and often serve as an impetus for the creation of a development program. But our purpose here is not to guide you through a defined strategic process, but rather to emphasize salient points about self-examination that can help a Catholic school establish a foundation on which to create a development plan.

An Appreciative Model for Assessing School Strengths and Weaknesses

As a starting point, I recommend a process that examines what is currently best about the school while also "dreaming" the school's ideal future. One such tool is known as *appreciative inquiry* (AI). AI is a method of inquiry developed to assess the life of an organization (Cooperrider & Srivastva, 1987). Rather than initially focusing on problem areas, AI's creators conceived of it as a process that initially focused on what an organization does best. The operational belief is that organizations spend a disproportionate amount of time on problem areas while neglecting to identify inherent strengths. Schools that adopt an appreciative approach to development will need to develop a data-gathering process that also takes into account the best that the school currently offers.

According to Ryan et al. (1999):

> AI can provide deeper understanding and appreciation of the school's mission and goals. By focusing everyone's attention about what is best about the school, the AI process often blends in with, and nourishes, the sense of possibility embedded in the school's mission. By involving so many of the school's stakeholders, AI also reinforces the likelihood that the school's mission will be embraced by an increasingly broad constituency. (Ryan, Soven, Smither, Sullivan, & Vanbuskirk, 1999, p. 6)

An appreciative approach is an appropriate template for schools beginning a development plan for several reasons. Consider that a struggling Catholic school with low enrollment and rising costs might naturally expend copious amounts of energy on problem solving. The result is often one change after another, with few tangible results. Members of such organizations become desensitized over time and eventually resist any effort to achieve substantive reform (Bridges, 2003; Hess, 1999). My examination of St. Leo School supports the belief that reform efforts without significant buy-in are often ineffective; repeated changes at St. Leo were met with skepticism by teachers and staff, even as the life of the school hung in the balance. Because AI involves a systematic inquiry that initially focuses on what an organization does best, relevant data with respect to the needs and hopes of a Catholic school community are able to be captured and built upon.

Another reason why AI is an appropriate starting point in development is that despite the current challenges before Catholic schools, there is much to be recognized as positive, even in struggling schools such as St. Leo. In some sense, terms such as *struggling, failing,* and *underperforming* are misnomers that more often than not create self-fulfilling prophesies that can expedite decline and eventual closure. My work with St. Leo School chronicled outstanding commitment and performance in different areas of the school program, despite the significant challenges.

Additionally, AI leads organizations to imagine their most desired future. For struggling Catholic schools, preoccupied as they are with survival, such images are necessary to begin to move beyond quick fixes toward true sustainability. According to Watkins and Mohr (2001):

> Appreciative inquiry is, in part, the art of helping systems create images of their most desired future. Based on the belief that a human system will show a heliotropic tendency to move toward positive images, AI is focused on the generative and creative images that can be held up, valued, and used as a basis for moving toward the future. (p. 30)

Using the Future to Create the Present

In addition to an appreciative orientation, school leaders must have a clear sense themselves of the best future for the school and should be able to articulate it in an effort to reorient present practices. As a new and compelling picture of the Catholic school is painted by leaders, the practices of members will begin to change in the here and now, charting a course to that better place in the future. What I am describing is a leadership practice known as the Future Creating the Present (Pascale, Millemann, & Gioja, 2000); it is a powerful problem-solving approach that creative leaders have tapped to reinvigorate flagging organizations, or ones whose message has fallen on deaf ears; the time is ripe for its use by today's Catholic school leadership.

Imagine the counter-intuitive vision needed to reverse the cycle of Catholic school closures in an impoverished, mostly non-Catholic community. Yet that is precisely what happened in the Diocese of Memphis, where seven Catholic schools reopened in 2000 with the help of local business (Zehr, 2003b). Located in some of the city's poorest neighborhoods, these schools had been closed for years as tuition rates grew beyond residents' ability to pay. Spurred by Bishop J. Terry Stieb's vision, Mary McDonald, superintendent, set out to secure the necessary funding to reopen these schools. She was able to garner financial support from local business leaders, who were White, non-Catholic individuals (who chose to remain anonymous) but were nonetheless committed to providing a quality educational experience for the mostly African American and impoverished children in the community. Why? Because they viewed their investment in terms of its benefit to the greater Memphis community. In the end they established a $38 million endowment to sustain those schools, as well as providing additional scholarships for students who went on to the local Catholic high school.

But none of it would have come to fruition if Bishop Stieb had not shared his vision with Mary McDonald, who recalls the moment (2007):

> When Bishop Stieb appointed me superintendent of schools in 1998, he laid out to me his vision of education and said, "Must our schools only be where all the Catholics are, or are we abrogating our mission to bring the Gospel where needed with what we do best? It has always been, and continues to be, the hallmark of the Catholic Church that we are with the less fortunate." With faith that with God all things are possible, and trusting in God's divine providence, I accepted Bishop Stieb's challenge in the name of all who serve in the ministry of Catholic education. (p. 35)

At the moment of that first encounter, the future began to create the present as McDonald began to conceive of and forge a new and exciting path for the diocese of Memphis. Her vision in turn was passed on to others, creating a domino effect of support for the idea of opening Catholic schools in a community that had seemingly given up on the notion that Catholic schools could exist, let alone thrive.

For those looking for specific development strategies, a focus on purpose may seem unnecessary, or an accepted given in the Catholic school. But as I found in my examination of St. Leo (Montejano, 2007a), it is important to collect the perspectives of stakeholders—teachers, staff, parents, parishioners and members of the community—in order to clarify and strengthen the mission among all stakeholders. The ability to garner necessary financial and other resources depends on a solid foundation and clear vision. Simply, school leaders—and to some extent all stakeholders—must first be able to clearly articulate the beliefs and values of the school before creating a plan for development.

GENERATIVE: THE CULTIVATION
OF RELATIONSHIPS BOTH LARGE AND SMALL

Once a purpose and vision is clearly understood and promulgated, a Catholic school community can begin to create the structures and processes that will support the school's financial mission. Central to any development plan is the cultivation of relationships with philanthropy and business, as well as with interested members of the community. In many cases, these efforts begin with ideas shared by a small group of people with a dream or vision. In the case of relationship building, no potential partnership is too small and no dream too big. We will see examples of both instances as we move through the remaining parts of this chapter. As schools begin to consider grants through such entities as foundations, it is helpful to understand what benefactors are looking for among the numerous grants and other philanthropic requests.

Partnerships With Business and Philanthropy

The opportunity for Catholic schools to partner successfully with business as well as garner the attention of philanthropists is perhaps greater than at any other time (Montejano, 2007b). Consider that many of those educated in Catholic schools now have the capacity to contribute time, treasure, and talent. Additionally, American business, cognizant of its flagging position in the world economy, now rests its hopes on the success of American education as a fundamental enterprise in revitalizing industry and commerce. And despite a recent economic downturn, grant giving on the part of foundations remains consistent, with education at or near the top of the list, according to a report of the Foundation Center in New York City (2009).

It is important then for Catholic schools to understand trends in the philanthropic community, where the current focus is on issues of organizational performance and accountability that result in measurable growth (Barton, Jones, DiMento, & Lewis , 2006; Thurman, 2006). At one time, people simply gave and hoped their contribution made a difference, but this is no longer the case. Benefactors who are able to track their donations and see results are more likely to be committed to the process of giving (Thurman, 2006). Thus, disaster relief efforts—such as those of Hurricane Katrina and more recently earthquake relief in Haiti—are less likely to attract large gifts from philanthropists precisely because of the difficulty in tracking where the money goes. According to Eugene Temple, Indiana's director of the Center on Philanthropy:

> When people make [large financial] gifts, they tend to want those gifts to be more permanent. Disaster relief is for taking care of pain and suffering right now, and the money gets spent. A donor's gift almost evaporates into thin air in front of them because sometimes the need is so large and it's hard to see where the $20-million went. (Barton et al., 2006, p. 4)

The challenge for Catholic schools is how to make inroads with potential funding sources after years of indifference toward foundations and philanthropists. Relying on their early success and the commitment of Catholic families, Catholic schools in the United States were hardly prepared for the changes that would rapidly and dramatically impact the way in which Catholic schools are funded. As a result, the hows and whys of philanthropy, as well as the potential pitfalls, have played a minor role in recent efforts to revive Catholic schooling (Montejano, 2007b). Catholic schools must position themselves as viable, creative, and effective entities in order to attract outside financial support.

A successful example in the field of Catholic education is Nativity/San Miguel schools—a collection of middle schools throughout the country that focus on struggling students by offering a rigorous curriculum and extended support system (Zehr, 2003a). The combination of small class sizes, committed teaching staffs, and an extended day has resulted in academic success across a variety of measures when compared to counterparts in traditional Catholic schools (Fenzel & Monteith, 2008). Innovative, and with a track record of academic success, this model is attractive to benefactors and effective.

The implications for Catholic schools at this point should be clear: Philanthropists are more likely to give to school programs with hope for the future, rather than to rescue a school in danger of closing. They are also more likely to show interest in innovative programs that target a specific need, such as those provided by the Nativity/Miguel Schools. Schools that perform and are of clear value to the community will also garner interest from outside benefactors. Finally, entities with a social mission are clear priorities of a philanthropic community interested in leveraging funding to effect social change (see Korten, 2009).

Additional evidence of the impact of philanthropy and business on Catholic schools also exists. Within the last decade, for example, individual benefactors and foundations have resuscitated Catholic schools (Borja & Branscom, 2005; Zehr, 2003b), built new ones (Reid, 2003), invested in innovative models (Zehr, 2003a, 2003b), and provided tuition awards to students from low-income families (Wittenberg, 2010). These individuals, foundations, and businesses responded to Catholic school leaders who outlined a plan beyond merely rescuing and maintaining Catholic schools; in each case, these leaders focused on one or more of the following areas important to potential financiers: the common good, civic needs, innovative programs, data showing excellent results, and a plan to insure sustainability and provide for growth over years.

In St. Louis, for example, Cardinal Ritter High School relied heavily on its reputation in the community to garner the interest of local business in refurbishing its dilapidated building and boosting dwindling enrollment

(Reid, 2003). Local philanthropists raised $30 million and built a new building that began accepting students in 2003. It was the city's first new private high school in the last 50 years. The school's excellent reputation (it was known for its academic rigor and perfect college acceptance rate in recent years) was motivation enough for the city's business leaders to commit multiple millions of dollars (Reid, 2003).

Boards in Catholic Schools

The addition of boards to the Catholic school landscape allows for a critical level of support in creating a development program (Haney, 2010). Boards in Catholic schools, of different configurations and levels of governance, allow for flexibility in creating an organizational framework that matches expertise with needs in the school community. It also creates a path for shared leadership. But data with respect to the establishment of boards in Catholic schools are mixed. The good news for Catholic schools is that most have a board of some configuration. In 2009–2010, 82.7% of Catholic schools reported having an existing board, commission, or council (McDonald, 2010). When restricted to high schools the number is higher, with 95% of respondents in a national survey reporting a board of some type (Gautier, Buck, & Cidade, 2009). But schools with low-income populations are less likely to have a board in place, according to survey data collected by O'Keefe et al. (2004); in schools where 90% of the students receive free lunch, the likelihood that the school has a board decreases by 20%. This number, while not surprising, is disheartening in that the very schools most in need of outside support are least likely to have it.

When Catholic schools are able to establish a school board that understands its charge and parameters—particularly in low-income communities—the results can be dramatic. An example is Philadelphia's Gesu School, which had been in decline for years but now thrives in part because of a newly created 57-member board of trustees who helped secure $1.7 million within three years (Borja & Branscom, 2005). The school population in this poor section of Philadelphia more than doubled between 1993 and 2005 as the school added a writing program, a counselor, and other enrichment programs. Additionally, the board also found donors to sponsor individual students.

Another creative example can be found with St. Anne School, which serves a mostly low-income population in Santa Monica, CA. With support from the Specialty Family Foundation,[1] St. Anne has created a development board that is a twist on the traditional model. Lacking the availability of expertise in their small parish community, they partnered with independent schools in Santa Monica to create the St. Anne School Support Council

(SASSC), according to Carol O'Day, the school's director of marketing and development (personal communication, January 21, 2011). Instead of relying on a set group of its own members, St. Anne has the capacity to call upon the expertise from partner institutions to serve the school in various capacities. According to O'Day, this model guards against "board fatigue" while at the same time giving service-oriented people the opportunity to contribute directly to a school of need. All of this, she states, has created a "community building spillover effect" in which the partnering institutions have increased their level of support as St. Anne has become better known to them. The SASSC has been able to raise enough money to offset the annual tuition deficit in each year of its existence. Further, St. Anne's success, with the help of O'Day and the SASSC, can be seen in its strong relationships with alumni, local preschools, and outreach to the business community.

Potential Pitfalls in Establishing Partnerships

To this point, only the potential benefits in reaching out to others for help have been discussed. But is there a downside for Catholic schools as they begin to rely less on the families who directly benefit and more on outside entities with their own needs and interests? Hendrie (2005) described an environment in which researchers need to question philanthropic activities in the educational arena. According to Hess (2005) and other scholars who contributed to a book on the topic, both researchers and media have been remiss in questioning the motives of philanthropists. Since $427 billion is spent annually on education, and only $1.5 billion comes from private benefactors, one can argue that a disproportionate amount of attention is given to reform efforts funded by foundations and wealthy benefactors (Hendrie, 2005). The role and needs of benefactors is something Catholic school leaders will need to understand, not only in terms of performance and accountability, as discussed above, but also with respect to educational philosophy and mission. Catholic school leaders should do everything to ensure the mission of Catholic schools and, as necessary, thoroughly educate potential benefactors about the nature and purpose of Catholic education.

Another area that must be considered is the impact of market-driven forces on education, which perhaps have more subtle implications with regard to partnerships among education and business. Apple (2001) referred to this as the "privatization, commodification, production, and marketing of goods and services" (Raduntz, 2005, p. 235). Its encroachment on education presents challenges for educational systems that have traditionally operated as democratic institutions; business leaders who set out to transform education into a profitable venture, he suggests, are likely to implant values that are counter to a democratic education (Apple, 2001).

The issues associated with outside assistance should be examined with a critical eye by leaders in Catholic education. Resource dependency theorists (Pfeffer & Salancik, 1974) have addressed the issue from the perspective of external control. They offer strategies such as resource diversification and employing measures to regulate outside influences, in order to guard against undue influence from outside the organization. External pressures, they postulated, can destroy or seriously alter an organization if outside forces are given too much control. In the case of Catholic schools, it might mean seeking funding from other sources if the goals and philosophies of benefactor and institution are far apart.

The above demonstrates that despite difficult circumstances, Catholic schools with a clear mission and purpose can garner interest in the philanthropic and business communities. They can also find ways to create boards that work to build and develop the school program. Both are critical components in initiating and implementing a development program in the school. But Catholic school leaders must be able to articulate clear lines of authority and communication when establishing partnerships. If boundaries are not clearly delineated, either by charter or other means, tensions can arise and inhibit development in the school (Montejano, 2007b).

SUSTAINABLE:
THE IMPLEMENTATION OF LONG-RANGE SUPPORTS

In this section we look at some of the development plans with long-range implications. The focus here is on efforts whose results might not be seen for years but are likely to have the greatest impact in helping schools weather unexpected changes, both within and outside the organization. In brief, these display characteristics that attempt to meet the survival demands of modern organizations by looking at the long-term goals and benefits. Examples in this area include the creation of new governance models, tithing, and endowments. Sustainability efforts of these kinds often require a deep change in the culture in order to build the resolve needed to secure the future. Therefore, careful planning is required in order to insure necessary buy-in.

New Governance Models

New governance models are a direct response to the financial problems plaguing Catholic schooling. They represent structural adaptations to the familiar parish school. These creative responses to the funding issue in-clude school sponsorships and consortia. Cimino (2010) notes that suc-cessful programs in this area share the following characteristics: work in the collective, carefully planned governance, commitment to historically marginalized populations, professional consultation, and attention to the Catholic identity in the school. Goldschmidt, O'Keefe, and Walsh (2004) identified different consortia throughout the United States and compiled relevant data about their shared aspects and what worked effectively. While each of the consortia varied in slight ways, they shared many common ele-ments. Each, for instance, turned to a consortium model to ward off im-minent closure. The administrators also shared the belief that their schools became stronger and more viable as a result of the move. An important ele-ment of the consortium model rests in its flexibility. As the authors noted:

> The strength of the consortium model is that there is no one formula and so it allows greater flexibility to meet the needs of the local Catholic community. Each consortium was designed to adapt to specific local realities (e.g., avail-able resources, local needs, size of the diocese, number of schools, etc.) and the wishes of its founders (i.e., the bishop, pastors, and the principals)....As dioceses tailor their consortia to their community, they seem to take a strong ownership in seeing it succeed. (Goldschmidt et al., 2004, p. 14)

An example of an effective consortium model is in Covington, Kentucky (Cimino, 2010). There, six urban schools are operated under one office structure. Financial and human resources are shared across these schools according to need. As well, a single school board oversees the development for each of the schools. This configuration focuses funding requests and alleviates the pressure of a single school having to secure significant fund-ing on its own. The loss of independence with regard to some aspects of the school program requires adjustments on the part of the school. The six schools in Covington represent a small and manageable number, but there may be a point when the addition of new schools to a consortium can financially overwhelm the structure (see Wuerl, 2008).

Tithing

Stewardship in the form of tithing is another area that has seen success in parts of the country but also requires a major shift in thinking about how the local Catholic school might be funded. This model "is one in which the parish assumes the entire cost of every student who seeks enrollment in the school and induces families to give sacrificially through the Sunday collec-tion" (James, 2007, p. 295). In the Diocese of Wichita, Kansas, the nearly 11,000 students attending 38 Catholic schools do so tuition free due to the support of Catholic school families through tax-deductible contributions to the Sunday collection (Karp, 2009). Parishes in Wichita can generate from tens of thousands to upwards of $100,000 weekly in support for the school, depending on its socioeconomic makeup (Karp, 2009).

The advantage of tithing, according to its proponents, is a strengthening of the relationship between school and parish (Karp, 2009). It also counters a market mentality in the typical parish school where "the affluent and influential purchase valuable access to leadership and decision-making" (Vobril, 2003, p. 14). Tithing further eliminates the reliance on outside donors and the itinerant problems with resource dependency discussed earlier in this chapter. In addition to the difficulty in cultivating the necessary financial commitment on the part of parishioners, tithing also requires a high level of affluence within the parish in order to raise enough money to support the school.

Endowments

To understand how an endowment is created, it might be helpful to consider a brief case study: the Catholic Education Foundation (CEF) in Los Angeles. Founded in 1986, the CEF annually provides tuition awards to students who qualify on the basis of financial need (Wittenburg, 2010). Using only the interest from its endowment, the foundation awarded $6.3 million to 6,800 students in 2009. In its 20-year history, the foundation has awarded over $71 million in tuition grants to 81,000 students. A study of the foundation's impact conducted by researchers at Loyola Marymount University (LMU) showed that 98% of CEF tuition award recipients go on to college (Wittenburg, 2010).

Wittenburg's (2010) chronicling of the CEF story indicates the importance cultivating relationships around a preferred dream. It also provides insight into how endowment goals are established and how an endowment's interest can be used to support key projects in an organization. In her account, she notes a meeting between Los Angeles' Cardinal Mahony and then-prominent business leader Richard Riordan to discuss a property transaction. As the two conversed, they learned of the other's passion for education. Mahony shared his vision with Riordan for a foundation with a goal of a $100 million endowment to support Catholic schools in Los Angeles, and Riordan—although surprised at the ambitious goal—expressed support. In a short time, the foundation was established with Riordan as its first president.

The first years of the CEF were used to establish a structure. The newly recruited trustees felt the need to get all the pieces in place while at the same time show others they intended to make good on the goal of a $100 million endowment. They initiated a Grant the Dream Campaign, whose purpose was to provide a Catholic education for financially disadvantaged children; the campaign netted $88 million in gifts and pledges from 1990–1994. The CEF was on its way to reaching its goal.

The CEF later funded other projects in support of Catholic education, such as a program to develop leadership in Catholic schools via an MA in leadership provided by local higher education institutions. But the funding of scholarships for needy students would always be at the core of its mission. Interestingly, one of the initiatives undertaken by the CEF was an alumni endowment appeal. Initiated in 2006, the foundation collected over $28,000 from current and former recipients of CEF funds. The CEF endowment peaked at nearly $140 million in 2007. And despite the recent economic downturn, the CEF remains above its original goal of $100 million.

On arriving at the goal of $100 million, Cardinal Mahony states (Wittenberg, 2010):

> I think that providing children and young people with a good solid Catholic education is the single most important thing the Church does in the lives of families. . . . We have to have Catholic schools and we have to have the financial resources to make them affordable. While the original goal of 100 million was out of nowhere, I am glad we picked a number that high. I hope we will get to 200 million before too long and then keep going. I see no limit to what we can do. (p. 99)

New models of governance, stewardship, and endowments are examples of long-range efforts to secure Catholic schooling. But the developmental process is time consuming and requires deep cultural change. In order to move Catholic schools beyond their archaic financial structures, the application of new thinking and creation of new models will have to be an organizational priority.

SUMMARY

This chapter reviewed the financial concerns and opportunities for development in Catholic schools. It began with an examination of the historical context and changing landscape as it related to financing the Catholic school. Because the archaic model of tuition-driven financing can no longer sustain Catholic schools, innovation and adaptation are necessary in order to secure the future. Various approaches to development as well as specific models were presented within a three-pronged framework of purpose, generativity, and sustainability. Catholic school leaders must consider each in order to understand the full-range of developmental options available, but they must also be aware of the challenging aspects of development, including culture change and the potential problems in involving outside benefactors.

NOTES

1. The Specialty Family Foundation developed a Catholic Schools Consortium to ensure the sustainability of selected Catholic schools in urban areas of Los Angeles. They are based in Santa Monica, CA.

REFERENCES

Apple, M. W. (2001). *Educating the "right" way: Markets, standards, God, and inequality.* New York, NY: RoutledgeFalmer.

Baker, D. P., & Riordan, C. (1998). The 'Eliting' of the common American Catholic school and the national education crisis. *Phi Delta Kappan, 80*, 11.

Barton, N., Jones, C., DiMento, M., & Lewis, N. (2006). How the wealthy give. *Chronicle of Philanthropy, 18*, 6–12.

Bellah, R. N., Madsen, R., Sullivan, W. M., Swidler, A., & Tipton, S. M. (1985). *Habits of the heart.* Berkeley, CA: University of California Press.

Borja, R. R., & Branscom, M. (2005). A spiritual investment. *Education Week, 24*, 34–38.

Bredeweg, F. (1980). *Catholic elementary schools and their finances—1979.* Washington, DC: National Catholic Educational Association.

Bridges, W. (2003). *Managing transitions: Making the most of change* (2nd ed.). Cambridge, MA: Da Capo Press.

Brown, C. L. (2005). *A recipe for change: Consolidation and restructuring in Catholic schools.* Washington, DC: National Catholic Educational Association.

Center for Applied Research in the Apostolate. (2006, Spring). *Primary trends, challenges, and outlook: A special report on U.S. Catholic elementary schools, 2000–2005.* Washington, DC: Georgetown University.

Cimino, C. (2010). The governance models. In D. F. Curtin, R. M. Haney, & J. M. O'Keefe (Eds.), *Design for success II: Configuring new governance models* (pp. 41–52). Arlington, VA: National Catholic Educational Association.

Cooperrider, D. L., & Srivastva, S. (1987). Appreciative inquiry in organizational life. In R. W. Woodman & W. A. Pasmore (Eds.), *Research in organizational change and development: An annual series featuring advances in theory, methodology, and research* (Vol. 1, pp. 129–169). Greenwich, CT: JAI Press.

Dolan, T. (2010). The Catholic schools we need. *America, 203*(6), 10–14.

Dwyer, T. W. (2009). *Catholic school strategic planning workbook.* Washington, DC: National Catholic Educational Association.

Fenzel, M. L., & Monteith, R. H. (2008). Successful alternative middle schools for urban minority children. *Journal of education for Students Placed at Risk, 13*, 381–401.

The Foundation Center. (2009). *Highlights of foundation giving trends*. Retrieved from http://foundationcenter.org/gainknowledge/research/Pdf/fgt09highlights.pdf

Gautier, M. L., Buck, A. C., & Cidade, M. A. (2009). *Dollars and sense: A report on Catholic high school leadership, governance & finance*. Washington, DC: National Catholic Educational Association.

Goldschmidt, E. P., O'Keefe, J. M., & Walsh, M. E. (2004). *Reconfiguring Catholic schools: A study of the Catholic school consortium model*. Boston College: Lynch School of Education.

Groome, T. H. (1998). *Educating for life: A spiritual vision for every teacher and parent*. Allen, TX: Thomas More.

Guerra, M. J. (2004). *Catholic schools: Gift to the Church, gift to the nation* [Monograph]. Washington, DC: National Catholic Educational Association.

Hallinan, M. T. (2000). Catholic education at the crossroads. In J. Youniss & J. J. Convey (Eds.), *Catholic schools at the crossroads: Survival and transformation* (pp. 201–220). New York, NY: Teachers College Press.

Haney, R. M. (2010). Why board and steps to start a board. In D. F. Curtin, R. M. Haney, & J. M. O'Keefe (Eds.), *Design for success II: Configuring new governance models* (pp. 5–20). Arlington, VA: National Catholic Educational Association.

Harris, J. C. (2000). The funding dilemma facing Catholic elementary and secondary schools. In J. Youniss & J. J. Convey (Eds.), *Catholic schools at the crossroads: Survival and transformation* (pp. 55–71). New York, NY: Teachers College Press.

Hendrie, C. (2005). Researchers ask tough questions of K–12 charities. *Education Week, 24*, 21–24.

Hess, F. M. (1999). *Spinning wheels: The politics of urban school reform*. Washington, DC: Brookings Institution Press.

Hess, F. M. (Ed.). (2005). *With the best of intentions: How philanthropy is reshaping K–12 education*. Cambridge, MA: Harvard Education Press.

James, J. T. (2007). Changes in funding and governance of Catholic elementary education in the United States. *British Journal of Religious Education, 29*(4), 287–301.

James, J. T., Tichy, K. L., Collins, A., & Schwob, J. (2008). A quantitative analysis of parish school viability. *Catholic Education: A Journal of Inquiry and Practice, 11*(4), 465–484.

Karp, S. (2009). Final exam: Can we reinvent Catholic schools? *U.S. Catholic, 74*, 12–17.

Kealey, R. J. (1992). *United States Catholic elementary schools and their finances 1991*. Washington, DC: National Catholic Educational Association.

Kealey, R. J. (2001). *Balance sheet for Catholic elementary schools: 2001 income and expenses*. Washington, DC: National Catholic Educational Association.

Korten, A. E. (2009). *Change philanthropy: Candid stories of foundations maximizing results through social justice*. San Francisco, CA: Jossey-Bass.

McClellan, J. A. (2000). Rise, fall and reasons why: U.S. Catholic elementary education, 1940–1995. In J. Youniss & J. J. Convey (Eds.), *Catholic schools at the crossroads: Survival and transformation* (pp. 17–32). New York, NY: Teachers College Press.

McDonald, D. (2010). *United States Catholic elementary and secondary schools 2009–2010*. Washington, DC: National Catholic Educational Association.

McDonald, M. (2007). Partners for quality in inner-city Catholic schools. *Momentum, 38*(4), 34–38.

McGreevy, J. T. (1996). *Parish boundaries: The Catholic encounter with race in the twentieth century urban North.* Chicago, IL: University of Chicago Press.

McGreevy, J. T. (2003). *Catholicism and American freedom.* New York, NY: W.W. Norton.

Montejano, F. (2007a). *Assessing the sustainability and possibility for transformation of The Catholic school: A case study of St. Leo School* (Unpublished doctoral dissertation). Loyola Marymount University, Los Angeles, CA.

Montejano, F. (2007b). Will philanthropy save Catholic schools? *Momentum, 38*(4), 6–11.

National Conference of Catholic Bishops. (1884). *The pastoral letter of 1884 (Third Plenary Council of Baltimore).* Retrieved from http://www.catholicculture.org/docs/doc_view.cfm?recnum=518

O'Keefe, J. M., Greene, J. A., Henderson, S., Connors, M., Goldschmidt, E., & Schervish, K. (2004). *Sustaining the legacy: Inner-city Catholic elementary schools in the United States.* Washington, DC: NCEA.

Pascale, R., Millemann, M., & Gioja, L. (2000). *Surfing the edge of chaos: The laws of nature and the new laws of business.* New York, NY: Crown Business.

Pfeffer, J., & Salancik, G. R. (1974). *The external control of organizations: A resource dependence perspective.* New York, NY: Harper & Row.

Raduntz, H. (2005). The marketization of education within the global economy. In M. W. Apple, J. Kenway, & M. Singh (Eds.), *Globalizing education: Policies, pedagogies, & politics* (pp. 231–245). New York, NY: Peter Lang Publishing.

Reid, K. S. (2003). City's movers and shakers rally to save Catholic school. *Education Week, 23,* 18–20.

Roberts, T. (2009). Saving a fragile Catholic school system. *National Catholic Reporter, 45,* 12–14.

Ryan, F. J., Soven, M., Smither, J., Sullivan, W. M., & Vanbuskirk, W. R. (1999). Appreciative inquiry: Using personal narratives for initiating school reform. *Clearing House, 72*(3), 164–168.

Ryan, M. (1964). *Are parochial schools the answer?* New York, NY: Holt, Reinhart & Winston.

Steinfels, P. (2003). *A people adrift: The crisis of the Roman Catholic Church in America.* New York, NY: Simon and Schuster.

Thurman, E. (2006). Performance philanthropy. *Harvard International Review, 28,* 18–21.

Vobril, B. (2003). Becoming rooted in the stewardship way of life. *Momentum, 34*(1), 14–16.

Walch, T. (1996). *Parish school: American Catholic parochial education from colonial times to the present.* New York, NY: Crossroads.

Watkins, J. M., & Mohr, B. J. (2001). *Appreciative inquiry: Change at the speed of imagination.* San Francisco, CA: Jossey-Bass.

Wincek, J., & O'Malley, C. (1995). *Taking hold of the future: The ABC's of strategic planning.* Washington, DC: National Catholic Educational Association.

Wittenberg, M. J. (2010). *An investment in children: The history of the Catholic education foundation.* Los Angeles, CA: Catholic Education Foundation.

Wuerl, D. W. (2008). How to save Catholic schools. *America, 199*(21), 16–18.

Youniss, J., & Convey, J. J. (Eds.). (2000). *Catholic schools at the crossroads: Survival and transformation.* New York, NY: Teachers College Press.

Zehr, M. A. (2002). Charters in some cities attract students from Catholic schools. *Education Week, 21*(37), 12.

Zehr, M. A. (2003a). Finding a way out. *Education Week, 22,* 22–28.

Zehr, M. A. (2003b). Memphis sees Catholic school renaissance. *Education Week, 23,* 6–8.

CHAPTER 7

RECRUITING
AND RETAINING STUDENTS

Barbara Stacy Rieckhoff

VIGNETTE

The new principal has just been hired for St. Mary's Academy. Current conditions are bleak, with the front gates of the school locked with a heavy chain due to the safety issues that prevail in the neighborhood. Local real estate agents spread the word that the school is closed. The neighborhood has been undergoing rapid gentrification. What was primarily a school and parish for Spanish-speaking families and children has become a neighborhood and parish for Caucasian English speakers. The families who have recently moved into the parish are building new large homes and demanding an excellent school for their children. They want to help create the vision for the school, but they also want guarantees that their children will have a rigorous education and be accepted into the top-tier Catholic high schools in this city.

Current enrollment in the school is declining. The preschool classrooms are half-filled, with one teacher who has an excellent reputation and one who is marginal. Parents request the excellent teacher and become upset when their child is placed in the class with the marginal teacher. Upper grades classes have small numbers, with combined grade levels at the 4th and 5th

Catholic School Leadership, pages 107–132
Copyright © 2016 by Information Age Publishing

grades and the 7th and 8th grades. At the same time, neighboring Catholic schools have waiting lists, families willing to pay extra, volunteer, and do just about anything to get their 2nd, 3rd, or 4th child into the school.

A new principal has been hired each year over the past three years, who then moves on to another position elsewhere. As a result, the pastor was forced to serve as the principal when he couldn't find anyone to fill the spot before the start of the school year. Already responsible for a large, urban parish, he attempted to run the school at the same time. The teachers are trying to lend their support, but there is no aligned message about the school. Many parents have volunteered to help but are unsure what they can do to help the school stay open and improve itself at the same time.

How would you mediate the two existing cultures? What steps would you take to manage the changes that have already occurred and those yet to come? How would you work with teachers, parents, and staff to bring them into the efforts to grow the school?

INTRODUCTION

The Catholic school principal has a number of responsibilities above and beyond that of the traditional school leader (Brownridge, 2009; Ozar, 2010; Schmitt, 2012). While the typical job description includes fostering and promoting the mission of a Catholic school environment, a key role attributed to the principal is recruiting and retaining students. This role demands close attention and has the potential to be an area of primary importance as it serves to keep the school doors open. Current economic conditions require a principal's attention to be focused on the school's enrollment; thus, the development and advancement of student enrollment should be a priority for a Catholic school leader. A principal needs to be aware of and understand the reasons that families select Catholic schools. This understanding of why families seek out Catholic schools links to specific strategies for building enrollment. There are a number of essential elements in a successful recruitment and retention plan. They are as follows:

1. Clear mission and vision
2. Strong academic and instructional program
3. Multi-tiered public relations system
4. Recruitment plan
5. Retention of current students
6. Knowledge of the local Catholic and civic communities
7. Partnerships with local universities and agencies
8. Demonstration of creativity and innovation
9. Use of data to inform stakeholders

10. Advancement process
11. Understanding one's leadership profile

> (*Source:* Adapted from the Office of Catholic Schools
> Marketing Committee, 2008)

WHY FAMILIES SELECT CATHOLIC SCHOOLS

There are numerous reasons a family selects a Catholic school for their child's education. While the primary goal of a Catholic school education is to promote the mission of the Church and its teachings, there are spiritual and nonreligious considerations for choosing a Catholic school. One of the primary reasons a family chooses a Catholic school is their commitment to their faith. The Catholic school environment embodies the values and discipline it instills in students. Parents associate Catholic schools with the development of strong moral values and discipline. Providing a safe, secure, and nurturing environment is among another of the reasons families select a Catholic school. Catholic schools are chosen for the religious education, better discipline, and the absence of disruptive students (Cain & Goldberger, 1983). Other unique qualities, such as school size and opportunities for involvement, further attract parents. Fewer layers of bureaucracy allow greater access and involvement to a child's education; parents are typically working with a single institution rather than a multilayered organization.

Related to decentralization, the smaller size of a parish school promotes better interaction between students, parents, and staff (Walch, 1997). Moreover, within the Catholic school setting, parents, students, and faculty share in a broad set of beliefs giving each school a moral purpose. This shared code of conduct stresses human dignity and the belief that human reason can discern ethical truth (Bryk, Lee, & Holland, 1993). Within this shared philosophy, teachers serve as role models and mentors because of the multiple functions they play in their students' lives each school day.

Minority families opt for Catholic education for the attention it gives their children (Hamilton, 2008). Catholic schools have a long history of respect for cultural differences, first among Europeans and later among people from all parts of the world. Additionally, Catholic schools in the United States have a proud legacy of providing educational opportunities to children from low-income, poorly educated families (Sander, 1996; Sander & Krautman, 1995; York, 1995). Following Vatican II, Catholic schools rededicated themselves to intensifying and expanding educational service to the disadvantaged (Hunt, Joseph, & Nuzzi, 2001; Riordan, 2000). There is a distinctive approach to Catholic education, one that is substantive, comprehensive, and integrated. Concern for the common good is an integral feature of a Catholic philosophy of education; "Catholic schools aim to develop in pupils the desire and ability to contribute constructively to worldly affairs, simultaneously with their readiness to respond to the call to conversion" (Sullivan, 2001, p. 176).

Academic excellence serves as another important reason to select a Catholic school. Coleman, Hoffer, and Kilgore (1982) were among the first to document private schools' academic success in *High School Achievement: Public and Private Schools*. Their study concluded that a private school education, including Catholic schools, results in higher cognitive outcomes than a public school education. The achievement gap in Catholic schools is smaller and students demonstrate higher academic achievement than students from similar backgrounds in public schools (Jeynes, 2007; Marks & Lee, 1989; Sander, 1996). Using data from the *High School and Beyond Survey*, Black inner-city students who attended Catholic high schools were more academically successful than their peers who attended public schools (Coleman & Hoffer, 1987). Bryk et al. contend that "Catholic high schools manage to simultaneously achieve relatively high levels of student learning, distribute this learning more equitably with regard to race and class than in the public sector, and sustain high levels of teacher commitment and student engagement" (1993, p. 297). The prevailing perception is that a Catholic education will provide better academic quality along with strong discipline to better manage students for optimal learning.

Understanding the reasons families select a Catholic education help the principal to build upon these qualities or characteristics and further utilize them as a means for recruiting new students and informing ways to retain existing students. Whether parental selection is based on one of these components or a combination thereof, the end result is that the principal will want to expand in understanding the factors parents are seeking out for their child's Catholic education. Knowledge of parental expectations is useful to the school leader to form and shape school culture in a continuous improvement cycle, building upon the school's strengths, while monitoring and targeting areas for future growth and development.

THE ROLE OF THE PRINCIPAL
IN RECRUITMENT AND RETENTION EFFORTS

What is the role of the principal in a school's recruitment and retention efforts? The principal must have an appropriate balance of knowledge regarding the process and her own involvement in the implementation phase. When interviewed about these areas, Catholic school principals cited the top three priorities of their work as spiritual formation, student learning, and teacher support (Glynn, 2006). While Glynn identifies the responsibility of increasing enrollment as fifth on a principal's priority list, it was work connected and undertaken by various groups, committees, or boards within the local Catholic school community. Therefore, it is useful for the principal to consider enrollment and recruitment initiatives as other school-wide efforts; the school leader needs to be involved and provide oversight of the process, while the implementation phase can engage key stakeholders from the community. While the Catholic school principal is charged with the responsibility of building school enrollment, the work needs to be shared with others who can move recruitment and retention efforts forward quickly. Consideration should be given to parents, teachers, and alumni who can inform and share in the process, the communication, and the intended outcomes. Depending upon the available resources of the school, its board, and the community, recruitment efforts can and should be delegated to these groups. It is crucial to share the important work of growing the school with the all of the parish community, with considerations for the prevailing culture and utilization of time, treasure, and talent that exist.

ELEMENTS FOR SUCCESSFUL
RECRUITMENT AND RETENTION

Principals need to ensure the presence of certain fundamental elements in order to meet with success in the recruitment and retention of students. What those specific elements look like and how they will be implemented depends upon the make-up and composition of the school, its resources and its culture. However, there is no substitute for having these key elements in place to further the school's growth and development. Most importantly, the principal must view recruitment and retention efforts within the context of how these relate to the broader role of supporting teachers and students, and serving as a faith model for all.

1. Clear Mission and Vision

A key element in the process of recruiting and retaining students is the development and articulation of a clear vision for the school. A school leader is required to articulate the vision and mission of the school to all stakeholders (Barth, 1990; Fullan, 2001; Interstate School Leaders Licensure Consortium [ISLLC], 2008; Sergiovanni, 1996). The significance of this step cannot be overstated; if not done correctly and consistently, this step has the potential to disrupt the other elements in the process of building a successful school. Equally important to the work of the leader is the process of maintaining and constantly reiterating the vision across multiple settings and contexts, with internal and external constituents, in the school community. The principal's ability to articulate and share the mission and vision is essential to a school's success. The vision must be clear and compelling, with authentic references to it in the day-to-day work of administrators and teachers. Vision has been defined as "the capacity to create and communicate a view of the desired state of affairs that induces commitment among those working in the organization" (Ubben, Hughes, & Norris, 2004, p. 15, Norris, 1990). A common mission statement might read: "Our mission is to ensure that all students can be successful." One way the school integrates this mission is to monitor the children's academic and behavioral success on a regular basis. For internal stakeholders, the vision and mission serve to model and reinforce the work of the faculty and staff inside the school. For example: "The mission of our school is to further spread the word of God and help each child reach his intellectual and spiritual potential." For external stakeholders, a transparent mission and vision provide a continual reinforcement or correction to the perception that outsiders have of the school. This clear and consistent message will align with the larger goal of building enrollment (Boyle, 2010).

As consideration is given to developing a school's mission and vision, one may already be in existence. The Catholic school leader may want to restate the commitment to that mission or consider updating it for current conditions. The parish or larger religious community may drive the mission for the school. If this is the case, consider creating one that is just for the school alone or utilizing the parish mission statement to help further articulate the vision for students (Boyle, 2010; Office of Catholic Schools, Archdiocese of Chicago, 2009). An exercise to assist with this process poses questions to stakeholders, such as: What does a graduate of our school have to know and be able to do? A graduate of our school will be able to demonstrate his knowledge, serve others, help the community, and become a life-long learner. A conversation with stakeholder groups using such a visioning activity will reinforce the mission throughout the school community (DuFour, 1998, 2001; Eaker, DuFour, & DuFour, 2002). Parishioners may view a graduate of the school through one lens, while internal stakeholders might have a different perspective. The dialogue helps to bridge differences that may exist and further create a shared understanding of the goals for the school. Although creating and revising mission and vision statements takes considerable time and energy, the process of deliberation and discussion establishes a foundation for identify priorities for the work of key stakeholder groups within a Catholic school. Questions to be considered for this process may include the following: What do we want our school to be known for? Is there a particular niche designated for our school, such as fine arts, excellence in academics, parish school, or other type of specialization? As today's Catholic schools are not all alike, many fit into a particular niche or specialty area. It is important to have these conversations with the local priests, school board and faculty, and all internal constituents so there is agreement and further reinforcement about the school's mission. Depending upon funding, the relationship between a parish or church and the school population served will dictate and direct the mission. The final, agreed-upon mission and vision statement will provide both a positioning and differentiating document for the school (DuFour, 1998). For the principal and members on the team, this compels all to consider what they believe personally on behalf of the school. This process aligns with the national expectations for the work of a school leader, illustrated by Interstate School Leader Licensure Consortium Standards (ISLLC, 2008), Standard 1: "A school administrator is an educational leader who promotes the success of all students by facilitating the development, articulation, implementation and stewardship of a vision of learning that is shared and supported by the school community" (ISLLC, 2008, p. 14).

A second step in the mission and visioning process is the identification of clear and measurable clear goals for the school. These may be derived from a strategic plan or other long-range plan that identifies long- and short-term goals. "Leadership involves purposes and direction. Leaders know the end toward which they are striving. They pursue goals with clarity and tenacity, and are accountable for their accomplishments" (Leithwood & Riehl, 2003, p. 7).

School leaders and boards should create, implement, and monitor a strategic plan with specific goal statements, objectives, strategies, and tactics. The strategic plan should support long-range plans in the areas of enrollment, communication, marketing, development, curriculum, technology, and finance (Wincek & O'Malley, 1995). For enrollment efforts, concentration on goals already identified for the school's evaluation or archdiocesan accountability reporting will be useful. This goal alignment with areas already being evaluated or assessed will ensure that priorities are maintained. A separate set of goals or subset within these main goals can include recruitment and retention efforts. Research suggests limiting the number of goals to three to five, as successful schools have shown to set priorities for a few items (Fullan, 1991; Hopkins, 1994). This is not just related to Catholic school enrollment issues; rather, this era of high-stakes accountability requires that all schools put enrollment at the forefront of what is best for children and prioritize these needs first. Materials and resources can help to monitor the mission by way of the school board or even a committee dedicated exclusively to this purpose, such as the mission enhancement committee, a group charged with the duties of translating the mission, identifying data to support it, and collecting the appropriate data to monitor its growth and progress (DuFour, 1998, 2001; Fullan, 1991).

2. Strong Academic and Instructional Program

Effective schools have strong instructional programs, with evidence and data to support this fact (DuFour, 2001; Elmore, 2000; Marzano, 2003). An excellent instructional program is a nonnegotiable requirement that provides for the needs of all students. The knowledge that academic quality is one of the three reasons parents send their children to Catholic schools further underscores the importance of this element. Schools with effective instructional programs continually attend to this goal. Effective schools are constantly evaluating, updating, and further refining their academic and instructional programs. How does a school get to this point and what are the hallmarks for a principal to look for? Researchers have identified factors to describe an effective school (DuFour, 2001; Kowalski, Lasley, & Mahoney, 2007; Marzano, 2003; Schmoker, 1996, 2001, 2006). Marzano's meta-anlysis of successful schools has further identified school-level factors for success, suggesting that effective schools have five school-level factors or elements in place. These include a guaranteed and viable curriculum, challenging goals and effective feedback, collegiality and professionalism, a safe and secure environment, and parental involvement. Other research has identified basic characteristics of effective schools; this includes data to diagnose problems and find solutions; challenging, realistic, and measurable goals; and assessment and continuous evaluation that is both formative and summative. Regardless of the model used for framing goals for academic improvement, effective schools employ a process that is ongoing and continuous (Bauer & Brazer, 2012; Bernhardt, 2002; Boudett, City & Murnane, 2005; Schmoker, 1996, 2001).

A Catholic school leader typically guides and leads the instructional program in addition to the many other roles held. While not mandated to report academic results and progress as public schools following No Child Left Behind Act (NCLBA, 2001), Catholic schools do need to share instructional and academic results with appropriate audiences and stakeholders. Catholic schools are not exempt from demonstrating evidence of student learning through reporting of standardized testing results or mastery of learning goals and standards. On the contrary, schools that have demonstrated academic success are those that have been involved in a continuous cycle of school improvement, identifying various data points for analysis along with targeted goals for improvement. The National Catholic Education Association recognizes a Catholic school's demonstrated growth in student achievement via the No Child Left Behind Act Blue Ribbon Schools Program, which honors public and private K–12 schools that are either academically superior in their states or demonstrate dramatic gains in student achievement:

Our nation has a responsibility to help all children realize their full potential. Schools honored with the Blue Ribbon Schools award are committed to
achievement and to ensuring that students learn and succeed. Their work
reflects the conviction that every child has promise and must receive a quality education. (U.S. Department of Education Press Release, 9/7/12 2012
National Blue Ribbon Schools press@ed.gov)

Along with reporting results, the importance of the principal's role as
the instructional leader for the school cannot be overstated. The principal
as a factor impacting on student learning is second only to that of the classroom teacher (Leithwood, Harris, & Hopkins, 2008). This impact comes
from knowledgeable school leaders who understand their instructional
programs and can articulate academic programmatic goals and priorities.
Within a Catholic school, the content includes the religion curriculum,
which in many ways serves to guide other instructional areas along with
the socioemotional and affective learning domains. While the religion curriculum and student socioemotional learning provide a strong foundation
for the teaching and learning that occurs in a Catholic school, these areas
cannot replace the need for a strong academic program across all content
areas. Academic, spiritual, and affective learning must be rigorous and
meet state and local standards while honoring developmental stages and
milestones (Fullan, 1991).

Rigorous academic programs are central to sustaining student enrollment. Enrollment losses occur for a multitude of reasons; the prevailing
perception may hold that the academics are stronger elsewhere. Elementary schools need to recognize critical developmental stages by working
with feeder programs at entry and exit points; this includes monitoring
student performance upon entry to the system and measuring success on
high school entrance tests and placement in advanced classes. High school
considerations should include data on college entrance, results of ACT and
SAT tests, along with success rates in Advanced Placement or International
Baccalaureate classes. Tracking and monitoring statistics and factors that go
beyond the actual elementary school's academic program can make a huge
difference in a school's success with recruiting students. Perceptions of a
school's academic program that are strong and rigorous, combined with
data on the number of students accepted into prestigious high schools or
colleges, will greatly promote positive recruitment efforts. While other factors require close consideration, successful entrance to the next educational level directly impacts enrollment. Student acceptance into high-perform-
ing high schools reinforces the strength of a school's academic program.

Parental knowledge of the school's academic program that occurs with
regular, ongoing communication of facts and data further supports recruitment and retention efforts. Standardized test scores should be publicized
and analyzed in relation to national, state, and local norms. Parent nights,

open houses, and regular face-to-face, online, and paper communication with families are part of the process of disseminating the instructional program. Report cards, midterm assessments, and classroom-level test results are generated at the teacher level. Recent technologies allow parents an increasing level of access to information on the school's website or portal in a timely, concise manner, thereby emphasizing their critical role in supporting their child's success. Curriculum revisions, new program implementation and materials can be made available on the school or teacher website. Communication and parent feedback about new program implementation further support parents' importance and partner role. Finally, the school's efforts in recruiting and retaining students connect directly to the instructional program. Data and frequent updates about the success of the program must be shared with various stakeholders. Potential parents and external partners will want to know the facts about the school as well as how to access key information and understand the cycle of ongoing improvement that exists (Sullivan, 2001).

3. Multi-Tiered Public Relations System

Catholic school leaders are charged with spreading the good news about their schools. These marketing efforts can have a dramatic impact on the recruitment and retention efforts. In spreading the good news, principals have to maintain credibility as a leader and member of the community. Standardized test scores may not be at desired levels; a more compelling notion to potential parents may be knowledge that an annual school goal seeks to increase student achievement test scores by a targeted number of percentage points over the next two to three years. This further serves to communicate the priorities of the school.

The responsibility of spreading the good news and serving as public relations agent does not rest exclusively with the principal. As a school leader serves in multiple roles, the one of marketing agent is certainly a shared role, as good news about the school resonates with programs, current and former students, parents, and teachers. Catholic schools benefit from publishing a profile of graduation rates, results of parent satisfaction surveys, and other perceptual or satisfaction data. The principal is in the position of modeling for teachers and staff how this information can best be shared. While there is no limit to the amount of information distributed, the most effective method is through regular venues, formally and informally, at the diocesan or system level, school website, weekly newsletters to parents, and quarterly updates to parishioners. An annual report provides a more formalized delivery of the accomplishments, achievements, and hallmarks of the school. News can be shared with school partners, community members, local chamber of commerce members, and those without a direct connection; an even more powerful process occurs when students, parents, and teachers share news of the school through their own networks (Burke, 2009).

The practice of making the school newsworthy requires participation in outside events and school activities. Student participation in competitions, pageants, school fairs, or public relations events at the local and state levels provide news for such a purpose. Relationships with public school colleagues can facilitate access and entry to such venues and further increase school recognition. An updated website accompanied with quality marketing materials will communicate these multiple opportunities for students' achievement and interests. Marketing materials should be concise, align with other information, and reinforce the stated mission and vision. The desired message should emphasize the welcoming and inviting community, one that is open and available to visitors after Mass for open house tours and during regularly scheduled times. Coordination with the pastor may involve a plea from the pulpit to invite parishioners to visit and continue their support of the school. Schools without parish connections should tap into alumni databases and involve former students to assist in this important work. Alumni help can be enlisted in traditional ways such as fundraising efforts, but also nontraditional ways, such as coordinating tours of the school, developing historical or archival materials, and most importantly, getting information about the school to new venues. If no formal alumni group exists, energy and time should be spent tracking alumni, determining where they are located and what they have accomplished. Every school has successful graduates who would be honored to return to the school and provide support when invited.

4. Recruitment Plan

A well-articulated plan for recruiting students is an essential element in the Catholic school leader's overall responsibility of recruiting and retaining students. Within this plan is the necessity to complete in-service training for teachers, staff, and administrators with regard to their roles in marketing the Catholic school for image and for building enrollment. Involvement of teachers in recruitment efforts from the committee level to actual implementation stage will help faculty understand the challenges related to enrollment and connect the importance of their role in the process. The recruitment plan links to the mission and vision of the school, with active involvement of current, satisfied parents and teachers serving as ambassadors for welcoming new families. Revisiting the plan annually to assess its effectiveness will safeguard against activities not meeting the goals and criteria. As the recruitment plan stems from the school board's strategic plan, such data help determine the appropriateness of adding a new section of a grade level each year, adding new school partners, or inviting school board members to expand resources for the school. Regardless of the specific details of the plan, the significant message of a recruitment plan communicates the school's growth and attention to that growth. Too often, Catholic school enrollments fluctuate based on increases in tuition or changes in teaching or administrative staff, which contributes to a negative image; this can be upsetting and worrisome to current families and risks communicating failure to outside groups. The strategic planning process helps to determine the maximum or preferred student enrollment for each grade with action steps for reaching these goals. Tuition increases should align with the strategic plan and delineate class size and the portion of tuition to be spent on operating expenses.

Strategic steps in the recruitment efforts can facilitate growth of the school. Begin by filling up the classes with the youngest students in the building; if the entry point is preschool, consider a Mom and Tots program from the parish base so that families can become acquainted with the school and other families. If the entry point is high school, develop a junior high program that brings students to the school for a single academic class, an athletic program, or a refresher course to prepare them for the transition to high school. The recruitment plan may call for adding a section each year to the school's enrollment, but safeguards must be in place against the critical points when students typically transfer out of school, such as during the middle grades, when they are trying to gain entry into high school. Consider enrollment projections in the process; three full preschool classes will transition into two kindergarten classes (Picciano, 2006). School presence and staff attendance at the local school fairs provide an opportunity for teachers and parent volunteers to speak directly with prospective parents. Open house tours held on a regular, more frequent basis than annual Catholic Schools Week celebrations allow outsiders multiple opportunities to visit the school. Classroom walkthroughs provide an opportunity to observe the teaching and learning process, religion instruction, and other hallmarks of the school. In this way, teachers play a significant role in presenting a positive image all year long. Students also share in the process, demonstrating their academic work, their behavior, and their pride in the school to visitors. Current parents can coordinate school tours, with parent-to-parent conversations providing good credibility. While the principal should be present and visible at many of these events, other members of the school community should organize and coordinate them. The principal can welcome prospective families at the start of the tour and then rejoin at the end of the visit to take questions or meet individually with prospective parents who have specific needs. School visits or tours should be followed with up notes, calls, or emails, using the method most befitting the local culture. Invite school board members, alumni and community members to join in this process. Finally, enlist the help of students to greet visitors, check coats, or serve coffee to further reinforce the mission of the school and the spirit of service to others that prevails (Dumas, 2009; Pritchard & Whitehead, 2004).

5. Retention Plan

Historically, retention among Catholic schools students is particularly healthy, especially for minority students enrolled in Catholic schools. Minority students in Catholic schools are less likely to drop out of school than minority students in public schools (Convey, 1992). What then is the principal's role in retaining current students, building upon the successes and understanding why some families do opt out of Catholic schools? Attention to keeping current students enrolled is often overlooked in the recruitment and retention plan. Clear strategies to enhance student retention must be in place. The first step for any school is to assess the retention situation, identifying past records on retention, to determine the reasons families are attracted to the school and identify steps for changing or enhancing the retention data and statistics. Begin by determining if students leave due to academic, disciplinary, personal, or financial reasons or some combination thereof. All too often, the focus is on recruitment of new students and not retention of current students. This is an imperative; if the retention of current students gets the attention it needs, it automatically serves to fulfill recruitment efforts. Problems with student retention will continually make the recruitment efforts more difficult and will signal the existence of a negative perception that needs to be addressed. The retention plan will serve to pose questions such as: Why do families leave a school voluntarily? and What process is in place to collect information about the reasons for leaving? Invite families to complete exit surveys or exit interviews, encouraging them to be candid about their reasons for leaving the school. However, school improvement is based on growth and development, with particular attention to the improvement of weak areas. The retention plan will provide a system for obtaining feedback from current families and from those who leave the school; the fact that the school cares about this information further communicates this concern to internal stakeholders and those who may consider joining the community. A school satisfaction survey that all parents complete will identity perceived strengths and weaknesses. This multipronged approach to school evaluation will capture parent perceptions so they can be addressed within the context of school improvement. Such tools for collecting parent and student satisfaction data are often linked to school-wide evaluations and can inform the process and provide facts on multiple levels (AdvancEd, 2012).

In addition to understanding why families leave a Catholic school, retention efforts should focus equal attention on the families who opt to stay in the Catholic school. At its basic level, retention relies on satisfied students and parents. School personnel will want to make a conscious attempt to survey constituent satisfaction, to modify programs and activities where appropriate, and to involve current students and families in the life of the school. As important stakeholders in the community, current students and parents require a voice and share in the decision-making processes of the school. Designated roles for parent participation can include formalized roles on boards and committees or informal roles such as planning single and annual events. Each opportunity for parents to have a voice and be knowledgeable about their child's school will serve as a positive impact. "Parents must be given considerable role in the development of policy for Catholic schools" (Convey, 2000, p. 81). Consider ways to help smooth the transition of families into the school regardless of entry point for the child. Students who transfer from another school frequently struggle with the adjustment to the new school. Efforts to welcome new families and closely monitor their transitions academically, socioemotionally, and spiritually will reinforce the mission and vision and create a sense of belonging for all students.

Additional strategies to support retention efforts may involve placement of teachers and staff. Placing the strongest teachers at critical points or grades where the school is losing students may help to minimize or address such losses. The goal of involving all parents in the school in some capacity will strengthen the bond and connection with the school. Share the retention and recruitment efforts; dispel any perception that an elitist group makes important decisions for the school. Finally, consider incentives or ways to reward and recognize families who do remain at the school for a long time, in the form or awards, services, or special privileges. This positive impact on current families will in turn be projected to the larger community.

6. Knowledge of the Local Catholic and Civic Communities

An awareness and understanding of school and parish norms and traditions is an effective means of supporting the recruitment and retention efforts in the school. The school leader must be aware of the traditions upon which the school has been built. This may cut across cultural, ethnic, and religious traditions. It may revolve around the ethnic diversity present within the parish and school culture, or it may revolve around traditions established by the parish and school groups such as the Mothers' Club,

Fathers' Club, Rosary Society, or Parent–Teacher Association. Each of these groups will have its own set of traditions and celebrations and may play a role in fundraising efforts for the school. Efforts to engage such groups and reinforce their connection to the school will prove beneficial; they are key stakeholders who can serve as ambassadors and continue to share the good work of the school. The principal's role is to be aware of these different groups and recognize their contributions to the school. While some events or longstanding traditions may have limited connections to the current day-to-day functioning of the school, they play a role in the success of the school. Certificates of appreciation and volunteer appreciation luncheons are ways to honor such traditions from the past and foster present day commitment. The principal will want to continue to forge and strengthen relationships with individuals who are loyal to the school and who will do whatever is needed to support its continued existence (DuFour, 1998, 2001).

Principals are required to be knowledgeable about the history of the school; how it was founded, when, and by whom; and take time to support and celebrate various anniversaries and celebrations of its existence. If the school or parish is connected to a religious order, learn about and share this information with teachers and staff members so all can honor the work, history, and traditions of these groups. New teacher orientation should include the background and history of the parish and its culture (Hood, London, & Rieckhoff, 2011). The richness of Catholic schools can be found in these traditions, and connections can be tied to fundraising themes and slogans. The Catholic Church and schools are institutions that are built upon strong traditions. It serves to honor the traditions that are the foundations for Catholic schools.

7. Partnerships With Local Universities and Agencies

The need for school partnerships and collaborative efforts has never been stronger; all schools benefit from connections with local universities and agencies as a way to share resources and further develop their strengths as an organization (Darling-Hammond, 2010; Teitel, 2003). Financial realities require Catholic schools to reach out to partners across a variety of settings to include local businesses and community partners. Civic leaders and local government agencies are also beneficial for making connections and sharing resources. Feeder schools or competitors, whether public, private, or charter, can enhance collaboration. Contacts in the public schools can foster professional relationships or support special education needs. Partnerships with other Catholic schools from a different economic status or area can be an asset. If the school is economically challenged, partnering with a more financially stable school may be a good fit. If the school has many resources, partnering with a school in need can develop an ongoing relationship to share assets and learning experiences. Affiliations with other schools can include joint field trips or other academic events. True partnering is reciprocal in nature; it has more depth than just one school giving and one school receiving, regardless of their differences. School partners will want to determine how both can benefit from the experience and how the partnering experience can enrich each partner. At the student level, partnering can engage students in a joint activity to help them become acquainted. While this requires extra time for planning and coordination, the end result is a richer, more in-depth life-learning experience for students as they learn about other schools and cultures (Payne & Edwards, 2010).

Potential untapped partners for Catholic school consideration can be found in local colleges and universities. A direct connection with the college of education in the local college or university can provide additional benefits to both parties. Institutions of higher education look to schools for student teaching placement sites, for service, or for research sites for faculty. Student teachers provide an additional resource to teachers and students, offering extra support and introducing current knowledge and pedagogy into classrooms. As with all collaborative relationships and partnerships, there is an aspect of give-and-take within shared roles and responsibilities. The professional development school (PDS) model provides specific guidelines for the relationship of higher education in collaboration with local schools for the purpose of improving student learning. PDS partnerships have a fourfold mission: preparation of new teachers, faculty development, inquiry directed at the improvement of practice, and enhanced student achievement (Darling-Hammond, 2010; Teitel, 2003). Within this kind of partnership, new roles emerge, in the form of teacher leaders who help with mentoring and coaching preservice teachers and university faculty who become immersed within the culture of the school and are members of the school's professional community (Damore, Kapustka, & McDevitt, 2011; Rieckhoff & Larsen, 2012). PDS partners come together to share responsibility for all parts of their mission and serve to bridge the gap between theory and practice. While facilitating renewal at the university and school levels, they can enhance teacher and student learning. Catholic schools would be well served to gather information about professional development school models and other school–university partnerships that may exist within their local area (Gemo, Meskel, & Rieckhoff, 2009). If a full-fledged partnership is not a possibility, consider inviting university faculty to serve on the school board or assist with science fairs, debates, and other special projects within the school. Other associations can include local school-government days, with students serving in mock roles within the community government, the local media, chamber of commerce, real estate agents, or other local businesses in the community.

Developing partnerships will raise a school's prominence and awareness in new settings and will acquaint others with the school. These types of affiliations will help to further reinforce the mission and vision of the school and expand the number of people who know about the school. Expanding partnerships and associations with outside groups will enhance the internal organization by contributing to its growth and development. As a recruitment tool, these new relationships will further broaden the network of groups who may not already know about the school but will want to take the time to do so.

8. Demonstration of Creativity and Innovation

The ability for a Catholic school to demonstrate current and innovative practices can be a daunting task with limited resources, but can serve as another way to communicate positive news about the school. The best starting point for such a process is the expressed willingness to be innovative and creative. This overlaps with the openness to partner with various groups and attempt new learning opportunities. As long as the leader in a faith-based school ensures consistency with the mission and vision, opportunities to test new materials and be creative should be pursued. Creativity and innovation may be in the form of providing service to others or providing help using technology; any method is suitable, provided it shows the school is living its mission. The perception versus reality is true in this case; work toward making the school's perception a positive one, so that outsiders see it as a potential place for their children and as a place where exciting, innovative learning occurs.

A school's openness and willingness to be innovative and implement new up-to-date technology and curriculum materials demonstrates the desire to stay current and pursue best practice. Historically, technology has been an area in which Catholic schools have lagged behind. In the last two decades, Catholic schools have made significant gains in their acquisition and use of technology for instructional purposes (Hagelskamp, 2002). However, there is still a need for technology to be used to promote higher-order thinking skills. A survey of technology use in nonsectarian and religious private schools suggests only minimal differences exist and both type of schools had adequate and up-to-date equipment. Students and teachers studied had access to labs, media centers, and technology-rich classrooms, suggesting that the tools are available to integrate technology. However, principals reported a majority of teachers do not use the technology to promote higher-order thinking (Dosen, Gibbs, Guerrero, & McDevitt, 2004). "Catholic school teachers are using technology primarily for preparing to teach, rather than as a teaching tool.... [I]t seems that teachers use technology as a preparatory tool for their lessons, but not as a tool for their students to engage more deeply in the subject matter at hand" (Gibbs, Dosen, & Guerrero, 2008, p. 190). Inner-city Catholic high school teachers receiving technology equipment in combination with the training did increase their use of technology along with their students. However, results suggest the professional development needs have to be geared to a diverse audience, with attention to all levels of skill development (Gibbs, Dosen, & Guerrero, 2009). Principals need to be aware of this gap and continue to strive for ways to integrate technology as an instructional tool to impact student learning. Use of social media or classroom web pages and blogs all suggest the school and teachers are innovative and up-to-date with technology use.

9. Use of Data to Inform Stakeholders

Current school accountability trends require the use of data to inform and implement decisions in managing schools and maintaining their viability. Today's Catholic school leaders need to be transparent with the use of data and the means for sharing it with stakeholder groups (Guerra, 2004). Darling-Hammond (2004) suggests five conceptions of accountability in American education: political, legal, bureaucratic, professional accountability, and market accountability. Each conception of accountability presents a necessary framework for informed decisions to move the school forward. Catholic schools have not been required to share and report standardized testing in the manner required by public schools as mandated by the No Child Left Behind Act (NCLBA, 2001). Regardless, the transparency in reporting data sends a positive message to stakeholders about the work taking place in the schoolhouse. The principal's use of data can directly support recruitment and retention efforts with enrollment and attendance projections. As the school moves forward with strategic planning and increases to enrollment, such data can inform the school board and decision makers. Student demographic information can inform funders and outside groups. Budgetary and financial management data can enlighten financial planning decisions. A far more powerful use of data is in measuring a school's academic progress, growth, and goals for improvement. Standardized testing data provides information about student progress, instructional coverage, and achievement goals (Bernhardt, 2003; Boudett et al., 2005; Preuss, 2007).

There are numerous models and frameworks for a school to collect, maintain, and analyze data. Grounded in the cycle of continuous school improvement, such models are intended for the school community to develop skills in analysis and in using data for a variety of decisions. Bernhardt (2002) presents a model that suggests four multiple measures of data for schools to collect—demographic, perception, school process, and student learning data. This framework provides key areas for schools to analyze the impact of current programs and processes on their students and decide what to change for desired results. These data can also assist schools in understanding the root causes of problems as opposed to just focusing on symptoms. Boudett et al.'s Data Wise model (2005) provides a step-by-step guide to using student assessment results to improve teaching and learning. Central to this model is the creation of a data team who will take ownership of the process of analyzing data and begin to connect student learning data with the teaching process. A data overview helps the school develop a clear picture of the various types of data collected and how each is used to make instructional decisions. Picciano (2006) applies a decision-making model to each aspect of the school leader's work. That is, data collected should include student data, demographics, and enrollment for planning current and future needs. Community and school members should provide data to better inform opinions and perceptions of the school, while financial and budgetary data support decisions made for allotting and determining resources. Classroom-, school-, and district-level assessment data can inform the learning process along with individual student results. In addition, collecting data to capture professional development needs and events will connect with expectations of a teacher's expertise and, in turn, prove useful in the teacher evaluation process.

Practical realities exist with the expectation that data are to be used throughout the various aspects and contexts of a school. Considerations begin with whether or not the school has the necessary resources to capture, collect, and analyze the data. Updated and efficient software, hardware, and web-based tools are required to collect and maintain files and identify patterns and trends in longitudinal data. Appropriate staff and faculty will need training to capture and then understand how to use the data to make decisions that impact possible changes to instruction.

Data supply the focus and target for school improvement efforts. The Catholic school principal's facility with and use of data will impact on coordinating recruitment and retention of students. In a broader sense, however, the school leader's overall use of data, in all contexts of her work, will communicate to stakeholders the outcomes and end results that make the school effective.

10. Advancement Process

Most Catholic school principals fully expect to be responsible for fundraising efforts in their schools, but many do not have the personnel and resources to operate and manage an effective development program. There are a number of points where marketing and enrollment practices and advancement practices intersect. Many marketing techniques are employed in a comprehensive advancement program to communicate the school's mission, vision, and message to identified constituents. One key intersection is at the very outset of a school's relationship with a new family and their children during the enrollment process. Advancement efforts rely on establishing relationships and building upon them by communicating and engaging families in the school's mission and vision for the purpose of securing charitable contributions in support of the school's mission. At the start of a new relationship with a family, systems should be in place to capture and share information critical to advancement efforts. To begin with, establish policies and guidelines governing data sharing between the admissions and advancement efforts. The school has to determine the documents and information to gather and share across efforts and then determine who will be responsible for collecting and distributing the information gathered.

While there are numerous lists of fundraising ideas, and most Catholic schools have many already implemented, the broader development picture helps to coordinate and track these efforts. Classroom- and school-level fundraising should be coordinated with the school board and PTA's requests. Larger-scale pleas to parents, alumni, and school contacts to support scholarships, building renovations, and the annual fund drives should be well coordinated as part of long-range development efforts. Schools can develop several tiers of funders to draw upon and invite to make donations to support various endeavors. The broader development view of school fundraising considers ways to grow funders along with the school, increasing the level of giving over time while remaining sensitive to frequent requests to the same groups of donors.

The relationship of the development efforts and fundraising campaigns of the larger parish school community are important for the principal to know and understand. Connections to recruitment and retention efforts are critical so that all can stay on message and be consistent with communicating the mission, vision, and goals of the organization (Burke, 2009).

11. Understanding One's Leadership Profile

School leadership is challenging work, and within that is the importance for a Catholic school principal to have an understanding of self and an understanding of others. Goleman (1997) suggests that self-understanding is a life-long process, essential to effective human relations. Without this clear understanding of oneself and the beliefs, values, and strengths within, it is difficult to lead any group or organization (Green, 2009). Leadership learning provides an opportunity for the leader to examine strengths and areas for growth and then apply this understanding to relationships with others. Green's (2010) framework presents a valuable lens through which to view leadership development using four dimensions to describe the work of the principal: understanding oneself and others, understanding the complexity of organizational life, understanding relationships and their importance, and engaging in best practices. This model aligns with the ISLLC standards; however, the true essence of leadership effectiveness emerges when all four dimensions are working simultaneously. If any one of the four is missing, leadership is seriously challenged. Dimension One emphasizes the leader's understanding of her own beliefs and values as well as the beliefs and values of others, enabling the emergence of a shared vision and goals. Dimension Two emphasizes a principal's role in understanding the complexity of organizational life, including the culture, climate, and interactions that exist. Awareness of the social interactions of others allows the leader to assess conditions and develop plans for goal attainment, while establishing and retaining a quality teaching faculty is included within this dimension as the leader assesses needs in teaching capacity. Dimension Three focuses on the leader's understanding of relationships that exist within and across all stakeholders in the school community. Such knowledge assists the leader in better understanding how to build capacity and develop a professional learning community, while acknowledging the importance of a school's internal and external partners. Dimension Four emphasizes the principal's role in identifying and using best practice to improve and transform the school. The leader's understanding of communication, decision-making, and change encompasses this dimension and leads to a model of school improvement for all students (Green, 2010). All aspects of this model align with the work of a Catholic school leader and compliment the mission of Catholic schools, while attending to the academic aspects of a principal's role.

Donaldson's (2008) leadership development model presents three domains for leadership knowledge and action: interpersonal, cognitive, and intrapersonal. This framework provides the language to assess leadership demands and successes, while considering processes to improve performance. The principal's awareness and understanding of core knowledge areas will provide information on areas that are developed and those that require additional growth. While Donaldson's model does not attempt to prioritize one area over another, the school leader's performance is equally important across all areas. What is critical for the Catholic school principal is to determine the areas that align more closely with the mission and vision of the school, along with the mission of the Church and its teachings. This reflective process is a growth process, thereby providing the leader with a better understanding of what is involved in her work as a leader.

SUMMARY

The role of recruiting and retaining students is not the reason most individuals decide to become principals. However, in a Catholic school this responsibility is clearly attributed to the principal. Effective principals will understand that this role is instrumental in keeping the school enrollment strong and by doing so connects with many other areas of an effective school. It is in the best interests of the school and its well-being for the principal to have a recruitment plan mapped out with clearly articulated goals and objectives. While it isn't necessary to implement the entire process, the principal is responsible for overseeing and contextualizing this work. There are specific elements to a recruitment and retention plan that will support the growth and development of the school enrollment and raise its prominence in the community. A strong academic and instructional program will also serve to attract families who want the best for their children (Meyer, 2007). Connections with local agencies and partnerships with university provide another way for the school to market itself while growing and developing its programs. Creativity and willingness to try out innovative materials and technology will, in turn, market the school to audiences who may not be familiar with it. Using data and benchmarks to share progress and target future goals will communicate the school's efforts toward improvement and advancement. These elements, when connected to the mission and vision of the school, will serve to further articulate and communicate the good work that compliments a Catholic, religious education.

REFERENCES

AdvancEd. (2012). *Advanced education accreditation process.* Alpharetta, GA: Author.

Barth, R. (1990). A personal vision of a good school. *Phi Delta Kappan, 71*(7), 512–516.

Bauer, S., & Brazer, S.D. (2012). *Using research to lead school improvement.* Thousand Oaks, CA: Sage Publications.

Bernhardt, V. (2002). *The school portfolio toolkit.* Larchmont, NY: Eye on Education.

Bernhardt, V. (2003). *Using data to improve student learning.* Larchmont, NY: Eye on Education.

Boudett, K., City, E., & Murnane, R. (Ed.). (2005). *Data wise.* Cambridge, MA: Harvard Education Press.

Boyle, M. (2010). *Monitoring the mission.* Chicago, IL: Loyola University, Archdiocese of Chicago.

Brownridge, J. (2009). *Effective Catholic school principals and what they do* (North American Edition). Ajax, Ontario: Educator Administrator Associates.

Burke, R. (2009, January). Managing successful Catholic schools in difficult financial times. *Catholic School Management Letter.*

Bryk, A. S., Lee, V. E., & Holland, P. B. (1993). *Catholic schools and the common good.* Cambridge, MA: Harvard University Press.

Cain, G & Goldberger, A. (1983). Public and private schools revisited. *Sociology of Education, 56*(4), 208–218.

Coleman, J., & Hoffer, T. (1987). *Public and private high schools: The impact of communities.* New York, NY: Reed Business Information, Inc.

Coleman, J., Hoffer, T., & Kilgore, S. (1982). *High school achievement: Public and private schools compared.* New York, NY: Basic Books.

Convey, J. (1992). *Catholic schools make a difference: Twenty five years of research.* Washington, DC: National Catholic Education Association.

Convey, J. J. (2000). Views of bishops and priests concerning Catholic schools. In J. Youniss, J.J. Convey, & J. A. McClellan (Eds.), *The Catholic character of Catholic schools.* Notre Dame, IN: University of Notre Dame Press.

Damore, S., Kapustka, K., & McDevitt, P. (2011). The urban professional development school network: assessing the partnership's impact on initial teacher education. *The Teacher Educator, 46*(3), 182–207.

Darling-Hammond, L. (2010). *The flat world and education.* New York, NY: Teachers College Press.

Darling-Hammond, L. (2010) Standards, accountability and school reform. *Teachers' College Record, 106*(6), 1047–1085.

Donaldson, G. (2008). *How leaders learn: Cultivating capacities for school improvement.* New York, NY: Teachers College Press.

Dosen, A, Gibbs, M. Guerrero, R., & McDevitt, P. (2004). Technology in nonsectarian and religious private schools. *Journal of Research on Christian Education, 13*(2), 289–314.

DuFour, R. (1998). *Professional learning communities at work: Best practices for enhancing student achievement.* Bloomington, IN: Solution Tree.

DuFour, R. (2001). How to launch a community. *Journal of Staff Development, 22*(3), 50–51.

Dumas, M. (2009). Ten years later . . . and miles ahead. *Momentum, 40*(3), 14–18.

Eaker, R., DuFour, R., & DuFour, R. (2002). *Getting started—reculturing schools to become professional learning communities.* Bloomington, IN: Solution Tree.

Elmore, R. (2000). *Building a structure for school leadership.* New York, NY: Albert Shankar Institute.

Fullan, M. (1991). *The new meaning of educational change.* Ontario, Canada: Ontario Institute for Studies in Education.

Fullan, M. (2001). *Leading in a culture of change.* San Francisco, CA: Jossey-Bass.

Gemo, R., Meskel, N., & Rieckhoff, B. (2009). Increasing teacher leadership through Catholic university and elementary school collaboration. *Momentum, 40*(1), 32–35.

Gibbs, M., Dosen, A., & Guerrero, R. (2008). Technology in Catholic schools: Are schools using the technology they have? *Catholic Education: A Journal of Inquiry and Practice, 12*(2), 176–192.

Gibbs, M., Dosen, A., & Guerrero, R. (2009). Bridging the digital divide: Changing the technological landscape of inner-city Catholic schools. *Urban Education, 44*(1), 11–29.

Glynn, C. (2006). *Case study in Catholic school leadership strategy: The role of elementary school principals in recruiting students* (Unpublished doctoral dissertation). Indiana University, Bloomington, IN.

Goleman, D. (1997). *Emotional intelligence.* New York, NY: Bantam Books.

Green, R. (2009). *Practicing the art of leadership.* Boston, MA: Pearson.

Green, R. (2010). *The four dimensions of principal leadership: A framework for 21st century schools.* Boston, MA: Pearson.

Guerra, M. (2004). Accepting accountability. *Momentum, 35*(4), 4.

Hagelskamp, J. (2002). Technology. In T. Hunt, E. Joseph, & R. Nuzzi (Eds), *Catholic schools still make a difference: Ten years of research 1991–2000* (pp. 147–162). Washington, DC: National Catholic Education Association.

Hamilton, S. (2008). *Who will save America's urban Catholic schools?* Dayton, OH: Thomas B. Fordham Institute.

Hood, G., London, H., & Rieckhoff, B. (2011). The care and feeding of new teachers: What principals need to know and do. *Illinois Principal Association Building Leadership Bulletin, 18*(9), 1–5.

Hopkins, D., Ainscow, M., & West, M. (1994). *School improvement in an era of change.* New York, NY: Teachers College Press.

Hunt, T., Joseph, E., & Nuzzi, R., Ed. (2001). *Handbook of research on Catholic education.* Westport, CT: Greenwood Press.

Hunt, T., Joseph, E., & Nuzzi, R. (Eds.). (2002). *Catholic schools still make a difference: Ten years of research 1991–2000.* Washington, DC: National Catholic Education Association.

Interstate School Leaders Licensure Consortium. (2008). *Candidate information bulletin for school leader assessment.* Princeton, NJ: Educational Testing Service.

Jeynes, W. H. (2007). Religion, intact families, and the achievement gap. *Interdisciplinary journal of research on religion, 3*(3), 1–24.

Kowalski, T., Lasley, T., & Mahoney, J. (2007). *Data driven decisions and school leadership.* New York, NY: Allyn & Bacon.

Leithwood, K., Harris, A., & Hopkins, D. (2008). Seven strong claims about successful school leadership. *School Leadership and Management, 28*(1), 27–42.

Leithwood, K., & Riehl, C. (2003, April). *What do we already know about successful school leadership?* Paper presented at the Annual Meeting of the American Educational Research Association, Chicago, IL.

Marks, H. M., & Lee, V. E. (1989). *National assessment of educational progress proficiency in reading: 1985–86, Catholic and public schools compared.* Final report, 1989. Washington, DC: National Catholic Education Association.

Marzano, R. (2003). *What works in school: Translating research into practice.* Alexandria, VA: Association for Supervision and Curriculum Development.

Meyer, P. (2007). Can Catholic schools be saved? *Education Next, 7,* 12–20.

National Catholic Educational Association. (2012). Retrieved from www.ncea.org

No Child Left Behind Act of 2001, 20 U.S.C. 6319. Retrieved from http://www.ed.gov/policy/elsec/leg/esea02/index.html

Norris, C. (1990). Developing visionary leaders for tomorrow's schools. *NASSP Bulletin, 74,* 6–10.

Office of Catholic Schools. (2009). Archdiocese of Chicago, Chicago, IL.

Office of Catholic Schools Marketing Committee. (2008). *Wheels and wings.* Metuchen, NJ: Diocese of Metuchen.

Ozar, L. (2010). Voices from the field: Interviews with three prominent Catholic school educators about leadership and collaboration. *Catholic Education: A Journal of Inquiry and Practice, 14*(1), 114–127.

Payne, K., & Edwards, B. (2010). Service learning enhances education for young adolescents. *Phi Delta Kappan, 91*(5), 27–30.

Picciano, A. (2006). *Data-driven decision making for effective school leadership.* Upper Saddle River, NJ: Pearson Education.

Preuss, P. (2009). *Data-driven decision making and dynamic planning.* Larchmont, NY: Eye on Education.

Pritchard, F., & Whitehead, G. (2004). *Serve and learn.* Mahwah, NJ: Lawrence Erlbaum.

Rieckhoff, B., & Larsen, C. (2012). The impact of a professional development network on leadership development and school improvement goals. *School-University Partnerships, 5*(1), 57–73.

Riordan, C. (2000). Trends in student demography in Catholic secondary schools, 1972–1992. In J. Youniss & J.J. Convey (Eds). *Catholic schools at the crossroads: survival and transformation.* New York, NY: Teachers College Press.

Sander, W. (1996). Catholic grade schools and academic achievement. *The Journal of Human Resources, 31*(3), 540–548.

Sander, W., & Krautman, A. (1995). Catholic schools, dropout rates and attainment. *Economic Inquiry, 33*(2), 217–233.

Schmoker, M. (1996). *Results: The key to continuous school improvement.* Alexandria, VA: Association for Supervision and Curriculum Development.

Schmoker, M. (2001). *The results fieldbook.* Alexandria, VA: Association for Supervision and Curriculum Development.

Schmoker, M. (2006). *Results now.* Alexandria, VA: Association for Supervision and Curriculum Development.

Schmitt, W. (2012). Survey of principals by Remick Leadership Program sees challenges. Alliance for Catholic Education: University of Notre Dame. Retrieved from http://ace.nd.edu/news/survey-of-principals-by-remick-leadership-program-sees-challenges

Sergiovanni, T. (1996). *Leadership for the schoolhouse.* San-Francisco, CA: Jossey-Bass.

Sullivan, J. (2001). *Catholic education-distinctive and inclusive.* Dordrecht, The Netherlands: Kluwer Academic Publishers.

Teitel, L. (2003). *The professional development schools handbook.* Thousand Oaks, CA: Corwin Press.

Ubben, G., Hughes, L., & Norris, C. (2004). *The principal: Creative leadership for excellence in schools.* New York, NY: Pearson Education.

Walch, T. (1997). From doubt to affirmation: Reflections on the recent history of Catholic parochial education. *Catholic Education: A Journal of Inquiry and Practice, 1*(2), 120–129.

Wincek, J., & O'Malley, C. (1995). *Taking hold of the future: The ABC's of strategic planning.* Washington, DC: National Catholic Educational Association.

York, D. E. (1995). The academic achievement of African-Americans in Catholic schools: A review of the literature. In J. J. Irvine & M. Foster (Eds.), *Growing up African American in Catholic schools* (pp. 11–46). New York, NY: Teachers College Press.

RECOMMENDATIONS FOR FUTURE READING

DuFour, R., & Fullan, M. (2013). *Cultures built to last: Systemic PLC's at work.* Bloomington, IN: Solution Tree Press.

Kanold, T. (2011). *The five disciplines of professional learning community leaders.* Bloomington, IN: Solution Tree Press.

Robey, P. (Ed.). (2012). *A practitioner's guide to Catholic school leadership* (NCEA Catholic School Leadership Series, Vol. 1). Arlington, VA: National Catholic Educational Association.

Rowe, D. (2003). *A straight-talking guide to running a school.* Washington, DC: National Catholic Educational Association.

Schmoker, M. (1999). *Results: The key to continuous improvement.* Alexandria, VA: Association for Supervision and Curriculum Development.

CHAPTER 8

FACULTY DEVELOPMENT

Sr. Patricia Helene Earl

A SCENARIO

You are a new principal in St. Mary Catholic School, committed to your faith, bursting with great ideas, filled with lots of enthusiasm to implement all of the theories that you have studied in your school administration courses, and eager to get started working with your faculty, parents, and students. After the first month of classes, you realize that there are several issues that keep arising. The teachers seem to lack enthusiasm in their own practice of the faith and often make mistakes in what they teach about Church doctrine. The children seem to be lethargic and disinterested in learning about their religion. The school is known for its academics, yet a review of recent test scores shows that the students generally are below average in both math and reading scores. The teachers are sloppy in their lesson plans, often giving only page numbers in books. The students, especially in the upper grades, seem to be out of control both in classes and as they change classes, and there is a subtle evidence of bullying to which the teachers seem oblivious. What can you do to provide for improvement and faculty development in each of these areas?

Catholic School Leadership, pages 133–150
Copyright © 2016 by Information Age Publishing
All rights of reproduction in any form reserved.

INTRODUCTION

One of the most important roles of the principal is to provide appropriate and relevant faculty development. This is not only invaluable for mentoring and retaining new teachers but also vital for deepening faith formation, promoting excellence in curriculum, and engaging students with the best pedagogical and classroom management practices.

In her work on the responsibilities of a principal, Ciriello (1994) identifies three major dimensions that are significant in a Catholic school: namely, the spiritual, instructional, and managerial roles of the principal. The spiritual role focuses primarily on the faith formation of students, faculty, and parents. The instructional role focuses on solid curriculum development, instructional practices, and appropriate supervision. The managerial role focuses on the long- and short-term daily operations of the school. Adapting this model, this chapter will approach faculty development in a Catholic school from spiritual, instructional, and managerial perspectives. However, a review of some basic theories on faculty development will provide a foundation for practical activities.

OVERVIEW OF THEORY

The Leader's Role

Tallerico (2005) notes that "school-based administrative support and guidance are key to building coherence among multiple improvement initiatives. And important among these initiatives is teachers' professional development" (p. xiv). The effective school leader is able to create a community of learners including teachers, students, and parents. Sigford (2006) draws on the work of DuFour and Eaker (1998) to identify five aspects of the role of the leader: to lead through a shared vision and value instead of rules and procedures; to be involved in curriculum, knowing what is taught, how it is assessed, and how to gather data and use it for effective instruction; to provide staff with needed information and training on how to make decisions regarding professional needs; to provide support and follow-up for new curriculum adoption and activities to support continuous improvement; and to provide training, resources, and time for reflection on professional practice.

> By creating the professional learning communities, the effective school leader creates a community that is energized, focused, and self-renewing. When the community is focused toward a common goal and energy is devoted to it, teachers get excited, empowered, and creative. (Sigford, 2006, p. 113)

Fulghum (1988) views the educational leader as a professional developer. "There are those who depend on us, watch us, learn from us, take from us. And we never know. Don't sell yourself short. You may never have proof of your importance, but you are more important than you think" (p. 80).

Content

From a theoretical perspective, several authors (Glatthorn, Jones, & Bullock, 2006; Sigford, 2006; Tallerico, 2005) use the National Staff Development Council (NSDC) standards as a framework for professional development. These standards include three areas: context, process, and content. Briefly, context standards refer to the *learning community* that organizes adults whose goals are aligned with those of the school or district, the *leadership* to provide for continuous improvement, and the *resources* to support learning and collaboration. Process standards refer to *data-driven* practices to determine priorities, monitor progress, and maintain improvement; *evaluation*, which uses various methods to guide improvement and demonstrate its impact; *research-based* strategies to reach established goals; *learning*, which applies knowledge on adult learning and change; and *collaboration*, which provides knowledge and skills to collaborate. Content standards refer to *equity* in appreciating all students, creating safe and supportive learning environments and holding high expectations for academic performance; *quality teaching*, which deepens teachers' knowledge, provides research-based teaching strategies, and prepares them in using assessments appropriately; and *family involvement*, which offers educators knowledge and skills to involve families and others (see Table 8.1 for complete NSDC standards).

Killion (2002) proposes eight components for professional development:

- Involves the acquisition of research-based knowledge and skill
- Has clear expectations about the implementation of the new learning
- Creates a desire to implement the new learning
- Allows for opportunities to apply the knowledge and to practice the new skills with feedback
- Is grounded in the belief that the practices are valuable
- Has ongoing assessment of the effectiveness of new educator practices by examining student work and reflecting on and refining instructional practice
- Facilitates consistent application of the practices in the classroom
- Utilizes a systematic support for continuous improvement (p. 19)

TABLE 8.1 National Staff Development Council Standards (2001)

Context Standards

Staff Development That Improves the Learning of All Students:

- Organizes adults into learning communities whose goals are aligned with those of the school and district. (Learning Communities)
- Requires skillful school and district leaders who guide continuous instructional improvement. (Leadership)
- Requires resources to support adult learning and collaboration. (Resources)

Process Standards

Staff Development That Improves the Learning of All Students:

- Uses disaggregated student data to determine adult learning priorities, monitor progress, and help sustain continuous improvement. (Data-Driven)
- Uses multiple sources of information to guide improvement and demonstrate its impact. (Evaluation)
- Prepares educators to apply research to decision making. (Research-Based)
- Uses learning strategies appropriate to the intended goal. (Design)
- Applies knowledge about human learning and change. (Learning)
- Provides educators with the knowledge and skills to collaborate. (Collaboration)

Content Standards

Staff Development That Improves the Learning of all Students:

- Prepares educators to understand and appreciate all students, create safe, orderly and supportive learning environments, and hold high expectations for their academic achievement. (Equity)
- Deepens educators' content knowledge, provides them with research-based instructional strategies to assist students in meeting rigorous academic standards, and prepares them to use various types of classroom assessments appropriately. (Quality Teaching)
- Provides educators with knowledge and skills to involve families and other stakeholders appropriately. (Family Involvement)

These components not only address the acquisition of knowledge and practical application, but they also include concrete ways in which the leader can supervise and assess faculty development and growth.

Design

There are many models for designing faculty development. In most cases, whichever model one chooses, it often grows out of the principal's supervision, and the effectiveness of that professional development can be assessed through supervision. Hess (2008) suggests a simple three-pronged model for professional development. It includes "(1) universal literacy strategies across the content areas, (2) subject specific content strategies, and (3) skills for success that benefit all teachers" (p. 63).

"Teachers vary significantly in their competence and professional development and thus can benefit from a supervisory approach that respects and responds to those differences" (Glatthorn et al., 2006, p. 33). They identify four major models linked with school development (See Table 8.2).

In Model 1, the focus is on various forms of school learning. A general session on the nature of learning could be offered to the whole faculty with breakout sessions related to specific subjects taught. Glatthorn et al. (2006) suggest that this model "would be implemented when the principal and other leaders believe that teachers in general are ignoring principles of learning" (pp. 44–45). They caution that this approach may be too theoretical and should allow for discussion on "the implications for teaching" (p. 45).

In Model 2, the focus is on teacher development. This approach could be used in conjunction with a differentiated supervision program. It would be useful when there are new teachers on staff or when school leaders see a general need for all "to make significant improvements in their teaching." In Model 3, the focus is on school improvement. This approach works when faculty has decided on a school-wide improvement program. "Each topic would be developed in depth and presented in a manner that resulted in informed action" (p. 45). Peer coaching with an emphasis on feedback for success would follow staff development.

TABLE 8.2   Staff Development Models

Model	Typical Agendas
Model 1: Learning	Adult learning Psychomotor learning Science Learning Language learning and reading Math Esthetic learning, creativity
Model 2: Faculty Development	Assessing present skills Developing a knowledge base Using peer coaching Using student feedback
Model 3: School Improvement	Continuous improvement Focused curriculum Conveying high expectations Safe, orderly environment Parent involvement
Model 4: Curriculum Alignment	Scope, sequence Organizing units Long-term plans Aligning tested, taught

Source: Glatthorn, Jones, & Bullock, 2006, p. 44

In Model 4, the focus is on curriculum alignment. This would be used when a new curriculum is adopted or when the principal's observations show that teachers have problems in putting the curriculum into practice. Many sessions would involve helping teachers to produce materials to aid them in their planning.

These models provide administrators "with a structure to determine which type of staff development matches the needs of the faculty" (Glatthorn et al., 2006, p. 46). Having predetermined faculty needs through surveys, focus groups, observation, interviews, test data, and feedback from parents and students, and having chosen from these a model based on knowledge, skills, and teacher dispositions, "the models are developmental in nature, moving from a knowledge-based model to a more evaluative model through school improvement" (p. 46).

Glatthorn et al. (2006) present another model related to staff development. The "differentiated model" recognizes teacher differences. It involves two stages: first, the informal observation stage and second, staff development. In the informal observation, peers, administrators, and supervisors drop into each class. They suggest that if an administrator set aside one hour a day and spend 5–10 minutes in a class, he or she could visit 20–30 teachers a week. The purpose is to allow the principal an opportunity to offer timely praise as well as to detect early problems. It increases the principal's visibility as well as his or her ability to monitor curriculum. As a result, teachers feel less isolated and develop a sense that their classroom is important. The principal can look for signs of learning and then follow up with positive as well as negative feedback. These observations do not take the place of the formal observations scheduled regularly throughout the year. The second stage of this "differentiated model" is staff development which is considered "the keystone . . . since it serves as a cohesive force in what otherwise might be a fragmented faculty" (Glatthorn et al., 2006, p. 35). All teachers take part in staff development, "which designates professional development opportunities provided in-house to groups of teachers" (p. 35).

After choosing a model that works best for the school, Glatthorn et al. (2006) suggest strategies for successful implementation (see Table 8.3), drawing from a variety of sources (see Darling-Hammond & McLaughlin, 1995; Gall & Vojtek, 1994; Sparks, 1995).

It is important to recognize that not all of these strategies will fit every school or faculty. However, they provide a good starting point to consider in implementing a model for staff development.

Seyfarth (1999) discusses eight criteria for professional development using a model developed by Fenstermacher and Berliner (1983). Successful professional development should be relevant, have clear objectives, offer attractive incentives, be easily applicable in the real classroom, offer

TABLE 8.3   Effective Staff Development Programs

1. Center on critical activities of teaching and learning (planning, evaluating, developing curriculum), emphasizing job-embedded learning. Keep the focus on student learning.
2. Grow from investigations and involve teachers as action researchers.
3. Are built on substantial professional discourse that fosters analysis and communication about practices among colleagues.
4. Reflect sound principles of adult learning.
5. Honor the individual learning styles and needs of the professional educator.
6. Allow for and foster reflection and mindfulness.
7. Are supported by adequate resources.
8. Recognize that teachers are at various stages of readiness for new programs and approaches and respond individually to staff development.
9. Provide sufficient time for follow-up and collaboration; do not interfere with teachers' other responsibilities.
10. Provide opportunities for teachers to develop knowledge in depth about the subjects they teach and means of helping students acquire that knowledge.
11. Are supported with reasonable incentives, such as credits, reimbursement of expenses, and released time.
12. Are structured with clear, specific, and meaningful objectives, with programs designed to meet those objectives.
13. Are planned, developed, and implemented by teachers.
14. Are evaluated systematically.

Source: Glatthorn, Jones & Bullock, 2006, p. 46

maintenance or support to teachers, include knowledgeable instructors who can present clearly, be appropriate for the teacher's instructional style and classroom circumstances, and provide time for participants to practice what was learned.

Evaluation

In order to assess the effectiveness of any faculty development, some type of evaluation must take place and be included in planning the professional development process. Glatthorn et al. (2006) suggest there are two evaluation tracks: namely, intensive evaluation and standard evaluation. The intensive process uses multiple data sources including multiple observations; analysis of student test scores; assessment of teacher work samples such as lesson plans, tests, and record book; and anecdotal reports on performance of duties. The standard process involves compliance with state and local policies, with the principal making the minimum number of observations and completing the required forms.

Stiggins and Duke (1988) suggest a three-track system. The accountability track is based on performance standards for nontenured teachers annually and tenured teachers every three to four years. The assistance system is provided for tenured teachers who are deficient in performance standards. Finally, the professional development system relies on individual goals, set by the teachers with their principals, for competent tenured teachers.

Several supervisory options parallel these models of evaluation. Glatthorn et al. (2006) suggest intensive development for new and marginalized teachers followed by intensive supervision, where the supervisor provides several cycles of conferencing, diagnostic observation, focused observation on a specific aspect of performance, feedback, coaching, and knowledge development. This is time consuming but is generally provided for a small number of teachers. Cooperative development is offered to competent tenured teachers who work in teams toward a common goal. The team uses several strategies to develop their knowledge and skills, such as, action research, curriculum development, peer review, dialog, and development of instructional materials. In this approach, "the principal needs to monitor progress, without being intrusive" (p. 36). Self-development is offered to the experienced competent teacher who identifies a particular goal related to student achievement, creates a plan to achieve the goal, performs the actions needed to accomplish the goal, and evaluates his/her progress at the end of the school year. In this approach, the principal serves more as a facilitator.

Tallerico (2005) notes the importance of each school developing its specific goals and priorities for student learning to motivate adult learning. It is also essential to state student-learning priorities in concrete and measurable terms in order to provide clear targets for improvement. These become the standards against which progress can be assessed. Thus, evaluation planning functions as a second and complementary means of determining the content for adult professional development. Guskey (2000) suggests five interdependent stages of questioning to arrive at the evaluation of professional development. These include teachers' reactions, teachers' learning, organizational support and change, teachers' use of new knowledge and skills, and student learning outcomes.

In reviewing some of the theory related to professional development, it is evident that content, design, and evaluation are important aspects to consider in devising any faculty development. An effective principal needs to know the students' learning needs and the faculty instructional needs and learning styles. However, "for school-initiated staff development efforts to be effective, the school staff must be able to identify and commit to a mission and to solve problems encountered in pursuit of that mission" (Seyfarth, 1999, p. 259). The next section will look at faculty development in relation to the vision and mission of the school.

Thomas Guskey (2003) analyzes 13 well-known lists of characteristics of effective professional development, including the NSDC Standards for Staff Development. His review showed that while there was some overlap, the lists were not identical. "The most frequently mentioned characteristic of effective professional development is enhancement of teachers' content and pedagogic knowledge" (p. 9). Helping teachers understand the content they teach and the ways students learn that content, along with higher order thinking skill, are vital aspects of professional development. "Another consistently noted characteristic is the promotion of collegiality and collaborative exchange" (p. 12). Educators value working together and exchanging ideas. Other common characteristics included the inclusion of evaluation procedures, offering school- or site-based opportunities, and building leadership capacity. Drawing from Kifer (2001), Guskey (2003) notes that analyzing student learning data generally shows "that greater variation exits between classrooms within a school than between schools or between districts" (p. 16). This leads Guskey (2003) to conclude that

> Visionary leaders who find ways to help these successful teachers share their practices and strategies with their colleague in a positive and supportive environment provide a basis for highly effective professional development.... Nevertheless, by agreeing on the criteria for effectiveness, considering the unique contextual elements of each school and the community of learners in that environment, and continually directing efforts toward improvements in student learning outcomes, visionary school leaders can do much to guarantee sure and steady progress in educators' and researchers' efforts to improve the quality of professional development endeavors. (pp. 16–17)

SCHOOL VISION AND MISSION IN FACULTY DEVELOPMENT

At this point, our discussion of faculty development has only focused on professional development. We begin to see that this parallels the intellectual and managerial approach to leadership noted by Ciriello (1994), with the content being similar to the instructional role of the principal and the pedagogy and collegiality being parallel to the managerial dimension of daily tasks of implementation. However, the role of the visionary leader leads us to look at the importance of a shared vision in the school, especially in Catholic schools, which in turn will lead us to look at the spiritual dimension of faculty development that is a vital key to the purpose of any Catholic school.

Huffman (2003) surveyed a variety of studies (DuFour & Eaker, 1998; Senge, 1990; Sparks, 1999) that described a professional learning community. Generally, this is a place where teachers pursue a clear purpose for student learning, work collaboratively to achieve the purpose, and collectively take responsibility for students' learning. School improvement can require change, which is time consuming and never easy and requires that all stakeholders share a common vision. Huffman (2003) states: "The task of the leader is to share and combine the personal visions of faculty members into a collaborative vision molded and embraced by all . . . [a]nd . . . based on common values and beliefs" (p. 22). DuFour and Eaker (1998) studied the shared vision concept and stated: "The lack of a compelling vision for public schools continues to be a major obstacle in any effort to improve schools. . . . Building a shared vision is the ongoing, never-ending, daily challenge confronting all who hope to create learning communities" (p. 64). While not directed to a Catholic school, DuFour and Eaker (1998) continue: "What separates a learning community from an ordinary school is its collective commitment to guiding principles that articulate what the people in the school believe and what they seek to create" (p. 25). These guiding principles cannot simply be promulgated by the principal; "they are embedded in the hearts and minds of people throughout the school" (p. 25). Huffman (2003) notes that Sergiovanni (1991) described schools as "nested communities" where people are united by common values which lead to shared rights and responsibilities (Huffman, 2003, p. 24). When values are defined and serve as the foundation for the school, communication and sharing of opinions is easier. There needs to be "an organized or structured mechanism to identify and inculcate desired values" (Huffman, 2003, p. 24). Thus, it is important to work collaboratively to create a vision statement for the school. Thus, in addition to providing professional development for faculty in the areas of subject content, pedagogy, learning styles, and collaboration, it is vital that a principal works with the faculty to first create a vision statement and then to revisit it annually so as to implement it and integrate it into the very fiber of the school. "It is critical, however, to understand that the emergence of a strong shared vision based on collective values provides the foundation for informed leadership, staff member commitment, student success, and sustained school growth" (Huffman, 2003, p. 32). The vision statement is almost like the spiritual soul of the school.

Kotter (1990) adds:

> The principal's most significant effect on student learning comes through his/her efforts to establish a vision of the school and develop goals related to the accomplishment of the vision. Sharing leadership and aligning people to a vision is crucial and leads to "leadership-centered culture . . . the ultimate act of leadership." (p. 11)

FACULTY DEVELOPMENT AND FAITH FORMATION IN THE CATHOLIC SCHOOL

Having looked at various theories to support how one chooses the content for professional development, the process for creating it, various designs for implementing it, and the importance of first creating a vision from which all professional development should flow, we recognize that each of these is vital for the success of any school. However, in Catholic schools, the concept of professional development must expand to the broader notion of faculty development. This takes us beyond the professional development of instructional content, pedagogical tools and classroom management, and the managerial process for implementation. Consistent with a Catholic philosophy of education, which seeks to develop the whole child spiritually, intellectually, physically, emotionally, and socially, faculty development looks to this holistic development of the educator. This raises the questions of why should we assist educators in Catholic schools in their own faith formation, what is faith formation, how can we do this, and how will this help them in their work with their students and their understanding of the mission of catholic education.

Through the sacrament of baptism, a person receives a call to holiness. Beginning with Scripture, we read:

> For this reason, I remind you to stir into flame the gift of God that you have through the imposition of my hands. For God did not give us a spirit of cowardice but rather of power and love and self-control. He saved us and called us to a holy life, not according to our works but according to his own design and the grace bestowed on us in Christ Jesus before time began, but now made manifest through the appearance of our savior Christ Jesus, who destroyed death and brought life and immortality to light through the gospel. (2 Timothy 1:6–7, 9–10, New American Bible)

Since Catholic school educators assume the vocation to teach and to share in the faith formation of their students, it is important that they themselves understand this baptismal call first in their own lives. With the decline in religious vocations and the increasing responsibility that the laity have for preserving the Catholic identity of their schools, Catholic school educators also need to be prepared not only in providing their students with an excellent academic education, but also in providing for "the formation of students' spiritual life through the Catholic faith and following the example of Christ" (Earl, 2008, p. 13). This is what has made the Catholic school unique and distinct. The United States Catholic Bishops (1972) in their document, *To Teach as Jesus Did*, stress the importance that Catholic schools have in integrating religious truths and values with life. The Catholic school shares in the Church's obligation "to provide for its children an education by virtue of which their whole lives may be inspired by the spirit of Christ" (Paul VI, 1965, No. 8, p. 730). Teachers in Catholic schools should also "bear testimony by their lives and by their teaching to the one Teacher, who is Christ" (Paul VI, 1965, No. 8, p. 733).

The spirituality of the teacher is a vital teaching force, especially when matched by the parents' spirituality (Keating, 1990). Real formation occurs when parents and teachers together show the child how to grow and develop in faith. The aim of catechesis is to develop understanding of the mystery of Christ in the light of God's word. Saying "yes" to Christ involves accepting God's word, but then endeavoring to know it better (John Paul II, 1979). The task of the catechist is to explain the truths of faith and Christian morality and to encourage the practice of virtue (Pius X, 1905). Formation, therefore, must be a part of and complement to the professional formation of the Catholic school teacher (Sacred Congregation for Catholic Education, 1982). The goals of this religious formation must be personal sanctification and apostolic mission, two inseparable elements in a Christian vocation. It requires a human and well-rounded formation, as well as a formation in spirituality and doctrine (Congregation for the Clergy, 1997). (Earl, 2008, p. 35)

Understanding why faith formation is so integral both to the formation of the faculty as well as the students in Catholic schools, what are some key elements in faith formation? In his talk on the importance of religious imagination, Bishop Morneau (1995) "highlights the reality that faith formation is important for all those who hold a set of beliefs in any particular faith. He speaks of the relationship that exists among images, attitudes, and behavior" (Earl, 2008, p. 25). A study on faith formation and the influence of virtue and spiritual seminars (Earl, 2008) "suggests that for us to share the faith without students, we must first have a deeper understanding of its meaning and value for us personally. Then the images and activities that we use to teach our students will be rich in meaning" (p. 26).

Throughout the United States, many Catholic dioceses create requirements for teachers to obtain religion certification. The specifics may vary. However, all draw on the *Catechism of the Catholic Church* (U. S. Catholic Church, 1992) and its four pillars of our faith: namely, Church doctrine, sacraments, morality, and prayer as well as sacred Scripture and teaching methods as major components. *The National Directory for Catechesis* (United States Conference of Catholic Bishops, 2003) also provides information on adult faith formation, the value and role of the Catholic school and its teachers along with the primary role of parents, and the needed pedagogy to accomplish this. Recognizing the importance of being formed in our Catholic faith, not only for each of us personally in living out our baptismal call to holiness but also in our responsibility as Catholic school educators to assist in the faith formation of our students, the Catholic school principal must try to show teachers that religion certification should not just be one more set of seemingly never ending requirements. Thus, the principal should include the importance of faith formation in the initial interviews with prospective teachers and continue to integrate this into faculty meetings as well as professional in-service days. Building on the idea that you cannot give what you do not have, the principal of the Catholic school, as the spiritual leader of the school along with the pastor and priests, will look for creative ways to foster a love for our faith, a desire to learn more about our Church and its teachings, and opportunities to grow in a personal relationship with Jesus Christ.

In the study (Earl, 2008) on a series of seminars given to teachers on virtue and how to teach it to students, as well as spirituality and how to cultivate a personal relationship with Christ and lead students to this same lifelong relationship, it became apparent that there are two important dimensions to faith formation. We need to know, understand, and appreciate what our Catholic Church teaches: namely, its doctrine, sacraments, moral principles, and the value of prayer. In coming to understand prayer, then we also come to recognize the importance of developing a personal relationship with Christ. Jesus, Himself, asked the apostles two questions: "Who do people say that I am?"—the faith content—and "Who do you say that I am?"—the person of Jesus Himself.

> The results of this study suggest that, in addition to the necessary educational and theological content, teachers also need guidance to develop their spirituality. Teachers attending the Spirituality and Virtue Seminars felt renewed. They learned to recognize the need to develop their own personal relationship with Christ, which, in turn, motivated them. They not only felt that they did a better job of teaching the content of the Religion, but they also discovered the importance of their own underlying relationship with Christ. They no longer taught just a subject called Religion, they taught a way of life. They grew in understanding how to live this Christ-centered life and were, therefore, enthusiastic in sharing this with their students. (Earl, 2008, p. 205)

Thus, when looking at faculty development, the Catholic school principal needs to plan for the spiritual development of faculty, their growth in the knowledge and understanding of Church teachings, and their ability to share prayer and faith, not only in the religion class but as an integral part of the whole classroom experience.

A RETURN TO THE OPENING SCENARIO

With some understanding of the scope of faculty development, we need to consider our opening scenario and look for some ways to handle the challenges that it presents. Several aspects of the scenario pertain to content. The teachers in this school obviously lack knowledge of the teachings of their faith. This may contribute to their incorrect teaching, lack of enthusiasm, and, thus, the students' lethargic approach to their religion classes. If the reading and math scores are declining, there is evidence of a lack of either knowledge of the subject or appropriate teaching methods to assist the students' attainment of the needed learning outcomes in these areas. This also shows itself in the lack of good lesson planning. There are also discipline issues as noted in the students' behavior changing class as well as the growing bullying problem. This principal has many areas for faculty development. Obviously, the principal needs to make the faith issues of faculty and students a top priority so that the school does not lose its Catholic identity. There are also issues of other academic content, teaching methods, classroom management, and behavior.

Addressing even one issue requires a process. The principal may decide to address some of these issues as part of an ongoing process during faculty meetings. While the principal may wish to do some presentation on special areas of personal experience, he or she may also want to begin to empower the teachers to take some ownership by setting up some small committees to research various content areas, behavior issues, and management issues. Perhaps a speaker could be engaged to motivate the faculty, or teachers might attend workshops and then come back and share what they have gained with the faculty. Peer observations and good mentoring as well as formative and summative evaluations can all contribute to good faculty development. All of these are part of the process of addressing the needs.

Several models have been presented for professional development. Realistically, these are examples that a principal may use or combine according to the dynamics of the faculty and their levels of need in various areas. Deciding on a model may be something discussed with the vice principal or with a group of principals in the diocese, especially if similar problems exist in several schools. What is most important is that teachers realize that the school will only be as good or effective as its teachers. By encouraging collaboration, consensus building, creativity, and sharing of ideas in team meetings of grades or subjects, faculty will be more attuned to learn, grow, implement changes, and achieve greater success. This, in turn, will build staff morale so that more teachers will want to be involved. The principal needs to recognize that change takes time. While teachers in a Catholic school are engaged in a ministry to teach the young and share the faith so that Christ becomes a focal point of their lives, the principal needs to make an effort to recognize even the smallest signs of growth. A word of praise for a job well done, a note of thanks for a well-planned lesson in the plan book, and setting a good example by taking part with the faculty in all aspects of the faculty development makes the teachers feel appreciated. Whatever model one adopts, the principal needs to look at the personalities among the faculty and then dialogue with some team leaders to hear the faculty needs, so that whatever design the faculty development takes, it becomes one that invites all to participate and motivates all to want to succeed in the total school improvement. It will not happen in a day, or perhaps even in a year since completed goals will be replaced in time with new and ever-changing goals. However, it can begin with time spent as a group and as individuals deciding perhaps on one spiritual goal, one academic goal, and one pedagogical or classroom management goal on a yearly basis.

Regardless of the various content, process, design, and goals, the central issue is first to revisit the school's vision and mission. Once this is affirmed or reaffirmed by at least an annual faculty look at what it states and what this means for the group and for each teacher personally, then this becomes the foundation and motivation for exploring how to handle all of the other issues.

The issue of faith formation is one that must become an integral part of the yearly faculty development. Beginning the year with a faculty retreat or having a mid-year retreat shows the entire staff that our mission to lead our students to Christ is at the heart of all that we do. Encouraging faculty to come together for a morning prayer and to pray for each other's intentions helps teachers to recognize more the need for a spiritual life. This may open the door for a faculty Scripture study or a book discussion to evolve as a periodic afterschool activity. The principal or volunteers among the faculty may give a short teaching in the faculty meeting on each liturgical season as it begins, deepening their appreciation and giving them motivation to have an Advent wreathe and prayer in their classroom, to want to enliven the students' participation at school Masses, to enter the Lenten season with a desire to teach the students about Lent or why they might attend the Stations of the Cross. Creating a virtue program by renewing their understanding of the theology of virtue as a response to our Baptismal call to grow in holiness and become the image of God and looking collectively at how a class or the whole school might focus on a particular virtue and some ways to practice it can create peace and harmony in the school and, over time, help to control the growing issue of bullying (Earl, 2006).

There is no one-size-fits-all answer to the questions posed in this scenario. However, becoming aware of areas for growth, both personal and school-wide; working with the faculty to collaborate and empower them to put the school vision into practice; and emphasizing the importance of witnessing to Gospel values and promoting the Catholic identity of the school provides the start for valuable, ongoing, lifelong learning through faculty development.

CONCLUSION

Faculty development for a Catholic school encompasses not only teachers' professional development but also their faith development. It really begins the moment you interview an applicant, share the school's vision and expectations as a Catholic school, and hire the person whom you feel will give witness to Gospel values, provide excellence in academic instruction, nurture and care for the students entrusted to them, and recognize that teaching in a Catholic school is not just a job. It is a vocation. "*The Declaration on Christian Education* (1965) addressed the role of the teacher, viewed as a vocation, requiring special qualities of mind and heart, careful preparation, and readiness to accept new ideas and to adapt to the old" (Earl, 2008, pp. 34–35). Faculty development is vital to the ongoing Catholic identity and academic excellence in our Catholic schools. It calls us to listen and observe all aspects of our schools. It challenges us to seek excellence in how we live out the Gospel and prepare our young people to do this while developing the academic proficiencies, physical and emotional abilities, and social qualities to fully develop and live the life God gave them and contribute to the local and global needs of society in the future. As the spiritual, instructional, and managerial leader of your Catholic school, you set the tone and, along with your faculty, develop the culture and climate to make our Catholic schools a success through your ever-evolving plans for faculty development.

REFERENCES

Ciriello, M. J. (Ed.). (1994). *The principal as spiritual leader: Expectations in the areas of faith development, building Christian community, moral and ethical development.* Washington, DC: United States Catholic Conference.

Congregation for the Clergy. (1997). *General directory for catechesis.* Washington, DC: United States Catholic Conference.

Darling-Hammond, L., & McLaughlin, M. W. (1995). *Doing what matters most: Investing in quality teaching.* Kutztown, PA: National Commission on teaching and America's Future.

DuFour, R., & Eaker, R. (1998). *Professional learning communities at work: Best practices for enhancing student achievement.* Bloomington, IN: National Education Services.

Earl, P. H. (2006). *Building the builders: Faith formation in virtue.* Washington, DC: National Catholic Educational Association.

Earl, P. H. (2008). *Faith formation of the laity in Catholic schools: The influence of virtues and spirituality seminars.* Charlotte, NC: Information Age Publishers.

Fenstermacher, G., & Berliner, D. (1983). *A conceptual framework for the analysis of staff development.* Santa Monica, CA: Rand.

Fulghum, R. (1988). *All I really need to know I learned in kindergarten: Uncommon thoughts on common things.* New York, NY: Villard Books.

Gall, M. D., & Vojtek, R. O. (1994). *Planning for effective staff development.* Eugene, OR: University of Oregon Press.

Glatthorn, A. A., Jones, B. K., & Bullock, A. A. (2006). *Developing highly qualified teachers: A handbook for school leaders.* Thousand Oaks, CA: Corwin Press.

Guskey, T. (2000). *Evaluating professional development.* Thousand Oaks, CA: Corwin Press.

Guskey, T. (2003). Analyzing lists of the characteristics of effective professional development to promote visionary leadership. *National Association of Secondary School Principals Bulletin 87*(637), 4–20.

Hess, R. T. (2008). *Follow the teacher: Making a difference for school improvement.* Lanham, MD: Rowman and Littlefield Education.

Huffman, J. (2003). The role of shared values and vision in creating professional learning communities. *National Association of Secondary School Principals Bulletin 87*(637), 21–34.

John Paul II, Pope. (1979). *On catechesis in our time.* Boston, MA: Daughters of St. Paul.

Keating, J. R. (1990). *A pastoral letter on Catholic schools.* Arlington, VA: Diocese of Arlington.

Kifer, E. (2001). *Large scale assessment.* Thousand Oaks, CA: Corwin Press.

Killion, J. (2002). *Assessing impact: Evaluating staff development.* Oxford, OH: National Staff Development Council.

Kotter, J. P. (1990, May-June). What leaders really do. *Harvard Business Review,* 3–11.

Morneau, R. F. (1995). *The importance of religious imagination: A talk.* Canfield, OH: Alba House Cassettes.

National Staff Development Council (NSDC). (2001). *NSDC Standards for staff development.* Retrieved from http://www.learningforward.org/standards/index.cfm

Paul VI, Pope. (1965). *Declaration on Christian education.* Boston, MA: Daughters of St. Paul.

Pius X, Pope. (1905). *On the teaching of Christian doctrine.* Boston, MA: Daughters of St. Paul.

Sacred Congregation for Catholic Education. (1982). *Lay Catholics in schools: Witnesses to faith.* Boston, MA: Daughters of St. Paul.

Senge, P. M. (1990). *The fifth discipline: The art and practice of the learning organization.* New York, NY: Currency Doubleday.

Sergiovanni, T. J. (1991). *The principalship.* Boston, MA: Allyn & Bacon.

Seyfarth, J. T. (1999). *Principalship: New leadership for new challenges.* Upper Saddle River, NJ: Prentice-Hall.

Sigford, J. L. (2006). *The effective school leader's guide to management.* Thousand Oaks, CA: Corwin Press.

Sparks, D. (1995). Focusing staff development on improving student achievement. In G. Cawelti (Ed.), *Handbook of research on improving student achievement* (pp. 163–169). Arlington, VA: Association of Supervision and Curriculum Development.

Sparks, D. (1999). Real-life view: Here's what a true learning community looks like. *Journal of Staff Development, 20*(4), 53–57.

Stiggins, R. J., & Duke, D. L. (1988). *The case for commitment to teacher growth: Research on teacher evaluation.* Albany, NY: State University of New York Press.

Tallerico, M. (2005). *Supporting and sustaining teachers' professional development.* Thousand Oaks, CA: Corwin Press.

U.S. Catholic Church. (1992). *Catechism of the Catholic Church.* New York, NY: Catholic Book Publishing.

United States Conference of Catholic Bishops. (1972). *To teach as Jesus did.* Boston, MA: Daughters of St. Paul.

United States Conference of Catholic Bishops. (2003). *National directory for catechesis.* Washington, DC: Author.

RESOURCES FOR FURTHER STUDY

Acheson, K. A., & Gnalls, M. A. (1997). *Techniques in the clinical supervision of teachers* (4th ed.). White Plains, NY: Longman.

Covey, S. (1991). *Principle-centered leadership.* New York, NY: Simon and Shuster.

Glatthorn, A. A., & Shields, C. R. (1983). *Differentiated supervision for Catholic schools.* Washington, DC: National Catholic Educational Association.

Glickman, C., Gordon, S., & Ross-Gordon, J. (2004). *Supervision and instructional leadership: A developmental approach* (6th ed). Boston, MA: Pearson Education.

Groome, T. (1998). *Educating for life: A spiritual vision for every teacher and parent.* Allen, TX: Thomas More.

Sergiovanni, T. (1990). *Value-added leadership: How to get extraordinary performance in schools.* San Diego, CA: Harcourt, Brace, Jovanovich.

CHAPTER 9

UNDERSTANDING THE ROLE
OF THE PASTOR

Barbara Stacy Rieckhoff

VIGNETTE

The new principal works from early in the morning until late at night to make sure he is learning how to do his job as leader of the school. He responds to emails and phone calls and stands in the front driveway at the start and end of the school day to meet and greet students and parents. He attends all meetings, has established a good relationship with the parent–teacher organization, and is working well with the school advisory board. After the first marking period and fall parent teacher conferences, he is feeling very proud of himself and takes a half day off of work to attend to some personal matters with his wife. He is hoping to take her out to dinner for the first time since he took this job. When his cell phone rings at 4:00 p.m. that Friday afternoon in November and it is the pastor calling, he realizes his evening may not go as planned. The pastor shares that 20 parents showed up at the rectory a short time ago demanding to talk with him about their dissatisfaction with their children's report card grades. They insisted that the pastor must take action immediately and are threatening to get more parents involved if the problem is not addressed quickly. How must the principal respond to this situation? Is he the leader of the

Catholic School Leadership, pages 151–163
Copyright © 2016 by Information Age Publishing
All rights of reproduction in any form reserved.

school or is the pastor? What can and should he do to remedy this immediate situation and what can be done to prevent future situations like this from occurring? What does the principal need to understand about the role and relationship between the pastor and principal in a Catholic school?

INTRODUCTION

The position of the pastor within the Catholic parish school is an important and complicated role. As the leader of the parish and spokesperson for all that occurs within the faith community, the pastor is in an exclusive position to greatly impact the school and its success. In today's current reality of declining Mass attendance and school enrollment, the pastor has been thrust into a role he may not feel adequately prepared for. While the most devoted pastor can have tremendous impact on helping a school grow and flourish, a pastor who has no patience for the challenges of the schoolhouse with limited educational and financial training can negatively impact the situation in such a way to drive families away.

The principal is also in a unique position to work alongside the pastor leading the school and helping it grow. When done harmoniously, the parish and school can flourish and draw parishioners and students from miles away. However, when strife is apparent and the principal is at odds with the pastor, even the family living down the block can be forced to find another Catholic church and school for their family to attend.

The pastor–principal relationship is a complex one that requires an understanding of the multiple layers and stakeholders involved. Essential to understanding the role of the pastor in the parochial school is becoming familiar with the background and historical perspective of how this role evolved over time and the immense challenges that exist for pastors. The various types and styles of pastors are described as well as strategies for principals to use in order to work with their pastors effectively. This chapter will focus on the evolution of the role of the pastor, the changes in school governance that have occurred, and some of the models of pastor behavior in supporting parish schools. This review aims to assist the principal in understanding how to effectively work with the pastor to support the school's growth and development. Strategies for successful pastor principal relationships are shared, with the intent of creating a collaborative culture where parish and school goals are met and the mission and spirit of the Catholic faith are ever present.

HISTORICAL PERSPECTIVE

The role of the pastor is complex, multidimensional, and changing over time. Changes in school governance in the last 25 years have impacted the pastor's role and how the school and parish leadership is shared with others. Tracing the history of the pastor's role and how it has evolved provides a good context for appreciating current roles and accompanying expectations in parochial schools and how these roles have grown in depth and breadth.

Catholic schools were typically situated within a single parish where boundaries defined the neighborhood, with the First Plenary Council of Baltimore in 1852 urging bishops in the United States to have a Catholic school in every parish (Haney, 2010). As a result, the pastor's role was to establish a Catholic school and encourage parishioners to send their children to the school. Over one hundred years later, by the mid-1960s, there was a trend for schools to move away from the parish structure so they would become more autonomous and professional and less insular. While the 2009 Catholic school enrollment data show that most schools are still parish schools, there were some changes in board roles and responsibilities that indicated a shifting of power, decision making, and authority. Situated within these changes are the responsibilities and expectations of the principal and how they have been impacted along with way.

Current Catholic schools, both elementary and secondary, operate in one of three basic board types. These include Advisory, where the school board's role is advisory to the decision makers, Consultative, where the board participates in the policy making process and the board is in a consulting role, although not the decision makers, and Board of Limited Jurisdiction, which is a policy-making board. In this case, the board is delegated the authority to enact policy in certain areas of institutional operation (Haney, O'Brien, & Sheehan, 2009). Haney suggests that boards are distributed as follows: 43% Advisory, 35% Consultative, 20% Boards of Limited Jurisdiction and 2% Boards of Trustees (Haney, 2010).

The impact of these board changes has been felt at the leadership level. While the pastor and principal are the final decision makers for the school, the noted shifts in board roles have changed how the process works with the required involvement of board members added to these decisions. Previously the pastor and principal could make decisions on their own, but more recently others have become involved in some aspect of the process. While these new procedures have involved invested stakeholders, they have also impacted how the pastor and principal can function; some pastors and principals may not see these board changes as positive as the involvement of more players in the decision making process can be time-consuming, involve more questioning and explanation regarding decisions, and, at times, be perceived as challenging their authority.

ROLES OF PASTOR IN PRACTICE

The actual day-to-day functioning of the pastor in a Catholic school can range from a great deal of involvement to limited or almost none. While the 1983 Code of Canon Law that governs the Catholic Church indicates the pastor is ultimately the leader of an elementary school, since the school is a ministry of his parish, Caruso (2012) indicates there is no seminary experience or training to prepare pastors for this role. Some dioceses may offer continuing education; however, most of the learning comes from on-the-job training (Caruso, 2012). Regardless of the knowledge and preparation, Traviss reminds of an important fact: "The pastor makes or breaks the assignment" (Caruso, 2012, p. 44). Four models have emerged to characterize the pastor's behavior or how the pastor might be perceived within the parish school community. Caruso suggests such characterizations might appear superficial, but they underscore the differences that exist in pastor behavior and levels of support for the school. "Father Hostile" is the pastor who prefers not to have a school as he sees it as a drain on resources and finances. He attends school functions reluctantly and does not lend support to the principal, students, or school families. Next on the continuum is "Father Schizophrenia," who accepts the presence of the school but is unpredictable and uneven in his support, his attendance at events, and willingness to participate in school functions and events. "Father Laissez-faire" accepts the presence of the school but does not see himself as the leader of the school community. While attentive to the financial and functional needs of the school, he empowers the principal to operate and manage the school. This pastor does not integrate his vision for the school and how it fits with the larger vision for the parish. "Father Engaged" represents the pastor who recognizes the school as an evangelizing agent and clearly sees himself as the leader of the school. His style is collaborative and he seeks the wisdom and expertise of others in helping the school grow and succeed. While the principal is empowered to lead the school, he sees himself as a member of a team, visible and in attendance at school functions, and offering and lending support in many concrete ways (Caruso, 2012).

Barrett (1996) provides a much different lens for viewing the pastor's role and behavior in relationship to the parish school. Acknowledging that the pastor's commitment to the school and its mission directly relates to the success of the school, he identifies examples of a pastor's presence, noting how each type of presence is necessary and provides a different kind of support to the school.

Spiritual presence describes how the pastor exhibits his leadership as he works with the principal, faculty, and director of religious education to ensure all are in agreement regarding the core mission of what it means to be Catholic. Further, he lends his expertise to the team regarding how religion is taught, sharing in planning faith development activities and closely monitoring sacramental preparation and other work connected to faith life in the school. Faculty and staff retreats provide the opportunity to connect with the adults in the school and support their faith life and development.

Financial presence is a different way the pastor supports the school. This encompasses more than providing the parish subsidy for the school; rather, it involves a thorough understanding of how the parish and school can work together so that mutual goals in the area of finance are attained. Fundraising and wise spending are connected in this area of financial presence. Marketing and recruitment efforts lead to a healthier financial outlook. Finally, this area of the pastor's awareness and understanding of the financial well-being connects to the true mission of the Catholic school and how it leads to faith development and evangelization of the Church.

Social presence describes the pastor's attendance at a variety of school activities and events. In particular, the socially present pastor comes to those events that are not required but which seem to impact the school community greatly. Clearly the time devoted to attend a variety of school events is a challenge, but this visibility sends a strong message to all stakeholders regarding the pastor's true commitment to the school.

Parish presence describes the integration of the school and parish together. The pastor can assist with connecting the two and providing opportunities for collaborative events, goals and opportunities.

Finally, the pastor brings intellectual presence to his role. He shares his expertise and understanding with the various parish groups he works with. Regularly scheduled time, both formally and informally, will provide the pastor with ways to share his ministry, his expertise, and his advice. Ongoing meetings and conversations with the principal, teachers, and various board members will continue to forge stronger relationship while helping constituent groups understand the mission and identify ways to integrate this mission in joint efforts (Barrett, 1996).

REALITIES OF PARISH SCHOOLS

The parish school continues to be the most common type of Catholic elementary school in operation across the United States today. Within that model, the pastor holds authority over the property and operations, and the principal serves at the behest of the pastor as the administrator over the educational functions of the school. There is variance within the range of duties and authority given to the principal. This is especially true in relationship to management of the budget. While the diocesan office and school boards assist with the identification of the principal candidate to be hired, the final authority and decision rests with the pastor (Goldschmidt & Walsh, 2013). Additionally, the pastor evaluates the principal and determines if he or she should be rehired for future employment.

Today's parish school depends upon a harmonious and collaborative relationship between the pastor and the principal. While pastors are given the message, "A good relationship with the principal is key to everything" (Archdiocese of Chicago, 2005), there are roadblocks that make this challenging even when the best of intentions are present. There isn't necessarily agreement about the actual role the pastor should take in offering support to the school and the principal. Gilbert (1983) suggests that when the pastor hires the principal to be the administrator of the school, he should permit the principal to be the leader of the school. That in turn requires the pastor to support the principal in this role, being available and willing to help the principal in any way possible. Geelan (2000) believes the most important work for the pastor is in policy making, while Drahmann (1985) suggests the key role for the pastor should be primarily focused on spiritual leadership and overseeing financial matters. Brock and Fraser (2001) cited principals having a preference for pastors with a background or experience in education. Pastors who were familiar with the inner-workings of the schools were able to serve in partnership with principals and understood the complex challenges the schools faced (Brock & Fraser, 2001).

The role of the principal in the Catholic school is complicated and multifaceted, with overlapping roles and responsibilities with some of the work done by the pastor. Divided primarily into three general areas of responsibility, the principal's role is to serve as spiritual leader, educational leader, and managerial leader (Ciriello, 1996). Gilbert (1983) refers to the principal as the pastor of the school, with responsibility for the faith development of the faculty and of the students. Additionally, Ciriello (1996) suggests that the spiritual leader role requires the principal to facilitate the moral and ethical development of students. As the educational leader, the principal is responsible for overseeing the academic program and how it is delivered in the schools. However, in addition, the principal is charged with developing a Catholic school culture while leading the work in areas of curriculum and instruction. The managerial role is the third area of leadership, which includes the operation of the school as well as finance, recruitment, and marketing. While the principal is the primary leader and decision maker in public and private schools, in the Catholic parochial school this role is shared with the pastor, who along with the principal is also designated as primary leader and decision maker (Schafer, 2004).

CHALLENGES

A variety of challenges emerge when attempting to bridge the gap for the pastor and principal to work amicably and support mutual goals for the parish church and school. The financial aspect is most challenging as the operational costs for the school and the church continue to grow. Invariably, asking parishioners and school parents to support one may take away the resources they can give to the other. In some parish schools, the parishioners and school families constitute the same group, in which case a plan may be developed that explains how to support both causes. However, in many schools and parishes today, these parishioners and parents represent two distinct groups. Overall, fewer parishioners attend Mass on a regular basis and fewer are in a position to share a portion of their income with the church. Parishioners don't always feel the sense of sharing to support the school; if they have already supported the school at an earlier time, they may feel that their have done their part to donate to the school, the church, or both. As a result, pastors believe that families need to be reminded that parish schools are not private schools, separate from the parish, but rather a ministry of the parish. This connection is not always clear, and when church and school are perceived as separate operations, both may lose out in financial and emotional support of their constituents.

Another challenge facing the pastor and principal has to do with the formation and demonstration of faith. Fewer families are attending Sunday Mass as a family and as a result, there is not as strong a connection with the faith taught in the school and the message from the pulpit on Sunday. Some families see the weekly Mass that their children attend with the school as a replacement for Sunday attendance. When pressured to attend Sunday Mass, with extra incentive points given at school, some parents drop their children off at Mass, treating it like an extracurricular activity that has little connection to their roles as parents and heads of the family. In addition, the parish spiritual events and activities may not be as well supported by school or church families. This places tremendous pressure on the pastor as he wants the school to be successful but doesn't see evidence of families teaching and modeling the Christian life for their children. Sunday Mass is competing with family time, sporting events, or busy schedules and may no longer be a priority in some households. As the pastor has to allocate money for the school or provide the school's deficits, it can be defeating knowing how hard he is working to build the parish resources and not feel supported in faith by the parishioners and not observe evidence of their faith in practice.

Communication can be a challenge for the pastor and principal. They have vastly different schedules and responsibilities and, sometimes, conflicting duties. Parents may reach out to the pastor in times of strife and discord in their lives and leave the principal out of the conversation, or they may reach out to the principal during a family crisis and leave the pastor out of the conversation. While the pastor and principal are not interchangeable, they both share leadership roles and can be instrumental in supporting families and children at various times in their lives. There is no singular way to communicate or create a flow chart of whom to call first, but the need for strong communication is evident. Communication can also be difficult as the pastor and principal come from different backgrounds and training. Most pastors do not have a background in educational administration; helping them frame some of the issues of the schoolhouse is linked to a need for clarity in communication and accepting that each comes from a different perspective and brings their own expertise to their positions (Urbanski, 2013). As a result, open lines of communication between the pastor and principal are important and can avoid unnecessary misunderstandings from occurring.

Principal retention and turnover can create another area of concern. The level of dissatisfaction with the job can present another challenge for the pastor in working with the principal. Conflict with pastors was cited as an issue in principal retention. "Principals viewed a harmonious working relationship with the pastor or governing body as a critical factor in job satisfaction" (Fraser & Brock, 2006, p. 427). Principals also reported on the interference of the pastor as a serious drawback of their positions as elementary school leaders (Fraser & Brock, 2006)

STRATEGIES FOR SUCCESS

As much as the role complexity and overlap can cause misunderstandings and challenges for principals and pastors, there are a number of ways both can work together to effectively support the mission of the parish and the school and collaboratively share leadership. While much of the research has studied principals' perceptions of the pastor, it is important to note that the shared pastor/principal leadership model requires both parties to have a demonstrated investment in the success or failure of their working relationship. Compared in a business model to the CEO and the president or operations manager, each has a share and investment in the working relationship and its success; their amicable collaboration will be in the best interests of the entire organization.

Pastors are reminded that the school serves as a vital parish ministry; the school's growth will simultaneously aid the parish's growth. Various strategies are provided to pastors to help them support the school and communicate that support to all stakeholder groups within the parish. Many of these strategies can apply to the pastor and the principal as they work to build the success of the school. The pastor can talk regularly about the school in homilies and in meetings and regularly attend functions at the school. Families who don't attend the school but are in the parish should be encouraged and invited to participate in events and activities both at the school and at the church so they are made to feel welcome as part of the parish community. The principal can be instrumental in reaching out to parishioners by speaking at Mass or inviting parishioners to get involved in the school as volunteers, tutors, or coaches. Sacramental preparation can be a bridge for those who attend the school and those who do not; having children prepare together provides a nice way to support both groups and not create divisions unnecessarily. The parish leadership team, on which the pastor and principal serve, can be a vehicle for sharing internal communication and reinforcing common goals. Regular meetings with the parish team help forge stronger relationships and keep all informed on the events and work being done (Archdiocese of Chicago, 2005).

Communication is a key element in successful leadership within any organization, but it is especially critical in this unique relationship. Within this communication needs to be an open loop whereby both the principal and the pastor are comfortable sharing and taking with each other about what is going on and sharing problem solving and decision making. A regular time to meet and discuss issues is critical to their roles and sends a clear message signifying to themselves and to others that they are working together and sharing their leadership.

Division of roles and responsibilities is tied to clear communication. Knowing exactly what is expected and who is responsible for what duties is helpful. A chain of command for communication with the outside world will help alleviate some misunderstandings or misperceptions. Parents and parishioners should know whom they should call for various questions, concerns, or needs. While the contact with the principal may end up with a meeting with the pastor, adhering to a clear communication plan will support all in their roles and responsibilities. When the pastor is contacted by a school parent, he can begin by asking if the parent has contacted the principal about the concern. He may redirect the parent to the principal, further supporting the school leader's role and jurisdiction. Particularly when roles overlap and constituent groups overlap in some instances and do not in others, these clearly defined roles and responsibilities may help. In addition, the role clarification would be useful not just for school parents, but for parishioners and those outside the parish as they navigate the parish church and school.

Trust is cited as another component that can have a positive impact on the pastor–principal relationship. "Trust develops when honest communication and support occur between principal and pastor" (Brock & Fraser, 2001, p. 91). This trusting relationship can help set the tone for the parish community and how work can be accomplished in a positive manner. The pastor and principal can share their journey of learning to work together as they come to understand each one's work styles and mutual goals. Together, they will be able to accomplish much more for the greater good of the parish when they are working in collaboratively than against each other.

As we look for the pastor to support the school, we too need to ensure that the principal is supportive of the parish and its accompanying goals and mission. That can be evidenced by attending Mass, participating in parish fundraising or spiritual activities, lending support, and volunteering. The idea of presence and visibility is so important within the Catholic school and parish culture. The principal's presence contributes to the overall perception of support and collaboration between the church and the school.

Paying attention to leadership transitions and how they occur is also an important strategy for a parish and school's growth. While the change of the pastor or principal may require adjustment, it also creates an opportunity for honest and much-needed dialogue to occur. Often a challenging time in a parish's history, changing leadership can signal problems or dissatisfaction or imply that something is wrong. Brock and Fraser suggest using the leadership transition period to dialogue on the following issues: educational philosophy, vision for the school, division of duties, expectations for each other and procedures for handling problems (Brock & Fraser, 2001). These conversations will lead to a better understanding of the needs and interests of the pastor and principal and organizationally, will keep lines of communication open during difficult times of transition.

Sharing leadership between pastors and principals has been a recurring theme identified by many. Greeley suggests that "the success and future of Catholic schools can be found in parish resources—human, organizational and financial. He recommends the pastor should work with laity to make them full partners in decision making and giving them more responsibility in the future of the school" (1992, p. 116).

Urbanski wrote about the successes in the Diocese of Raleigh, indicating the pastor–principal relationship can be a powerful one. "Working together can form a synergy that provides a system of checks and balances and a blend of secular and spiritual focus for the school community" (Urbanski, 2013, p. 34). The Diocese of Raleigh began a series of formal meetings organized by the school superintendent and the bishop. While these meetings attempted to more evenly distribute resources across the diocese, they also provided an opportunity to get groups of pastors and principals together to create and commit to an ongoing dialogue (Urbanski, 2013).

Collaboration by all members of the community represents an important component of Church governance. "The development of an effective educational ministry depends upon the ability of persons individually and in association to collaborate" (O'Brien, 1990, p. 18). "Collaborative ministry calls for the vision and gifts of others" (Gramick, 2001, p. 20). Much like a principal sharing leadership with teachers, this notion of distributing leadership in the Catholic school parish structure can have a positive impact on outcomes and help all meet their goals effectively (Spillane, 2006).

FUTURE DIRECTIONS

The roles of the pastor and principal will continue to be challenging, multilayered, and complex. However, moving forward at a time when both Catholic churches and schools face increasing challenges, it becomes more important than ever before for these two leaders to work together. First and foremost, it is necessary for the pastor and principal to find common ground and agree to work together. Upon interviewing and hiring, the principal should take time to meet with the pastor and meet with others who can provide insights about the pastor and how he operates and oversees his parish. More information heading into the relationship will help later so both can appreciate their work styles, strengths, and talents. As with any relationship, it will take time to get to know one another, to build trust, and to understand each other's perspective. This foundational work is important and will lead to stronger connections and a positive working relationship in the future.

Additionally, the leadership team should build upon the success of the new governance models. They should consider how they can authentically share leadership in a positive way that allows delegating responsibilities to others who can assist. This may include sharing with parish staff, school board members, or parish board members. The idea of trust and empowerment begins with the pastor–principal leadership team and has the potential to model for others how decisions can be made collaboratively and how leadership can be shared in an appropriate and meaningful way. The pastor and principal should talk about collaboration, its value and worth within a Catholic culture and setting. Brock and Fraser (2001) suggest the importance of developing complementary roles and supportive interactions between the pastor and the principal. Clearly, the work done in Catholic schools and parishes is in keeping with professional learning communities discussed by DuFour and others (DuFour, 2004). Consideration should be given to applying the professional learning community model as Catholic school identity is congruous and supportive of professional learning communities (PLCs). Community plays a large role in Catholic school identity and highlights the similarities between the PLC process and the character of Catholic school communities (Salina & Traynor, 2009).

Understanding the roles held by the pastor and the principal is an important step in better communication and helping all reach their goals. Continuing to dialogue and look for ways that support the shared efforts of the parish leadership team will be essential for Catholic schools and parishes to grow and flourish. The relationship between the pastor and principal has the potential to move the parish church and school to a point where all are working together with common goals and interests for the good of the parishioners and school families; they can reach a point where all feel welcome and all are modeling their work as an extension of their faith. The strength of the pastor–principal relationship will build a stronger Catholic faith for all.

REFERENCES

Archdiocese of Chicago. (2005). *Handbook for pastors*. Chicago, IL: Archdiocese of Chicago, Office of Catholic Schools.

Barrett, F. (1996). The role of the pastor in the parish with a school. In Maria Ciriello (Ed.), *Expectations for the Catholic school principal: A handbook for pastors and parish school committees* (pp. 115–126). Washington, DC: National Catholic Education Association.

Brock, B., & Fraser, J. (2001) Principals and pastors sharing leadership: Perspectives from Nebraska and New South Wales. *Catholic Education: Journal of Inquiry and Practice, 5*(1), 85–100.

Caruso, M. (2012). *When the sisters said farewell: The transition of leadership in Catholic elementary schools*. Lanham, MD: Rowman & Littlefield.

Ciriello, M. (1996). *Expectations for the Catholic school principal*. Washington, DC: United States Catholic Conference.

Drahmann, T. (1985). *Governance and administration in the Catholic school*. Washington, DC: National Catholic Educational Association.

DuFour, R. (2004). What is a professional learning community? *Educational Leadership, 61*(8), 6–11.

Fraser, J., & Brock, B. (2006). Catholic school principal job satisfaction: Keys to retention and recruitment. *Catholic Education: Journal of Inquiry and Practice, 9*(4), 425–440.

Geelan, T. E. (2000). *Pastoring Catholic education boards, commissions and councils: Witness of an experienced pastor*. Washington, DC: National Catholic Educational Association.

Gilbert, J. R. (1983). *Pastor as shepherd for the school community*. Washington, DC: National Catholic Educational Association.

Goldschmidt, E., & Walsh, M. (2013). Urban Catholic elementary schools: What are the governance models? *Catholic Education: Journal of Inquiry and Practice, 17*(1), 111–135.

Gramick, J. (2001). Catholic women: A contemporary style of leadership. *Muslim World, 91*, 19–29.

Haney, R. (2010). Design for success: New configurations and governance models for Catholic schools. *Catholic Education: Journal of Inquiry and Practice, 14*(2), 195–211.

Haney, R., O'Brien, S & Sheehan, L. (2009). *A primer on educational governance in the Catholic church.* (2nd ed). Washington, DC: National Catholic Educational Association.

O'Brien, S. (1990). *A primer on educational governance in the Catholic church.* Washington, DC: National Catholic Educational Association.

Salina, C., & Traynor, J. (2009). Creating and sustaining a structured professional learning community within a Catholic context. *Momentum, 40,* 32–35.

Schafer, D. (2004). Leadership role expectations and relationships of principals and pastors in Catholic parochial elementary schools: Part 1. *Catholic Education: Journal of Inquiry and Practice, 8*(2), 234–249.

Schafer, D. (2005). Leadership role expectations and relationships of principals and pastors in Catholic parochial elementary schools: Part 2. *Catholic Education: Journal of Inquiry and Practice, 9*(2), 230–249.

Spillane, J. (2006). *Distributed leadership.* San Francisco, CA: Jossey-Bass.

Traviss, M. P. (2001). Research in Catholic school administration. In T. Hunt, J. Ellis, & R. Nuzzi (Eds.), *Handbook of research on Catholic education.* Westport, CT: Greenwood.

Urbanski, C. (2013). The New Catholic school leadership: Principals and pastors working together. *Momentum, 44*(2), 31–34.

RECOMMENDATIONS FOR FURTHER READING

Alliance for Catholic Education. (2014). *Some ideas for what pastors can do.* South Bend, IN: University of Notre Dame. Retrieved from https://ace.nd.edu/catholic-school.../pastors 11/14/14

Bolman, L., & Deal, T. (2013). *Reframing organizations* (5th ed.). San Francisco, CA: Jossey-Bass.

Frabutt, J, Holter, A., Nuzzi, R., Rocha, H., & Cassel, L. (2010). Pastors' views of parents and the parental role in Catholic schools. *Catholic Education: Journal of Inquiry and Practice, 14*(1), 24–46.

Gallo, M. (2011). *Succession planning for the leaders we need.* Ontario, Canada: Lambert Academic Publishing.

Garrido, A. (2013). *Redeeming administration: 12 spiritual habits for Catholic leaders in parishes, schools, religious communities and other institutions.* South Bend, IN: Ava Maria Press.

Spillane, J., & Diamond, J. (Eds.). (2007). *Distributed leadership in practice.* San Francisco, CA: Jossey-Bass.

Weiss, S. (2007). Pastor-principal relationship in the parish school. *Catholic Education: A Journal of Inquiry and Practice, 11*(1), 7–22.

CHAPTER 10

OPERATIONAL VITALITY

Barbara Stacy Rieckhoff

VIGNETTE

The principal of the school is working with the business manager to develop the budget for the following academic year. She insists that raising tuition will have a detrimental effect on enrollment and strongly recommends against it, insisting the hard work focused on recruiting new students will have been in vain. The business manager pulls out the current monthly budget and shows the principal the latest balance sheet. "The school is $250,000 in debt and this is the only way to help correct this situation for next year. We can't continue to deplete the parish resources." The principal describes all of the fund-raising initiatives planned for the upcoming year. She tells him about the walk-a-thon, car wash, and various events sponsored by the parent association. She reminds him that last year's gala and silent auction raised over $100,000 with these funds dedicated exclusively for school use. From her perspective, the school should be operating in the black and should be acknowledged for repayment of debt to the parish. Her response to the business manager was as follows: "We promised the school board and parent association that tuition rates would be frozen for three years in a row. The tradeoff was that they would support a variety of fundraising events, commit service hours and encourage other parents to do the same. Parents even painted the school basement and donated their

Catholic School Leadership, pages 165–184
Copyright © 2016 by Information Age Publishing
All rights of reproduction in any form reserved.

time to repair some of the broken lunchroom tables." What information does the principal need in order to understand the connection between tuition, enrollment, and the school's financial situation? How does the connection with the parish subsidy impact the school, and what is the relationship between the parish and school? In her efforts to save money, has the principal realized any true gains for the school's financial situation?

INTRODUCTION

The Catholic school principal has a range of duties and responsibilities that are well documented (Ciriello, 1996) and are distributed in three areas of leadership: educational or instructional leadership, spiritual leadership, and managerial leadership. Each role is important in the successful operation of the Catholic school in meeting students' academic and faith needs while sustaining a school's fiscal viability. All require the principal's constant attention and energy; the various roles are equally important and integrate the work of a school leader on a daily basis. This chapter will focus on the managerial function of the Catholic school principal, which encompasses the operational vitality of the school. Operational vitality comprises the financial well-being of the school; it includes financial planning, both long- and short-term, human resources and personnel policies, facilities and management plans, and institutional advancement.

The *National Standards and Benchmarks for Effective Catholic Elementary and Secondary Schools* published in March 2012 cite "operational vitality" as one of the four key areas of standards and benchmarks along with (a) mission and Catholic identity, (b) governance and leadership, and (c) academic excellence. The operational vitality standards, Numbers 10, 11, 12, and 13, identify benchmarks to describe excellence in financial planning, effective human resource policies, well-maintained facilities, and comprehensive institutional advancement programs. The benchmarks call for collaboration and planning in order to achieve operational vitality.

FINANCIAL PLANNING

Financial planning is the most important area of a school's operational vitality. This plan or blueprint is critical to the success of the school; its development and thoroughness will integrate and impact other areas of a school's financial well-being. It will guide decision making and the financial implications of those decisions. The *National Standards and Benchmarks for Effective Catholic Elementary and Secondary Schools,* (National Standards, 2012) indicate the following: "An excellent Catholic school provides a feasible three to five year financial plan that includes both current and projected budgets and is the result of a collaborative process, emphasizing faithful stewardship" (National Standards, 2012, p. 14). Phelps suggests four key steps in Catholic school strategic planning that overlap goals in financial planning. These include clarifying mission, vision, and values; consulting with all stakeholders; gathering data; and developing processes for successful implementation of the plan (Robey, 2012).

While the principal serves as the primary driver of the financial plan, often it is a shared responsibility with others in the school or parish. New principals struggle to understand this fiscal role and responsibility, often being overshadowed by the business manager or other staff involved in financial decision making. "Acquiring and managing the school's financial resources may be the least appealing and most frightening and mysterious tasks for which Catholic school principals are responsible" (Konzen, 1996, p. 245). In some cases, the managerial duties that relate to financial planning are handled or overseen by parish or school business managers, the school secretary, or office assistant with direct responsibility for the collection of tuition, registrations, and other fees. Regardless of the amount of tuition charged or the way it is collected from parents, the principal must have the requisite knowledge and skills to oversee and coordinate this aspect of managing a school.

The financial state of the school extends well beyond the scope of tuition collection; it is a key driver and impacts the other decisions made in the school. Having a clear understanding of the budgeting process as well as the procedures will ensure data-based decisions in all areas. Budget development as it relates to financial planning, along with constant attention to modifications or changes, provides the principal with the tools needed to make decisions that further the school's success and financial well-being (Picciano, 2006).

It is never too early for the principal or president to learn about a school's financial well-being. Rowe (2003) suggests that a clear understanding of the school's financial situation is something the school leader should be aware of before taking on a leadership position. He recommends probing seven key areas of finance before accepting the leadership of the school; examples of these areas include a clear understanding the school's debt, knowing who holds financial expertise, and being aware of whether salaries are competitive. As a future leader, one can decide if the financial state can be managed or is in such a state of disarray that it would be difficult to change.

The principal needs to be vigilant in understanding and monitoring the financial plan, with attention to changes in direction, enrollment, and other factors that may influence the bottom line. Regular monitoring will allow the principal to communicate to all groups, ensuring best practices are in place and that the financial plan is clearly linked to decisions made in the best interests of students.

Tuition-Based Model

Today's economic uncertainties require a three- to five-year financial plan and allow an opportunity for the school's stakeholders to learn from past history and experiences while planning for the future. As such, a financial plan that projects future life of the school, with attention to local and community changes, enrollment dips, and trends, should be clearly communicated and understood by board and parents with all roles in the process outlined and defined. Most schools create such a plan relying heavily on tuition to provide the majority of the school's income. Harris suggests the present Catholic school funding model, where parents pay tuition bills that increase far in excess of inflation, leads inevitably to a future where some good Catholic schools will educate some Catholics (Harris, 1999). This model is not one that is sustainable and will alienate those who cannot afford the rising tuition costs. Bryk, Lee, and Holland (1993) report that high schools are becoming less tuition-dependent, with small increases in grants and bequests when compared to elementary schools. In some cases, high schools receive subsidies from their religious communities, thereby alleviating a portion of the financial burden. While there are positive trends in developing other funding sources, tuition remains the primary source of income, as 69% of secondary and 63% of elementary school income is derived from tuition (Byrk et al., 1993).

Closely related to the tuition rate is connecting actual costs associated with operating the school and the actual costs to educate a child; these costs need to be clearly outlined and communicated to parents and parishioners. Catholic school costs have increased greatly over the past decade for a variety of reasons. Significant increases in costs are in part due to increases in staffing to lower the pupil–teacher ratio. Inflation and the implementation of new curricula are also reasons that costs have increased (Harris, 2000). Current realities of employing lay staff and how they comprise today's Catholic school faculties suggests how important this aspect is. Heft (2011) recognizes the importance of finding the finances to pay faculties who are now predominantly lay people and, as a result, are employed at higher costs than previous non-lay or religious teachers and staffs. While at times school personnel are reluctant to connect actual costs to tuition rates, more transparent and direct connections will help all parties be aware of what is required to fund a quality Catholic education. Low tuition rates may attract families to the school initially, but in the end the school will need additional money to operate effectively, thus turning to other sources to support the school's operation.

The collaborative aspect of the financial planning process garners ownership and awareness needed for its future support. In a parish school, the parents of students as well as parishioners who do not use the school need to be aware of the current and projected costs to provide a quality Catholic education. Parents are obvious collaborators, but local community and/or parish members who do not have daily contact with the school should also be involved. School board members, parents, and parish representatives all share in developing the financial plan and monitoring its health and well-being. Tony Bryk and his colleagues concluded that the most important factor in the success of Catholic schools was the sense of community among teachers and students (Bryk et al., 1993). This same community must extend to parents and key stakeholders so the school's mission is well understood, valued, and shared in a way that all can financially support. The principal's role then, in this area, is to be transparent and open regarding costs, fees, and expenses that have to be met.

Stewardship

Faithful stewardship suggests all are responsible for more than developing the financial plan, but in supporting it as well. The U.S. Bishops' Pastoral Letter on Stewardship defines the role of a Christian Steward:

> As each one has received a gift, use it to serve one another as good stewards of God's varied grace (1 Pt 4: 10).

> A steward is defined as safeguarding material and human resources and using them responsibly are one answer; so is generous giving of time, talent, and treasure. But being a Christian steward means more. As Christian stewards, we receive God's gifts gratefully, cultivate them responsibly, share them lovingly in justice with others, and return them with increase to the Lord. (United States Conference of Catholic Bishops [USCCB], 2010, n.p.)

Here is one school's description of faithful stewardship:

> We emphasize stewardship at St. Mark Parish School because it is an essential quality of being an active disciple of Jesus. Every Catholic is called to be a good steward, whether or not they have school-aged children. Stewardship is very simple: as Christ gave His life for us, so we must give our lives to others. That involves giving of Time, Talent, and Treasure—but it starts with giving Jesus our hearts. (St. Mark Parish School, n.d.)

The concept of stewardship invites and encourages all to support, in name and in dollar amount, the education and faith development provided. It provides a template for supporting schools with all sharing in the costs. Stewardship is not a school funding model: it is a way of life, one that models the life of Jesus. Through the stewardship of each Catholic, people with children, people whose children are grown, people who give generously to fund all missions of the church can reduce the amount of adjusted tuition (Diocese of Kansas City, 2010).

While the stewardship model presents a possible solution for supporting Catholic schools, it is difficult to monitor and hold parishioners accountable. Some parishioners feel that they have already made their contributions to the school when they were active school parents; others do not share the sense of responsibility or duty toward garnering this support. Many parishes have opted to invite parishioners to contribute to a general school fund. This does not yield the same results as the stewardship model, but it is in keeping with the notion that all are responsible to support Catholic education.

Fundraising

Historically, fundraising has been a critical component in the financial plan in Catholic schools. From wrapping paper to candy sales and the many school and parish events held to build community, these efforts have grown considerably over the past decade. Fundraising in Catholic schools has gone from 11 to 15% of the school budget (Harris, 2000). Yet even increased fundraising can result in diminished returns and does not guarantee the solvency of Catholic schools. While intended to strengthen the sense of community between the school, parishioners, and local supporters, too often these efforts can wear down the energies and resources of well-meaning volunteers. Fundraisers are often perceived as single events not linked to the larger vision of the school, its needs, and its relationship to the financial plan. Unfortunately, poorly coordinated efforts can fail to raise the money needed and instead, instill negative feelings. While such efforts are important and can contribute to the larger financial plan, they must be well coordinated and planned in advance so they can be successful and provide much-needed dollars to the overall common good. Phelps suggests that schools maintain a checklist of fundraising approaches in order to assess and track the breadth and effectiveness of each one (Robey, 2012). Key constituents and supporters of the school should be familiar with the overall financial plan and the goals to achieve that plan. They will be more likely to be regular and ongoing contributors if they understand how their charitable donations will be used and, additionally, they can help get the message out to others.

Fundraising has changed in its method and style in recent years. The traditional bake sale has been replaced with sophisticated efforts to sell gift cards and certificates whereby the schools get a percentage of the money raised. Elaborate fundraising events comprised of silent and live auctions have replaced informal site-based events. While the potential to raise a substantial amount of money exists in these more sophisticated events, the reality is that the same group of parents is continually enlisted to support these efforts. In cases where parents have unlimited resources, this can work. Unfortunately, current economic constraints placed on families restrict their ability to provide unlimited support. Many parents are already financially strapped with higher tuition costs and cannot support additional fundraisers. The result can be loss of families to another school, perhaps public, where the financial pressures are not as great.

The principal's role in this process is an important one that includes communication of a clearly mapped out schedule of events and "asks" throughout the calendar year. This schedule includes dates and timelines for all parish and schools fundraisers, tuition, registration payments, and fees. An awareness of requests placed on parents to contribute is essential, and at times, the principal may have to step in and discourage groups from overextending parents' capabilities. Some schools develop a joint letter from the parish and the school; this regular and ongoing communication connects all of the fundraising efforts to a larger strategic financial plan that will directly support actual costs and provide constituent and stakeholder groups with a clear sense of how monies are being spent.

Parish Subsidy

The parish subsidy is the amount of support the parish provides to the school each year. This can be a fixed number or one based on the deficits and unanticipated budget expenses. Harris (2000) describes the current funding dilemma facing Catholic schools. While the parish subsidy has been the method for paying for the school's shortfall, rising costs make this amount difficult to guarantee. It can set up an *ex post facto* model for budgeting and covering costs. In effect, the parish "picks up the tab" for what the school cannot afford. Parishes have been less able to provide this support in recent years, so the costs are handed back to parents in the form of rising tuition costs. This system works when parents can afford to meet these rising costs. If parents cannot support the increases, then enrollment can potentially be impacted.

All of these efforts to support the local Catholic school are well-intended and heartfelt. Whether parishioners, parents, friends of the school, or local community members are providing support, the system does not always allow a clear path from revenue and expenses. Instead, in some cases it is a continual game of catch-up that starts over again each year with no predictability. The principal has to deal with the current financial reality, which ultimately impacts the needs of the school. Acquisition of new technology or science equipment for the academic program moves up and down on the priority list based on fundraising success rather than on the current conditions or need, on what has been budgeted, and on what money can be spent to further underscore its importance. Over time, Catholic school costs have continued to rise, and these increases are handed to parents. Unfortunately, this has impacted enrollment as families in need are not able to be part of this current funding model.

New strategies for funding Catholic schools continue to be explored and piloted. A tuition-aid program provides schools with a subsidy to be used for partial tuition in order to attract students who may not be able to afford the regular tuition. A consortium model involves a group of schools working together, sharing resources (Wuerl, 2008). Crimino (2008) offers an overview of new configurations that include regional schools (where groups of schools have used geographic data to broaden the user base), merged schools (where grade configurations have been separated into various buildings or many buildings have been merged into fewer sites), and the creation of systems (where K–12 education is available through a centralized structure). It is important to know that one model may not meet the needs of every locality; in fact, the operating principle behind this year's focus area was "one size fits one" (Crimino, 2008). For the principal, whether new or seasoned, the financial planning realm is one requiring constant attention and care. The school leader needs to be the key driver in the conversation, working collaboratively with parish, school, and community members so the best plan can be crafted for the school.

EFFECTIVE HUMAN RESOURCE POLICIES

Human resource policies represent another area that falls within the overall operational vitality of the school. The National Standards and Benchmarks for Effective Catholic Elementary and Secondary Schools (National Standards, 2012) regarding effective human resources policies is as follows: An excellent Catholic school operates in accord with published human resource/personnel policies developed in compliance with (arch) diocesan policies and/or religious congregation sponsorship policies, which affect all staff (clergy, religious women and men, laity and volunteers) and provide clarity for responsibilities, expectations and accountability (National Standards, 2012). Clearly, the policies and their development provide important guidance to the principal in operating the school effectively. In conjunction with the local diocese, adherence to policies and procedures must take place.

Hiring practices in Catholic schools have changed in many ways in recent years. Pressures to compete with public and charter schools have impacted Catholic schools' increased expectations regarding certification and licensure to ensure teachers have the necessary qualifications for the job. Job descriptions for each of the positions are more clearly defined with key elements of each employee's job description and a process for supervision and evaluation of staff. Teacher and staff accountability and expectations often present the most difficult task for the principal. Careful and ongoing supervision of each staff member, from building engineer to lunch personnel to teacher and office staff, has to occur. While Catholic teachers and staff consistently earn less than their public school counterparts, they are still expected to be successful in producing measurable student learning outcomes and faith-filled children. Overseeing their performance and providing ongoing feedback and direction support this development of human resources. Ciriello (1996) suggests time spent on this personnel aspect of leadership is time well spent and necessary to a school's success. "The success of the school relies on the competent and committed performance of many people" (Ciriello, 1996, p. 3).

While the principal may find it challenging to secure quality teachers, she must adhere to the required guidelines to find the individuals whose values and interests align with that of the Catholic school. Hiring should be done with forward thinking and a vision towards future goals and changes, and not just replacement lines for staff. Additionally, finding the best people for each position will be of benefit later, as each new hire represents an opportunity to make changes and improve upon area needing to grow.

Volunteers and their roles in a Catholic school environment have also undergone substantial changes. As an important component to the pool of Catholic school resources, volunteers now face clear expectations and policies regarding their roles in the school. They have to be vetted and trained in accordance with the Bishops' mandate with a clear understanding of their role in protecting children and serving as mandated reporters (USCCB, 2010). The good intentions of volunteers have been replaced with strict accountability and expectations closely aligned to the requirements for professional staff. Reflecting the church's response to the sex abuse scandal, safeguards have been put in place to ensure such events cannot happen in the future. All school personnel, regardless of training or position, are put under increased scrutiny in order to protect the safety and well-being of children. For volunteers, a period of mentoring and coaching can be a useful probationary time to ensure individuals are a good fit for the school environment and for work with children. A well-meaning volunteer who screams, yells, and behaves in a manner opposite the school's mission and vision provides no real help. Many schools have found success by enlisting a cadre of volunteers who undergo a period of training, utilizing parent mentors or teachers to work with them so they understand the goals and expectations of their volunteer efforts. Volunteers are key stakeholders who represent a valuable human resource; however, there is a certain way the school runs and operates that stems from beliefs about children and faith that must be adhered to.

Teacher accountability has also increased with more demands placed on teachers than ever before. New tools to observe, evaluate, and support teacher growth and development are available to measure a teacher's success and impact on student learning (Danielson, 2012). Danielson's framework has become the professional standard for evaluating teacher performance across all school settings. The rubric for teacher performance is divided into four domains, taking into account planning and preparation, the classroom environment, instruction, and professional responsibilities. A variety of measures are used to assess teacher performance, with the emphasis on student growth and evidence of learning outcomes. Standardized tests and other benchmark assessments provide good data to determine if teachers are meeting expectations for student learning.

Catholic leaders also evaluate the teacher's faith teaching, based on presenting the beliefs of the faith in religious instruction. Depending upon the age or grade level, the faith teaching includes sacramental preparation, church attendance, and knowledge of prayers. Most importantly, the principal evaluates how the teacher incorporates the Catholic values and beliefs into the classroom and teaching repertoire on a day-to-day basis.

The accountability and expectations for the work done in Catholic schools has increased in recent years. All members of the school team are held accountable for their work. The teacher is responsible for student learning while the marketing director is responsible for recruiting new students. School accountability efforts have increased across the board for all schools in the last decade, with Catholic schools being no exception. Performance evaluations and evidence-based reviews have impacted all employees. Whether teacher, building engineer, or development director, all are under increased pressure to succeed, perform, and achieve the goals aligned with their individual job description. While this accountability and expected job performance helps to "raise the bar" on expectations, there are implications for the principal. Each staff member has to be supervised, evaluated, guided, and mentored. In order to do this well, there is a tremendous expectation on the principal's time and energy.

Principals are responsible to hire the best candidates for their schools, while making sure each is a good fit for the core values and teaching in a Catholic tradition. In doing so, the leader follows the local and archdiocesan policies and procedures. Adherence to the policies is critical, as the hiring and supervision of staff has direct impact on children. Once hired, teachers and other staff need constant guidance, support, and supervision. The principal has to maximize time to do all of these duties and perform them well. When possible, delegating and getting assistance is useful. Creating a culture of visibility where the principal is seen throughout the school regularly rather than sitting behind closed doors helps enforce the expectations throughout the school. Furthermore, the principal can observe others at their jobs and collect informal data related to job performance. Technology tools such as iPads and smartphone devices help to capture events and observe the staff doing their work. The school leader should provide feedback to employees regularly and ask others for feedback about their performance; these procedures help to support a collaborative culture with all expected to learn and grow.

WELL-MAINTAINED FACILITIES

A school's facility and its physical condition communicate its overall well-being. The importance of a school's facilities is described in the National Standards and Benchmarks for Effective Catholic Elementary and Secondary Schools (National Standards, 2012) as follows: "An excellent Catholic school develops and maintains facilities, equipment, and technology management plan designed to continuously support the implementation of the educational mission of the school" (National Standards, 2012, p. 15).

Facilities

The condition of the school and accompanying facilities communicates the level of care that exists for it. Many consider the condition of the front entrance important in shaping perceptions others have about the school. A well-maintained and welcoming front entrance suggests a pleasant environment for children, further reinforcing the good work going on inside of the school. Unfortunately, many Catholic schools are housed in old buildings in dire need of repairs and upgrades. As a result, such facilities can be challenging and expensive to manage. The principal is faced with the ongoing task of ensuring that the school is maintained at its optimal capacity. In addition to whether the school is visually pleasing and inviting on an aesthetic level, the issue of facility compliance factors into the discussion of facilities. Old buildings may not readily meet with compliance regarding current safety codes; upgrades and standards reflect requirements that have changed over time. Classroom space needs to comply with local ordinances to protect the safety of children; this can range from occupancy requirements to an ordinance regarding early childhood classrooms that requires them to be located on the first floor closest to the exit of the school. Fire, asbestos, and health needs all factor into a school's facilities with constant attention to the accompanying cost factor to meet compliance standards.

Once facilities are upgraded, the challenge of maintaining them is also present. This involves ensuring that daily cleaning takes place in the school, whether through supervision of janitorial staff or contracted services of a cleaning agency. Regardless of the method and the expense, maintenance of the school is an area worthy of constant vigilance. Attention to restrooms, classrooms, early childhood napping areas, the faculty lounge, and lunchroom all require the principal's inspection on a regular basis; such actions set a high standard for how they are maintained. Managing and upkeep of the school is a daunting task even for veteran principals; however, its importance cannot be overstated as it contributes to the overall perception of the school sent to all stakeholders.

Equipment

School equipment comes under the broader heading of facilities and needs to be up-to-date and reflect the latest requirements and safety codes. Health equipment such as defibrillators and fire extinguishers require documentation of regular inspections or updates based on the local ordinance or standards of practice. Academic equipment may include safety material in the science and technology labs, or educational materials found in classrooms. Recreational equipment also has to reflect current standards for school use. Well-meaning donations of home play equipment cannot replace equipment intended for the level of use in a school. Compliance with city, local, and state ordinances must be met so the best interest and safety of children is clearly a priority.

Other types of equipment may not be required but may contribute to the well-being of the students and teachers. Air conditioners, ceiling fans, or other types of heating and cooling devices can make the school environment more comfortable. They still need to adhere to codes and regulations, being supported by proper electrical circuits.

Equipment throughout the school must be held to a high standard. Whether athletic equipment used for physical education and after-school care or science lab materials, the principal has a role in monitoring children's safety and well-being. The message to the teachers and parents has to be clear so that these stakeholders can assist with making this a priority. The school leader can work with key personnel, such as the athletic director, science department chair or lead teacher, and maintenance department, thereby communicating the priority that such matters receive the attention they deserve.

Technology Management Plan

The role of technology has become more prominent in all schools, but in a unique way in Catholic schools. There are a number of factors that contribute to a school's technology management plan and its successful implementation. Continued efforts to train and support teachers' use of technology have met with varied results. As a group, Catholic teachers' use of technology is focused on preparing to teach, rather than as a teaching tool. While echnology has changed teachers' lives in helping them develop materials, it has not had as much impact on engaging students in their learning (Gibbs, Dosen, & Guerrero, 2013). The digital divide still exists; these researchers found differences in low- and high-poverty schools in how teachers used technology for the developing instructional materials and use in communicating with parents. Schools of higher poverty were less likely to utilize such tools.

Technology has been utilized in recent years as a means to advance the school's image as a marketing tool. Most importantly, there has been a clear link to the principal's disposition toward technology and its successful implementation (Hunt, Joseph, & Nuzzi, 2002). The principal's strong interest in technology and belief that it can benefit students has led to overall support. Support from the principal has included allocation of resources, hiring of personnel, and staff development for training teachers.

The development of a written technology plan is the first step in the process toward technology implementation. An effective technology plan is based on the shared vision of educators, parents, community members, and business leaders who have technological expertise. It ensures that technology strengthens existing curricula and supports meaningful engaged learning for all students. It also specifies how the technology will be paid for and how its use will be supported (November, 1998). The principal serves as a key stakeholder along with the many others who will be involved in its support and implementation. Within a Catholic school, engaging school board members, parents, teachers, and community members to serve on a planning team initiates the process and communicates that technology is an important priority that must be embedded and integrated throughout the work done in the school.

INSTITUTIONAL ADVANCEMENT PROGRAMS

Developing a strong support system in the form of advancement is another key element to a school's success. An excellent Catholic school enacts a comprehensive plan, based on a compelling mission, for institutional advancement through communications, marketing, enrollment management, and development (National Standards, 2012).

Heft (2011) suggests that Catholic school leaders need to be more forward thinking about increasing their sources of financial support and begin to create a "development mentality." He references the 2008 Notre Dame study entitled "Faith, Finances and the Future," with specific recommendations for improving finances in Catholic schools. These include increasing revenues through capital campaigns, annual giving opportunities, keeping close track of alumni, writing grants, and approaching foundations. Engagement in these specific areas will lead to schools staying open and thriving. "Those schools with professional and energetic leadership in the areas of fundraising, marketing and planning will continue to thrive" (Robey, 2012, p. 15).

Institutional advancement is broadly defined as those activities undertaken by the institution to develop understanding and support among its various students, faculty, staff, alumni, parents, and friends. While high schools and higher education settings have active offices of institutional advancement, most parish elementary schools do not have the resources to establish such an area of focus. Regardless of school size, the idea of how the school will continue to gain support from past and current stakeholders is worthy of consideration. Some schools may be able to hire a director of development to undertake responsibility for this process. Ninety percent of Catholic high schools have a development director with an established position for that role (Tracy, 2001). However, in most parish schools, the process of advancement is left for the principal to oversee. There are a number of outreach activities that the parish school can undertake to stay in contact with stakeholders and enlist them in financial, emotional, and personal support of the school and its mission.

By its very definition, institutional advancement taps the pool of alumni who have graduated from the school. In such, enlisting alumni to assist and participate in the process is a powerful tool to reach others. Every school has well-meaning alumni who want to get involved. They can assist with updating the alumni database, contacting graduates, and planning events for this sector of the school population.

Related to the school's institutional advancement is the principal's comfort level in asking others for financial support. An ongoing task in her repertoire, the school leader has to readily communicate the current and anticipated needs, large and small, and be able to ask for support. While this is not skill taught in principal preparation programs, it is one that she will have to learn quickly. Stakeholders will look to the principal to be aware of the needs, the dollar amount, and the level of support required. Funders will require the leader to be well-versed in sharing long-term goals, with an explanation of how goals are measured and met; all are required to foster positive relationships with all potential donors.

Scholarship funds have become necessary to entice students to attend Catholic schools. The principal may share the scholarship decision making with the pastor, making the determination of which students receive support and the amount. Additionally, annual funds are monies the school collects to support what the tuition alone does not cover. Annual fund goals vary by school governance type and in many ways align with a school's development office.

Endowments represent another way that Catholic schools have supported their efforts. An endowment is an investment fund set up by an institution in which regular withdrawals from the invested capital are used for ongoing operations or other specified purposes. Endowments are funded by donations, which are tax deductible for donors.

STRATEGIC OPERATIONAL VITALITY

The principal's roles and responsibilities are vast and include a range of duties that are academic, spiritual, and managerial. Each of these roles is in competition for the school leader's time and attention and represents a critical area in a school's success and survival. Clearly, the demands are great and require some balancing and juggling from one role to another. There are some strategies that will support the principal in handling all of the duties and ensuring that a school's operational vitality gets the attention it requires.

The first strategy involves the school's governance structure. An assessment must be made to determine how the structure and relationship between pastor, principal, school board, and parent association are supporting a healthy operation within the school. Are there ways to structure the Catholic school so that all of these roles are clearly defined and delineated? Many schools have not considered the structure and model for operations. A review of the decision making, duties, and expectations is helpful to understand roles and responsibilities. While not rendering the power and authority away from the principal, this process can be helpful to see where shared decision making might be utilized.

Relationship building is another important strategy for the principal to utilize with colleagues. It is important for the principal to form strong relationships within the parish team. Working well with the business manager or financial agent as well as the director of religious education and pastor can facilitate shared duties and a better understanding of the pressures with which the principal must deal. The end result is that shared areas of leadership can reflect true collaboration. These relationships seem to succeed best when school mission and vision are central and the interests of the students are the priority.

Additionally, the principal has to learn to trust in others and delegate certain aspects of their work load. Utilizing a distributed leadership model can be an effective method for sharing leadership and supports leadership practice, rather than hard-and-fast roles and responsibilities (Spillane, 2005). The best leaders create a culture that empowers others to be part of the decision-making process. Ownership is part of developing a school culture that is shared and participatory. The principal has to be informed and involved in all aspects of the school and its operation, while making sure each receives equal time and attention. Doing so requires developing teacher leaders who can monitor and assume duties at meetings and office staff who can take on specific tasks and roles. The principal has to trust others to take on these roles and trust they are capable to accomplish what is required.

Clearly, principals need to attend to the various components of the school's operational vitality. This aspect of school management and leadership connects with critical support areas of running a school. Unfortunately, principals do not feel well equipped in areas of marketing and finance (Rieckhoff, 2014). Principals have to walk a fine line between getting support and delegating these areas, but still overseeing and managing the big picture. Burke (2013) has developed a checklist to correspond with each area of operational vitality. While items may not align with each parish school, the concept of itemizing and checking each task under the broader heading of operational vitality will assist in tracking and monitoring what is required as well as benchmarks for its success. All are clearly linked to the mission and vision of the school. The principal is the leader of that mission and vision, so ultimately these need to reside with her.

FUTURE DIRECTIONS IN OPERATIONAL VITALITY

The importance of operational vitality cannot be overstated in the survival and well-being of the school. Clearly, the principal's role and responsibilities in this area are vast and can potentially consume all the leader's time and energy. There are a number of changes, however, that could assist the principal in meeting with success in this area. Principal preparation programs, new principal training and mentoring conducted by dioceses and universities as well as continued professional learning for principals can all be improved upon so that principals feel well equipped to handle this critical aspect of their work.

The majority of the principal preparation programs provide candidates with a single course in each of the following areas—school finance, school law, and human resource management. While content coverage in these courses attempts to expose candidates to the key concepts, they by no means provide future school leaders with all of the tools they need for successful leading a school's operational vitality. Partnerships with Catholic schools where principals in training can train and gain more exposure to the day-to-day operation of a school would be of great benefit. Strong connections with practicing principals in the field serving as adjunct faculty and guest lecturers will continually provide them with the realities that exist and real-life case study examples. While coursework often contains field experiences, these can at times seem artificial when the principal candidate is not familiar with the context or setting. A more useful exercise would be for the candidates, individually or as a group, to problem solve and complete field hours in an authentic school setting solving actual operational vitality issues. When coordinating schedules to connect graduate students with school placements, the end result would be more confident candidates benefitting from the experience aspect provided.

Induction programs are utilized by Catholic school dioceses to train large groups of new principals at one time. Often, these programs center on the policies and procedures of the diocese as well as helping new principals gain familiarity with the central office staff who are able to support and assist them in their work. Principals meet on a regular basis throughout their first year of leadership and get an overview on a wide range of topics. The area of operational vitality is often presented in various sections, with so much of the reality dependent upon the parish's pastor, business manager, or the way things have been established with their context. Often the formal written policy and implementation of the policy do not match. Thus, it is dependent on the new principal to make sense of the actual practices and consider how they might be improved. Each system of schools functions differently and expects the principal to figure out where and when these align. It might be useful for the induction programs to include an onsite portion whereby the principal can learn the system that is in place within the school and parish and learn how to navigate it effectively. Pastors and business managers need to be part of the conversation and training so that the message is consistent and emanates from the diocesan policies and procedures.

Mentoring programs for principals continue to gain popularity in Catholic school systems as individualized training supports new leaders in their own setting. Often connected with a peer principal or local veteran principal from a neighboring parish, this method helps the principal learn within her own context as well as connect her with colleagues in the field. Although they are often competing for the same students, the more ways principals can work together and support each other, the better off all will be. In the same way, mentors must be vetted and trained through a process so that their work is driven by standards and benchmarks in the field rather than well-intended veterans who seem to have all of the answers.

Finally and most importantly, Catholic school systems need to ensure that there is a system to support principals' ongoing learning and development. Similar to teachers, professional learning for principals is the most powerful tool for changing practice within the field. Resources for principals to access as needed in areas of budget, finance, and institutional advancement should be available regularly. In that way, the principal from one school to the next will not be forced to use time to create and develop programs and practices that already exist and should be shared throughout the system.

REFERENCES

Bryk, A., Lee, V., & Holland, P. (1993). *Catholic schools and the common good.* Cambridge, MA: Harvard University Press.

Burke, R. (2013, February). *Operational vitality white paper.* Paper presented at the Diocese of Palm Beach Leadership Summit. Palm Beach, FL.

Ciriello, M. (1998). (Ed). *Principal as managerial leader, 2nd ed.* Washington, DC: United States Catholic Council of Bishops Publishing.

Crimino, C. (2008). Diocesan and local leaders use new models to enable schools to survive and thrive. *Momentum, 38*(4), 18–22.

Danielson, C. (2012). *Enhancing professional practice: A framework for teaching.* Thousand Oaks, CA: Association for Supervision and Curriculum Development.

Gibbs, M., Dosen, A. & Guerrero, R. (2013). Technology in Catholic schools: Are schools using the technology they have? *Catholic Education: A Journal of Inquiry and Practice, 12*(2), 176–192.

Harris, J. C. (1999). A plan to pay for Catholic schools. In R. Haney & J. O'Keefe (Eds.), *Creatively financing and resourcing catholic schools* (pp. 49–71). Washington, DC: National Catholic Educational Association.

Harris, J. C. (2000). The funding dilemma facing Catholic elementary and secondary schools. In J. Youniss & J. J. Convey (Eds.), *Catholic schools at the crossroads: Survival and transformation* (pp. 55–71). New York, NY: Teachers College Press, Columbia University.

Heft, J. (2011). *Catholic high schools.* New York, NY: Oxford University Press.

Hunt, T., Joseph, E., & Nuzzi, R. (2002). (Eds.) *Catholic schools still make a difference: Ten years of research 1991–2000.* Washington, DC: National Catholic Education Association.

Konzen, J. (1996). The principal's role in finance and development. In M. Ciriello (Ed.), *Expectations for the Catholic school principal: A handbook for pastors and parish school committees* (pp. 245–255). Washington, DC: United States Catholic Conference.

National Standards and Benchmarks for Effective Catholic Elementary and Secondary Schools. (2012). Retrieved from www.catholicschoolstandards.org

November, A. (1998). *Critical Issue: Developing a school or district technology plan.* Oak Brook, IL: North Central Regional Educational Laboratory.

Nuzzi, R. J., Frabutt, J. M., & Holter, A. C. (2008). *Faith, finances, and the future: The Notre Dame study of U.S. pastors.* Notre Dame, IN: Alliance for Catholic Education Press.

Phelps, S. (2012). Planning and development in a Catholic school. In P. Robey (Ed.), *A practitioner's guide to Catholic school leadership.* (NCEA Catholic School Leadership Series, Vol 1, pp. 15–26) Arlington, VA: National Catholic Educational Association.

Picciano, A. (2006). *Data-driven decision making for effective school leadership.* Upper Saddle River, NJ: Pearson.

Rieckhoff, B. S. (2014). The Development of Faith Leadership in Novice Principals. *Journal of Catholic Education, 17*(2). Retrieved from http://digitalcommons.lmu.edu/ce/vol17/iss2/3

Robey, P. (Ed.). (2012). *A practitioner's guide to Catholic school leadership* (NCEA Catholic School Leadership Series, Vol. 1). Arlington, VA: National Catholic Educational Association.

Rowe, D. (2003). *A straight-talking guide to running a school.* Washington, DC: National Catholic Educational Association.

Spillane, J. (2005). Distributed leadership. *The Educational Forum, 69*(2), 143–150.

St. Mark Parish School. (n.d.). Dodge City Diocese. Received from http://www.dcdiocese.org/stewardship/319-stewardship-404-time-and-talent-319-319

Tracy, M. (2001). *Mission and money: A CHS 2000 report on finance, advancement and governance.* Washington, DC: National Catholic Education Association.

United States Conference of Catholic Bishops. (2010). Charter for the Protection of Children and Young People, Washington, DC. Retrieved from http://www.usccb.org/issues-and-action/child-and-youth-protection/upload/2010-Child-youth-protection-resources.pdf/

Wuerl, D. (2008). How to save Catholic schools. *The National Catholic Review, 199*(21), 16–18.

RECOMMENDATIONS FOR FURTHER READING

Bambrick-Santoyo, P. (2010). *Driven by data: A practical guide to improve instruction.* San Francisco, CA: Jossey-Bass.

Bambrick-Santoyo, P. (2012). *Leverage leadership: A practical guide to building exceptional schools.* San Francisco, CA: Jossey-Bass.

Bimonte, R. (2008). *Financing the mission: A profile of Catholic elementary schools in the United States, 2007.* Washington, DC: National Catholic Educational Association.

Brennan, J. (1995). *The road to success: An orientation for Catholic school teachers.* Washington, DC: National Catholic Educational Association.

Danielson, C. (2009). *Talk about teaching: Leading professional conversations.* Thousand Oaks, CA: Corwin Press.

Gilroy, A., & Leak, L. (1996). The principal's role in personnel management. In M. Ciriello (Ed.), *Expectations for the Catholic school principal* (pp. 3–10). Washington, DC: United States Catholic Conference.

Hunt, T., Ellis, J., & Nuzzi, R. (Eds.). (2004). *Catholic schools still make a difference, ten years of research, 1991–2000* (2nd ed.). Washington, D.C.: National Catholic Educational Association.

United States Conference of Catholic Bishops. (2014). Retrieved from http://www. usccb.org/beliefs-and teachings/what-we-believe/stewardship/

AFTERWORD

Anthony J. Dosen and Ronald Hoover

In the course of my years at DePaul, I have taught several courses on Catholic School Leadership and have had my students from these courses go out and serve as administrators of Catholic schools in the Chicago Metropolitan Area. What follows are the reflections of one of my former students, Ron Hoover. I hope that you find his reflections on his life and work in Catholic education as inspiring as I have.

RONALD HOOVER

I am an accidental teacher. I bamboozled my way into my first teaching gig (with summers off—my deepest motivation) by parlaying my interest in world religions, my winning interview skills, and my willingness to work for a subsistence wage into an interview after a tiny ad (in a newspaper, of all things) for a theology teacher appeared in very, very late July. I could smell the desperation. I got the job. I did my time. This jack-of-all-trades suddenly had his own classroom! And, in time, I became very good at teaching. In time I'll tell you how.

Something unanticipated happened along the way. After resisting for a few years, I fell in love with the school, the Religious who sponsored it and were among my favorite colleagues, many of the lay folk, and the students. The authenticity of the place, the authenticity of the people, and the palpable sense of Presence in the building shattered my deafness. I was hooked.

Catholic School Leadership, pages 185–192
Copyright © 2016 by Information Age Publishing
All rights of reproduction in any form reserved.

I was home. The talk was walked, due in no small part to Religious, administrators, and colleagues who led with skill, love, and honesty. We rocked the mission. The particular charism of this high school was consciously and intentionally enfleshed and celebrated and informed the experience of all who entered its embrace. Despite my best efforts, I was not immune to its charm. It all began in 1993.

Fast forward 21 school years and here I am in my third year as the principal of another school, with a different charism, and in a very different place. How did this wise-cracking and clueless guy (the department chair who recommended my hiring later confided she assumed I was a one-year-hire) stay for 18 years? Call it grace, or conversion, a preferential option for downward mobility, or good sense on my part concerning where I needed to be. Said department chair became principal and invited me to be dean of students after a few years in her shoes as department chair. Along the way I also picked up the academic dean and vice principal roles, as tough times demanded wearing a whole lot of hats; through it all I kept teaching, too. In an after-the-fact progression, I picked up necessary degrees and certifications, milking every loophole available. See? An accidental teacher became an accidental administrator. Unless, of course, one is able to see the hand of Providence in life. I was invited to be principal of the school on a fine spring morning 16 years after I arrived. Hence, the theme of accidental, or at least a theme, that does not endorse career planning *per se*. The invitations came at the right time. I was primed to respond. Becoming a leader in a Catholic school is relational, volitional, and formed in a master–apprentice dynamic, as it seems to me.

Our current Holy Father talks about attending to the marginal, those on the periphery. I have spent my career in two peripheral Catholic high schools, places that do not quickly come to folks' minds when they hear "Catholic high school." Marginal students who, on paper, give evidence of very little ability or potential, come to flourish with authentically robust self-confidence and acceptances to colleges and universities that give one pause. We have our gifted for sure, and our typically successful students and their hearts are enlarged to match their intellect. What a gift to fly under the radar, to do good work unhampered by too human politics and competition and the drive for status and the tunnel vision of accountability and results as defined by test scores. There is freedom on the margin, and great challenge, and opportunities unimagined save by those who experience them. Without faith and the beauty of our deep and challenging and wonderfully nuanced Catholic heritage, it cannot be explained or understood—even to ourselves by ourselves.

But there is also tension (How can we survive? You want us to what? How can you ask me to do that with a clear conscience?) and fear (Payroll again? Another family lost their income? Downtown called and didn't say why?) and anxiety "for all the members," to borrow from St. Paul, and sometimes envy of the more resourced, the more wealthy. Being responsible for a learning community is essentially pastoral, thank God, and only secondarily—though importantly—administrative. One is called to be all things to all—impossible, of course, but the bar has been set high by the administrators I have known and admired. There is no typical day, there are no typical duties. The best image of the position for me is the fulcrum under a seesaw: Somehow I am carrying it all, am responsible for it all, even as the ship (to mix metaphors) lists from side to side, and sometimes flies, and often faces strong headwinds.

One of my mentors... often, daily, very often, I stop and wonder what the members of my pantheon of mentors would do in a situation I am encountering. (This paragraph was going in a different direction but I decided to write a few pages here at school, and kept track of the interruptions—17 in two hours, and so I forgot where I was going....) Anyone considering leadership in a Catholic school needs mentors, and networks, and friends who get it from the inside. Hearing after hours, as in after a ten-hour day, "What did you do today?" often reduces me to hysterical laughter. Friends and loved ones have learned not to ask unless they have some time blocked out for a response. Upon the conclusion of the litany, the appointed response tends to be, "Why do you put yourself through that?" The word *vocation* comes to mind. Yes, we the baptized, we the usually lay, we this generation of Catholic school administrators have a vocation to do what we do. No other explanation would keep our feet to the fire.

This reflection would be written on auto pilot if it could simply recount the tales and sayings of the mentors I have been privileged to know and observe. Some were formal mentors, the vast majority not. Just seeing them in action was, and is, both formative and informative. Some, now, are younger than I am—an interesting development! But in common they live out the art and craft, the science and technology of administration and faith-filled leadership—which, to quote one of them, are two different things. "We have lots of administrators, but very few leaders," one of them opines frequently. Leadership is based on character, and inspiration, and eliciting confidence based on the authenticity of oneself and the congruence of saying what one means and meaning what one says... clichés that are particularly apt in our settings. Knowing what you're doing helps too. When I retire (!) I intend to write a love song to the women and men who have formed me, and to create a compendium of their wise sayings. Alas and only half-jokingly, I will be 70 and most will be on to their reward when I get to sleep in daily. Tell your folks you appreciate them now!

One of my mentors often repeats: Tell your folks you appreciate them! I have found this to be so very true. And, as a good teacher would, compliment on concrete actions and words and initiatives that show you are watching. People continue to thank me for the smallest of acknowledgements, surprised when someone notices the good they do. Living in a stance of gratitude can and should come naturally even to the most distracted Catholic school administrator, and that gratitude notices all the good that is happening moment by moment in every school day, even if particular fires are burning and storm clouds are gathering and the toilets are overflowing (I had to work that in at least once) and vendors are demanding payment or else. Too, when being alert to the signs of the times within one's building, one sees what needs correcting, what needs encouraging, and who should be identified as future school leaders. Be on the lookout for our replacements!

There are mentors too who can feed the soul, though we have never crossed paths. Three come to mind that I simply must recognize. I cannot imagine my practice without them. They have been my mainstay now for decades. The first is St. Benedict. His *Rule* informed the life and practice of the school where I spent so many years, and animated in an existential way all that we did. The *Rule*, and the centuries of literature unpacking it, and the centuries of human experience formed and interpreted by it, speak to teaching, and community formation, and faith, and authority, and "listening with the ear of the heart." It provides an interpretive lens for all that teaching and leading is about. Like the Bible, it is an interesting piece of literature. Like the Bible, situated in the context of a believing community, it is formative and life giving. More cheekily, I consider it the first student handbook, and a practical application of the Gospel imperative.

A pair of writers and a single writer rounds out my Trinity of written inspiration. I happened upon each just at the time I needed them. Sitting in an initial administrative class some 20 years ago, one of our assigned texts was by the team of Sergiovanni and Starratt. They presented a perspective on supervision with which I resonated deeply. I entered the academic program with some reservation, expecting an emphasis on things quantitative and legal. Instead, I encountered a clearly researched and beautifully written text on supervision as moral act. "Yes, thank you," was my response as these authors put together the many inchoate thoughts I had long been harboring about leadership and supervision. They gave me permission to forge ahead in my studies while maintaining my sense of what was, and is, most important: the human and relational dimensions of all that we do. I continue to rest in their reminder that "supervision" includes vision, and looking up-and-over, and taking a prophetic stand when necessary, and pulling (not, note, pushing) an institution to where it needs to be. It also helped me identify a skill set that serves me well and that I would encourage administrators to develop: seeing. See the big picture, see the systems, see the beliefs, and see how they connect. This "vision" allows for competent and efficient decision making as well as effective leadership.

Finally, Parker Palmer is my man. I have never met him, but I feel like I know him. More, I feel like he knows me. He has the heft and the rigor that allowed me to confidently find my own teaching, and later, administrative voice, and gave me permission to work from where I am, rather than from some model or construct of what a school leader ought to be. He presents a path toward authentic and integrated teaching, leading, and being that brings together the many strands of what I have learned, what I know to be true, and what I still aspire to be. There is in his work, I think, a healthy co-mingling of the self and the act of administration. We lead as we are, and we craft our institutions—to some degree—as images of ourselves. That may sound grandiose, but it contains a truth about the power and centrality of one who carries the title of school leader. Coercion is of little lasting effect. What lingers, because it is deep and lasting, is placing oneself at the service of the mission and purpose of one's school in a healthy and balanced manner. We're called to be the roots, not the towers. One can dive in anywhere in the collection of P.² as I think of him, and will emerge a better person and leader.

To this point I have rarely alluded to skill sets, things to do, interpretation of testing data, school law, budgeting, human resource work, or plumbing and electric, shoveling and plowing. That is intentional. The great gift of working in a Catholic school is the permission and presumption that we will address what really matters: God, the human being in all her or his component parts, life in the Church, and the betterment of society. We are, happily, craftspeople and constant disciples, who bring to our craft and discipleship all the technical and pedagogical skills we can command—as a beginning, not as the end. So we work hard and long and thank God for the opportunity.

The theme I would suggest that binds this work together is to find one's own voice. That, in essence, makes me an excellent teacher and, maybe, a maturing school leader. That is the goal I have for my students, for my teachers and staff, for all whom I encounter . . . and for me. Finding voice, for me, speaks of authenticity, and liberation from parroting what I or others think I should be. Rather, grounding in oneself leads to powerful teaching, powerful leadership, and transformative administration. Education as liberation can be understood from this perspective as well. This assertion could, misunderstood, be interpreted as egotistical nonsense. But the journey of self-discovery, when authentic, leads instead to cooperation and the placement of oneself at the service of mission and purpose. At least it does on a good day. For those seeking to look more deeply into why I emphasize what I emphasize, full disclosure insists that I present myself as a 4 on the Enneagram and an INFP—with an ever ascending J thanks to this job—on the MBTI. Know thyself. And, for the love of God, choose as close advisors those who think such stuff is pointless and just want to get the job done. Conversely, if you are a Type A and get-the-job-done soul, hook up with a dreamer or two. Complementary types make for the strongest leadership.

I would conclude with a mention of the "three abilities": visibility, availability, and vulnerability. Taken together, these abilities allow one to be a human leader, an empathetic leader, and an honest leader. As a bonus, these abilities will cement their practitioner comfortably in leadership. For I have learned that the role of school leader is a necessary one, but also isolating and relentless. Keeping track of my practice of the three abilities has, I have learned, kept my constituents content and my bosses (the Presidents, the topic of another reflection someday, some way) satisfied. Give them a whirl—the concrete demands of the job will present themselves and not ever go away, though they can be tamed by sound practice and disciplined abilities.

Visibility cannot be over-emphasized. It is demanding, and time-consuming, and difficult to justify until lived experience proves its worth. Standing in the hall at passing time, working the cafeteria, popping into classes, being at the main door or parking lot a.m. and p.m., strolling through extracurriculars, managing to be seen at three home games simultaneously—or so it seems—make the rank and file happy. To this day I find it remarkable how one is noticed, and how one's absence or invisibility are noticed. Do nothing, speak when spoken to, notice everything, and make a list of people to compliment... we do work, even when clutching a favored coffee mug at 7:15 a.m. and a favored water bottle at 7:15 p.m. while valiantly attempting to remain upright. "It makes no sense," to quote some of my students through the years... but visibility is effective, and appreciated, and a central component of a school leader's job. That being said, well, be happy if you can at least do a walk-about. That's just the way it goes some days.

Availability is another trait to foster. When one is visible, one is a target. Lots and lots of folks will take advantage and share a word, a story, a concern, even a disclosure of personal illness or family challenge. Find a method to remember all you hear until you can get back to the office and do a data dump. Foster too those postures and habits that telegraph "I'm listening," even when you don't want to listen. And learn folks' names! Crucial.

Availability also means willingness to take meetings that you know will go nowhere, or will essentially be a sales pitch, or will be informed by complaints with no basis in reality. Listen, be kind, and gently move things along. Angels and mighty donors have been entertained unawares. When I am working—always, almost, with the door open, I make it a practice to put my pen down (or, to remove my hands from the keyboard) and stand myself up to greet any head that pops in to see if I have a minute. Be prepared for the line I find most (unintentionally, I am sure) offensive: "Are you busy?" No—I'm doing the Sunday Times crossword puzzle. C'mon in...

Finally, most distressingly, vulnerability. Being a school leader, some days, is being an emotional punching bag. Wait for it—yes, on rare occasions, even a physical punching bag as you place yourself between dueling students when it is necessary to do so. People will attack, and critique, and just unload their frustrations. Finding the resolve to encounter them well even when your personal concerns are large is one of the graces of the office, I do believe. In the world of survival worries, new ideas and initiatives must be constantly entertained, even when your strength is ebbing.

I had to live my own words when I was hired to a new position three years ago, grieving my former school even as I embarked on a most challenging new journey. New school, new people, new mission, new charism, new colleagues, new community. No stories in common, no inside jokes, a different ranking of the values we hold in common. The transition was much harder than I anticipated. With no credibility to build on, I had to earn my chops and my leadership from scratch. The work is still a work in progress. I had to let myself grieve, being vulnerable to my own sense of loss, even as I rolled up my sleeves and began a new ministry as principal. In today's world, when professionals are encouraged to anticipate a lot of transition and buy-outs and new positions, the Catholic school ethos still values relationships and community and stability in the ongoing pursuit of excellence. Students are ends, not means. This is one of the little candles we hold up in the throw-away world the Holy Father has warned us about since his election. (And, when you have a moment, get your hands on the work of Nel Noddings. I think her insight on "care" has so much to recommend itself as we compete with big guns both private and public.)

In summary, know that "charism" is not recognized by spell check, and the value of Catholic education is not recognized by a large segment of the population, even among Catholics. The bar is set high to prove our worth, to demonstrate our excellence, to entice enrollment and employment given that we cannot compete, for the most part, with other parts of the educational world, save in the intangibles. Our education is true because complete, our mission is heroic because undervalued and misunderstood, and our lives as school leaders will be poured out in service and challenge and care. Embrace that. The meaning will present itself.

Two nagging final thoughts: some of my favorite Catholic school administrators (shhhh) aren't Catholic, and "this is not your childhood's principalship." Even in my couple-of-decades of service, our little world has changed radically. With few exceptions, the Religious are gone and non-Catholics often value what we have to offer more than our own family of faith. Go with it. In my personal list of the top ten Catholic school administrators I have experienced, a little less than half are non-Catholic, or even unchurched. But they get it. They really get it. I have heard discussions of baptism by water, by fire, and by desire. In these latter days I am wont to advocate for baptism-by-tuition and baptism-by-salary. The boundaries of the Catholic school world have blown open, and all sorts of wild birds are settling in the branches. For that, thanks be to God.

Today's principal preparation seems, from the outside, so focused on results, accountability, and a very brief shelf life for the school leader. Hold fast to your dreams. We are so much more than that, though we incorporate all that research has to offer. We stand in a long line of school leaders about whom stories will be told, memories created, myths developed, and reunion-based encounters will be retold on social media. We hold tremendous and formative power in our hands. Pray God we put it to life-enhancing use. And, to conclude with my current reality and emergent voice, "Live Jesus in our hearts, forever."

I continue to be amazed at the dedication of my students to the mission of Catholic education. They truly see (or get, as Ron Hoover would say) that the work of Catholic education is more than a job, it is a vocation. God calls us, sometimes through the very mundane reality of finding a job, and encountering a Catholic school. But God calls, nonetheless. It is the vocation of teaching and administering that each of us in Catholic schools has been called to embrace. As Ron stated so well, it means more than just lesson plans, data analysis, and playground supervision. The vocation to Catholic education means growing in faith, while helping young people grow in their own faith. It means taking responsibility for leading the classroom or school community. Most importantly, it means being a guide on the journey of faith.

Ron used three words to describe his leadership: visibility, availability, and vulnerability. These words should not get lost in the words of this chapter or this book. The successful Catholic school leader is one who is seen around campus. Whether it is at the junior varsity basketball game, the kindergarten Christmas pageant, or just strolling down the hallway during class time, our presence is important. Our presence mirrors the loving Presence of the One who calls us. As important as visibility is, availability is even more important. We can be seen at events but be more distant than the moon when it comes to interacting with people. Each of us, introvert or extravert, needs to see our lives as being offered to those whom we serve. Therefore, we make ourselves available so that others may experience the Presence of the One who calls us. Finally, we must learn to be vulnerable. Our response to the worries and inevitable dumping that takes place on the leader of any school, but especially a Catholic school, makes us vulnerable. Caring makes us vulnerable, and we are called to care. It is not only being visible or available, but also vulnerable. It is in the vulnerability of the moment that we often express our sincerest care for the other. It is in that moment that we share in the cross of Christ, who showed us the way to complete vulnerability.

As Ron spoke of his mentors, know that we encourage you to find your own mentors. Perhaps in the pages of this text you will find a recommended text that will be of service to you. Perhaps you will find a mentor in one of your courses, or in the course of your wide reading. You may even find that special person in your region who can offer you the mentoring that you will need as a new principal. Take advantage of these mentors. Allow them in, and allow them to help you. Catholic school leaders work best in community—that is why we are a Church!

The editors and authors wish you well as you begin this journey! You certainly will be in our prayers. Continue to be the Presence of the One who calls us.

ABOUT THE CONTRIBUTORS

Fr. Anthony J. Dosen, CM, PhD, STL is a priest of the Congregation of the Mission and an associate professor of educational leadership at DePaul University in Chicago, IL. He has taught and held various administrative roles in Catholic secondary schools throughout the Midwest for fifteen years. He currently prepares students for administrative roles at both the building and district levels in both public and private settings.

Sr. Patricia Helene Earl, IHM, PhD, is a member of the Sisters, Servants of the Immaculate Heart of Mary, Immaculata, PA. With over 40 years in Catholic education, she has taught on the elementary and secondary levels, served as an elementary principal, was assistant superintendent of schools for the Diocese of Arlington, and is currently a professor of education at Marymount University in Arlington, VA where she directs the Catholic school leadership program, a MEd in Administration and Supervision PK–12. Her dissertation focused on the faith formation of the laity in Catholic schools. She has published several books, chapters, and articles and presented at conferences nationally and internationally on faith formation in virtue, spirituality, and Catholic school leadership.

Ronald Hoover, MEd, has been a high school teacher and administrator in the Archdiocese of Chicago since 1993. He is in his fourth year as principal of St. Joseph High School, a Lasallian ministry located in Westchester, Illinois. For 18 years he served at St. Scholastica Academy in Chicago, beginning as a full-time teacher in theology, as well as teaching international

Catholic School Leadership, pages 193–194
Copyright © 2016 by Information Age Publishing
All rights of reproduction in any form reserved.

baccalaureate philosophy and theory of knowledge. At St. Scholastica he held many administrative positions as well, in time becoming principal of the Academy. He is completing his doctorate in curriculum and instruction at Loyola University, Chicago.

Frank Montejano has spent a career in Catholic education as a teacher, principal, and regional supervisor within the Archdiocese of Los Angeles. He recently served on the faculty at Loyola Marymount University in the school's Center for Catholic Education. Currently, Frank is the principal of Holy Family School in South Pasadena, CA.

Barbara Stacy Rieckhoff, PhD is an associate professor at DePaul University and teaches in the principal preparation program. She has spent fifteen years as a public and Catholic school administrator. Her research interests include principal mentoring and school improvement planning.

INDEX

A

Accountability, 12, 94, 97, 113, 124, 172–174, 186, 191
Advancement, 9, 108–109, 125–126, 128, 166, 177–178, 182
Anthropology, Catholic, 24, 69
Apple, Michael, 97–98
Appreciative Inquiry, (AI) 91–92
Are Catholic Schools the Answer?, 87
Assessment, 66, 68, 71–73, 75, 114, 116, 125, 130, 135, 136, 139, 174
Augustine, St., 64–65
Authentic Leadership, 10, 13, 14–15

B

Baker, D. P. & C. Riordan, 82
Bass, Bernard M., 11, 17
Beutow, Harold, 28
Bimonte, Bro. Robert, 54, 60–61
Bloom's Taxonomy, 71, 78
Board Fatigue, 97
Boards (types of)
    Advisory, 43–44, 151
    Consultative, 43–44
    Limited Jurisdiction, 43–44, 153

Bolman and Deal, 5–6
Bryk, Anthony, 28–30, 33, 109–110, 168–169
Burns, James MacGregor, 10–11, 17

C

Canon 803, 28, 37, 47
Canon Law 28, 33, 36, 37, 48, 154
CARA (Center for Applied Research in the Apostolate), 88
Catechism of the Catholic Church, 144
Catholic School Superintendents, 35, 40, 160
Catholic Worldview, 20, 30, 67
Center of Evangelization, 25, 47
Christ and Culture, 64–66
Ciriello, Maria, 134, 141, 156, 166, 173
Civil Law, 37–38, 47
Co-curricular activities (*See* extracurricular activities)
Coleman, James S., 110
Collaboration, 12, 42–43, 46–47, 76, 121–122, 136, 139, 142, 146, 158, 160–161, 166, 179
Collins, Jim, 71, 78

Catholic School Leadership, pages 195–199
Copyright © 2016 by Information Age Publishing

Common Good, 11, 24, 36–37, 69, 95, 109, 170

Communication, 5, 9, 74, 98, 111, 113, 115–116, 127, 139, 142, 157–160, 162, 171, 178

Community, 3–5, 7, 9, 12, 14–16, 19–21, 23, 26–28, 30, 37, 42, 44–45, 47, 48, 52, 55, 58, 66, 77, 82, 90, 92–97, 99, 111–113, 116–122, 124–128, 134–135, 141–142, 152, 154, 159–162, 168–171, 177, 186, 188, 190–192

Consortium Model, 99, 172

Council of Baltimore, 50, 153,

Curriculum, 25, 29–30, 38–40, 59, 63–64, 66–71, 74–75, 95, 113–116, 123, 134, 137–140, 156

D

Data Driven Decision making, 57, 136

Development, 8, 11, 14, 45, 46, 48, 66–69, 75, 76, 77, 83–85, 88, 90–93, 96–99, 101, 108, 110, 111, 113, 115, 119, 120, 122–128, 133–148, 152, 155–156, 160, 169, 172–174, 177–178, 182

Declaration on Christian Education, 148

Dewey, John, 29, 33, 34

Diakonia, 27

Diocesan Bishop, 23, 28, 35, 37–39, 44, 47, 99, 160

Diocesan Office of Education, 40

Distributed Leadership, 13, 15–16, 18, 180

Drahmann, T., 156

Dygert, Bro. William, 45–46, 48

E

Earl, IHM, Sr. Patricia Helene, 77, 78

Eliot School Rebellion, 85–86

Endowments, 98, 100, 101, 179

Enrollments, Catholic School, 32, 42, 52, 54, 57, 59–60, 107–108, 110–111, 113, 115, 117–118, 124–126, 128, 191

Equipment, 8, 123–124, 171, 175, 176

Eucharist, 27

Evaluation, 39, 73, 113–114, 119, 125, 136, 139–141, 146, 173–174

Extracurricular activities, 59, 76, 89, 190

F

Facilities, 45–46, 166, 175–176

Faculty Development (*See* Professional Development)

Finances, 9, 55–56, 60, 81, 82, 154, 168, 178

Financial Planning, 46, 124–125

"Finding God in all things," 30, 78

Francis of Assisi (St.), 25–26

Fundraising, 45–46, 54–55, 77, 121, 126, 160, 166–168, 172

G

Gemeinschaft, 3–4, 18

Gesellschaft, 3–4

Ghetto, Catholic, 52

Gilbert, J. R., 156

Glatthorn, Allan, 135, 137–139

Goleman, Daniel, 18, 126

Gospel Values, 21, 24–26, 66, 147–148

Greeley, Andrew, 70, 160

Greenleaf, Robert, 13, 17, 47, 48

Grennan, Jacqueline, 25

Groome, Thomas, 24, 25, 27, 32, 34, 90

Guskey, Thomas, 140–141

H

Hallinan, Maureen, 88

Heft, S.M. Fr. James 33, 48, 168, 178

Herzberg, Frederick, 8, 18
Hesse, Herman, 13, 17
High School Achievement: Public and Private Schools, 110
Hobbes, Thomas, 4
Holistic education, 28–29, 36–37, 64, 70, 143
Hopkins, Gerard Manley, 70
Hughes, Bishop John, 50
Human Resources, 60, 81, 84, 99, 169, 172, 173

I

Identity (organizational), 19–25, 32–34, 45–46, 161
    Catholic identity, 24–25, 99, 143, 146–147, 161
Ignatius of Loyola (St.), 33, 66
Incarnation(al), 64–65, 69
Induction programs, 180–181
Instruction, 3, 36–39, 45, 55, 57, 66, 71, 73–77, 78, 108, 114–116, 134–136, 139–141, 143, 148, 156, 174, 177
ISLLC (Interstate School Leader Licensure Consortium Standards), 111, 113, 127

J

Jesus Christ, 10, 20–22, 24–25, 27, 64–65, 143, 145, 169, 191
John XXIII (St.), 87
(The) Journey to the East, 13, 17
Juridic Person, 28, 37, 43, 44, 48

K

Kenrick, Archbishop Francis Patrick, 50
Kerygma, 27
Kouzes, James & Barry Posner, 11, 18

L

Learning Objectives, 70, 113, 128
Learning Theory, 70
leitourgia, 27
Liberal artist, 72, 75
Literacy, 74–75, 136
Luther, Martin, 64–65

M

Mahony, Roger Cardinal, 100–101
Marketing, 45, 84, 97, 109, 113, 116–117, 126, 155–156, 174, 177–178, 180
McGregor, Douglas, 8
McLaughlin, Terence, 25, 32–34, 138
Mentoring, 122, 146, 173, 180–181, 192
Mission, 5, 19–33, 36–37, 40–41, 46–47, 50, 55, 60, 64, 66, 76–77, 78, 81, 83–87, 89, 90–91, 93, 95, 97, 98, 101, 108–109, 111–113, 117, 119, 120, 122–123, 126–128, 140, 141, 143, 144, 147, 152, 154–155, 158, 160, 166–167, 169–170, 173, 175, 177–178, 186, 189–191

N

National Catholic Education Association (NCEA), 19, 43, 66, 87
National Standards and Benchmarks for Effective Catholic Elementary and Secondary Schools, 19–21, 25, 34 66–67, 76, 166–167, 172, 175, 178
Neibuhr, H. Richard, 64, 78
No Child Left Behind, 57, 114, 124
Northouse, Peter, 5, 19
NSDC (National Staff Development Council), 135–136, 140

O

Ozar, Lorraine, 19, 66, 108

P

Palmer, Parker, 188
Parens Patriae, 39
Parish(es), 1, 35–38, 41–43, 47, 50,
    54–59, 86–88, 100, 107–109,
    111–113, 116–118, 120–121, 126,
    152–162, 165–172, 178–182
Partnerships, 83, 94, 97–98, 108,
    121–123, 128, 131, 161
Pastor, 21, 28, 35–37, 39, 41–44, 52–54,
    77, 99, 108, 117, 145, 151–162,
    179, 181
Pastor–Principal Relationship, 76, 152,
    158
Peterson, Kent, 5, 17
Philanthropists, 83, 85, 94, 96
Picciano, Anthony, 118, 125, 167
Pierce v. Society of Sisters, 39
Presence, 154–155, 160, 185, 192
President/Principal Model, 45–46, 48
Principal as
    Faith leader, 3, 23, 46, 75, 77, 145
    Instructional leaders, 3, 75, 77, 115
    Manager/Managerial leadership, 3,
        7–8, 156, 158, 166–167, 179
    Spiritual leader (*see* Faith Leader)
Professional Development, 40, 122,
    124–125, 133–148
Professional Learning Communities,
    134, 161
Protecting Children, 173
Public Law 94-142, 31

R

Recruitment, 45, 59, 73, 108, 110–111,
    115–120, 124, 155–156

Retention, 73, 111, 113, 115–116,
    119–120, 124–126, 128, 158
Ryan, Mary Perkins, 87–88, 91, 104

S

Sacrament(al), 7, 36, 69, 143–145, 155,
    159
Scanlan, Martin, 21, 34
Schmoker, Mike, 74, 78–79, 114
Scholarships, 54, 101, 126
(The) School and Society, 29, 33
Second Vatican Council (*see* Vatican
    Council II)
Sergiovanni, Thomas, 3, 18, 111, 142
Servant Leadership, 10, 13–14, 17,
    47–48
Seton, St. Elizabeth Ann, 51
Sisters of Charity, 51
Sisters of Loretto, 51
Social Justice, 90, 103
Spillane, James, 15, 18, 161, 180
Stewardship, 84, 99, 101, 104, 113,
    169–170
Stieb, SVD, Bishop J. Terry, 92–93
Sustainability, 81, 92, 95, 98, 101–102,
    104

T

Teaching the Tradition, 30, 34
Technology, 50, 113, 123, 124, 128, 171,
    175–177, 187
Thomas Aquinas (St.), 64–65, 67
Tithing, 98–100
To Teach as Jesus Did, 26, 34, 143
Tönnies, Ferdinand, 3, 4, 18
Transactional Leadership, 10
Transformational Leadership, 10–11
Traviss, M., 154
Tuition, 2, 42, 54–57, 60, 82–83, 88, 89,
    92, 95, 97, 99–101, 118, 165–172,
    179, 191
Tyler, Ralph, 67–71, 78

U

Understanding by Design, 68, 78–79
Ursuline Sisters, 50
Utilitarian individualism, 90

V

Vatican Council II, 87
Visibility, 138, 155, 160, 174, 189–190, 192

Vision, 3, 10–12, 41, 69, 89, 92–94, 100, 103, 107–108, 111–113, 116–117, 120, 123, 126–128, 134, 141–143, 147, 154, 160–161, 167, 170, 173, 177, 180, 186, 188
Volunteers, 118, 147, 159, 170, 172–173

W

Walch, Timothy, 85, 87, 104, 109
Wiggins, Grant & Jay McTighe, 67–68, 71, 73–74, 78–79

Made in the USA
Monee, IL
24 January 2020